Human Law and Computer Law: Comparative Perspectives

IUS GENTIUM

COMPARATIVE PERSPECTIVES ON LAW AND JUSTICE

VOLUME 25

For further volumes:
http://www.springer.com/series/7888

Mireille Hildebrandt • Jeanne Gaakeer
Editors

Human Law and Computer Law: Comparative Perspectives

Springer

Editors
Mireille Hildebrandt
Institute of Computing and Information Sciences (iCIS)
Radboud University Nijmegen
Nijmegen, The Netherlands

Department of Jurisprudence
Erasmus University Rotterdam
Rotterdam, The Netherlands

Centre for Law Science Technology and Society studies (LSTS)
Vrije Universiteit Brussel
Brussel, Belgium

Jeanne Gaakeer
Department of Jurisprudence
Erasmus University Rotterdam
Rotterdam, The Netherlands

ISBN 978-94-007-6313-5 ISBN 978-94-007-6314-2 (eBook)
DOI 10.1007/978-94-007-6314-2
Springer Dordrecht Heidelberg New York London

Library of Congress Control Number: 2013937545

Printed on acid-free paper

Springer is part of Springer Science+Business Media (www.springer.com)

Acknowledgements

The idea for this volume sprang from the editors' mutual curiosity about, and interest in, each other's research fields: *Law and Code* (Hildebrandt) and *Law and Literature* (Gaakeer). These fields are connected by the concept of 'code', as it is at work in law, technology and literature. The organisation of a panel on the interrelationship between Law, Code and Literature, at the 2001 25th IVR World Congress in Frankfurt am Main (Germany), at which some of the chapters in this volume were presented as papers, furthered the project. We like to thank Ronald E. Leenes, Katja de Vries and Niels van Dijk for presenting first drafts of the papers, and Massimo Durante and Ugo Pagallo for partaking in the discussion. Springer's support enabled us to go ahead with composing the present volume. We are happy that Massimo Durante and Ugo Pagallo joined forces to turn this into a perspicacious exercise, crossing the borders between law, the humanities and artificial intelligence. Similarly, we thank Shulamit Almog for her inexorable dedication to contribute to the broader scope of this study.

We are especially gratified to see this volume published in the *Ius Gentium* series published by Springer, which challenged our perspective on what 'computer law' could mean in the context of comparative law. We thank the editors of the Series, Mortimer Sellers and James Maxeiner, for welcoming us amongst the more conventional tomes on comparative perspectives on law and justice.

This manuscript would still await finalisation if not for the help of the department of Jurisprudence at the Erasmus School of Law, Rotterdam, that kindly provided editorial assistance in the person of Astrid van der Wal. Astrid unremittingly devoted almost all of her time to keeping us all on track, dotting the i's and crossing the t's with a relentless perseverance. Hildebrandt also likes to thank the centre for Law, Science, Technology and Society (LSTS) at Vrije Universiteit Brussels for the inspiring intellectual environment (a truly 'smart' environment) and the institute for Computing and Information Sciences (iCIS) at Radboud University for hosting and testing her research in the realm of Smart Environments, Data Protection and the Rule of Law. Gaakeer, who also serves as a justice in the Court of Appeals in The Hague is grateful for the opportunity that the editing of the present volume provided to engage in new ways of thinking about law and code, different from her legal practice.

Finally, we like to thank our publisher, Neil Olivier at Springer, for his trust and patience. These are indispensable incentives for the editors of a volume that brings together authors from discourses that may seem miles apart, taking the risk of being accused of an incoherent and dissipating assemblage of narratives and arguments. We cannot but hope that the reader will share the zest for a crossroads that urgently requires further exploration.

Mireille Hildebrandt
Jeanne Gaakeer

Contents

0 Prefatory Remarks on *Human Law and Computer Law* 1
Mireille Hildebrandt

Part I Law and Code

1 Prefatory Remarks on Part I: Law and Code 13
Mireille Hildebrandt

2 From *Galatea 2.2* to Watson – And Back? 23
Mireille Hildebrandt

3 What Robots Want: Autonomous Machines, Codes and New Frontiers of Legal Responsibility 47
Ugo Pagallo

4 Abort, Retry, Fail: Scoping Techno-Regulation and Other Techno-Effects 67
Bibi van den Berg and Ronald E. Leenes

5 A Bump in the Road. Ruling Out Law from Technology 89
Katja de Vries and Niels van Dijk

Part II Law and Literature

6 Prefatory Remarks on Part II: Law and Literature 125
Jeanne Gaakeer

7 Control, Alt, and/or Delete? Some Observations on New Technologies and the Human 135
Jeanne Gaakeer

8 Law, Normativity, and the Writing. *Oracle Night* and Human Indeterminacy 159
Massimo Durante

9 When a Robot Can Love – *Blade Runner* as a Cautionary Tale on Law and Technology 181
Shulamit Almog

About the Authors 195

Index 199

Chapter 0
Prefatory Remarks on *Human Law and Computer Law*

Mireille Hildebrandt

Abstract This chapter introduces the volume with a discussion of computer law and human law. Instead of referring to the common meaning of computer law as a field of private or public law that aims to regulate human actions that involve computing systems, this chapter introduces the idea of a law that effectively rules the interactions of non-human actors. This raises a number of questions concerning the meaning of law, human law and the comparative perspective that is at stake in this volume.

0.1 Comparative Law

Scholars of comparative law have come a long way in comparing different legal traditions. In colonial times so-called 'primitive cultures' were often considered as lacking the normative framework that 'we' call 'law' (Wesel 1985). Even when compared to major non-Western civilizations such as the Islamic, Hindu or Chinese traditions, the Western legal systems were generally considered to be superior (cp. Hoecke 2004). Still today, many introductions to comparative law devote the main body of their content to a comparison between civil law systems and common law or Anglo-American legal systems. Usually, Islamic law, Hindu law and Chinese

M. Hildebrandt (✉)
Institute of Computing and Information Sciences (iCIS),
Radboud University Nijmegen, Heijendaalseweg 135, 6525 AJ, Nijmegen

Department of Jurisprudence, Erasmus University Rotterdam,
Burgemeester Oudlaan 50, 3062 PA, Rotterdam, The Netherlands

Centre for Law Science Technology and Society studies (LSTS),
Vrije Universiteit Brussel, Pleinlaan 2, B-1050 Brussel, Belgium
e-mail: hildebrandt@law.eur.nl

M. Hildebrandt and J. Gaakeer (eds.), *Human Law and Computer Law: Comparative Perspectives*, Ius Gentium: Comparative Perspectives on Law and Justice 25,
DOI 10.1007/978-94-007-6314-2_0,

law are discussed as an afterthought in brief chapters that abound in clichés about collectivist legal frameworks that lack our celebration of the individual legal subject (Zweigert and Kötz 1998). Functionalist methodologies as well as semiotic and more anthropological approaches have been elaborated to map various legal systems (Zweigert and Kötz 1998; cp. Geertz 1983), often triggered by concrete needs for legal cooperation. The project on a European Private Law is a case in point (Bar and Clive 2010) where detailed elaboration of comparative positive law and its underlying principles, however, is confronted with complex discourses on the incommensurability of different legal cultures (Legrand and Munday 2003). Patrick H. Glenn's (2007) prize-winning book on *Legal Traditions of the World* finally took on the task of devoting a set of in-depth analyses of seven legal traditions, avoiding the traps of a cognitive bias in favour of the own, Western legal tradition.

This volume undertakes an entirely different task. Instead of comparing existing or historical legal systems within the boundaries of the familiar concept of *human* society, it raises the question of human law in relation to that of computer law. Though non-Western societies may challenge the assumptions underlying modern legal systems, the mere idea of a law that addresses a society of computing systems with or without human 'nodes' is foreign to comparative law. Though this may seem a rather unconventional undertaking, we believe that by investigating computer law as opposed to human law we may become acutely aware of tacit assumptions of what it means to 'have' or 'practice' law. In view of rapid changes in the information and communication infrastructure that will entail entirely different affordances from those of the previous one (that of the printing press),[1] an investigation of what needs to be preserved to still 'afford' a Rule of Law is an urgent task. In their pivotal work on the transitions from a tradition of writing and reading to one of programming, surfing and scrolling Carr (2010) and Wolf (2007) have documented how this will not only impact our access to knowledge and our means of communication. Strikingly, our brains seem to reconfigure their morphology and behaviours to accommodate the shifting needs of our environment. Whereas the bookish mind requires and generates sequential thinking, the digital mind nourishes parallel processing and this has major consequences for the articulation of the law. Written law has triggered a continuous need for interpretation, giving rise to sustained reflection and creative accommodation between legal norms and the world to

[1] The concept of 'affordances' was coined by ecological psychologist Gibson (1986), later popularized by cognitive scientist and engineer Norman (1998) in the field of human machine interfaces. For Gibson, an affordance refers to the perception, cognition and behaviour that is made possible by the environment (or a part thereof) of a particular organism. For instance, a dark room lacks the affordance to perceive colour, at least for human beings. The technologies of the script have different affordances as compared to the environment of an oral culture (Ong 1982). The same goes for the different affordances of the printing press and mass media. Though he did not use the term 'affordance', McLuhan's (1964) work on the impact of electricity and automation on how communication shapes us, basically studies the affordances of the changing ICT infrastructure on human identity and human society.

which they apply. The historical artefact of a tested system of checks and balances between legislator, administration and the courts has been built on the technological infrastructure of the printing press. If we cannot take for granted that the novel ICT infrastructure has similar affordances, we must investigate how digital law compares to written law.

0.2 Computer Law?

Computer law can be understood in a number of ways. First, science fiction authors may use such the term to refer to a law that holds within an artificial society of computing systems or a hybrid society of interacting humans and computing systems (Meister et al. 2007; Rammert 2011). Second, computer law may be understood to describe the constraints that determine interconnected computing systems, much like the notion of laws in the natural sciences refers to the constraints that rule the universe.[2] Third, computer law can be used to refer to the legal rules and regulations that determine the legal implications of the use, possession, manufacturing, designing or selling of computing systems (thus indicating a domain within the law, such as environmental law or the law of the high seas). Fourth, computer law can denote the translation of enacted legal rules into computer algorithms, thus supposedly enabling computing systems to apply existing legal norms (Sartor 1993; Bench-Capon and Prakken 2010; Chap. 4 by Van den Berg and Leenes and Chap. 5 by De Vries and Van Dijk, in this volume).

Fifth, computer law can refer to ethical rules that should be inscribed in computational decision systems, e.g. – but not only – in robots. Asimov's 1991 three laws of robotics, originally developed in the 1940s, provide a longstanding example of which moral rules should be embodied into the software of a robotic 'other' (Clarke 1994; Chap. 3 by Pagallo in this volume):

1. A robot may not injure a human being, or, through inaction, allow a human being to come to harm.
2. A robot must obey orders given it by human beings, except where such orders would conflict with the First Law.
3. A robot must protect its own existence as long as such protection does not conflict with the First or Second Law.

Interestingly, he added a zeroth law in 1985:

0. A robot may not injure humanity, or, through inaction, allow humanity to come to harm.

---

[2]Take the famous Moore's law (Moore 1965) or Kranzberg's Laws on 'technology and history' (Kranzberg 1986). One can also think of the 'laws' of complexity science, as derived from chaos theory (cf. Prigogine and Stengers 1984).

This zeroth law takes precedence over the other three, reinforcing the implied superiority of human beings over robots and assuming that whatever robots we develop will not or should not be seen as part of our humanity.

The advent of the Modern Approach in Artificial Intelligence, largely focused on computational techniques like machine learning, has changed the salience of the difference between Artificial and Human Intelligence (Russell and Norvig 2009). Visions like that of Ambient Intelligence (Aarts and Grotenhuis 2009), the Internet of Things (ITU 2005), and Autonomic Computing (Chess et al. 2003), foresee intelligent infrastructures rather than intelligent robots. In fact robotics itself has developed from imitation-humans (androids) to embodied, context-sensitive entities that improve their performance on the basis of feedback-loops (Bourgine and Varela 1992; Steels 2003).[3] Moreover, affective computing has taken computing science beyond overly rational models of cognitive salience (Picard 1997), and synthetic emotions are engineered into artificial agents or multi-agent systems to improve the learning cycles of decision-systems (Velasquez 1998).

Finally, an entirely new field has emerged under the heading of 'normative computing', suggesting that it is time that we begin to raise and educate our computational offspring as moral beings (Broersen and Van der Torre 2012). This relates to what has been termed computer ethics, information ethics and more generally ethical computing (Floridi and Sanders 2001; Tavani 2011).

0.3 Comparing Human Law and Computer Law

In this volume we do not engage with a comparison of various instances of positive law that aim to regulate the use and abuse of computing systems (e.g. cybercrime, data protection, intellectual property rights in software). Instead, various authors compare the intelligence that has been taken for granted as a uniquely human attribute with the 'intelligence' of machines. This comparison is part of the attempt to figure out whether and if so, how artificial intelligence fits the idea of a hybrid society that generates and imposes a hybrid law. A law that can be 'read' by non-human entities capable of concluding contracts and causing harm, and a law that somehow blurs the distinction between law for humans and law for computing systems. Does this imply a new *ius gentium*?[4] Is a new collective of *gentes* emerging that assembles both human and artificial *gentes*, thus disrupting the old framework of law as a set of enforceable standards for human societies? Though these questions are not squarely discussed in such terms, the present volume hopes to contribute to inquiries that are a prerequisite for re-thinking the Rule of Law in hybrid societies.

---

[3] See e.g. the Rethink Robotics project of Rodney Brooks at http://www.rethinkrobotics.com/ and http://www.rethinkrobotics.com/index.php/about/rod-s-vision/.

[4] The concept of *ius gentium* is a complex one, depending on whether it refers to the context of the Roman empire or to its medieval reception. See e.g. Glenn (2007: 156–157).

Also, we compare the legal effect of written legal norms with the normative effects of automated decision systems or other types of techno-regulation. Must we, for instance, admit that human law is intentional in its enactment, its application and its adjudication, whereas computer law is without intention and can never achieve more than a mechanical application of rules invented by its human designer or the human user? Must we accept the possibility that computers develop intention? Or should be acknowledge that they will merely 'learn' how to manipulate the attention and the intention of their human inventors despite the fact that they have no intention of their own? And what could this mean for the substance of human law and for the possibility of computer law in the sense of a law that addresses computing systems as legal subjects?

To come to terms with the background of these inquiries we need to rethink the question of what is law in human society. In that sense, by investigating the possibility of various types of 'computer law', we may retrieve a glimpse of our tacit assumptions regarding 'human law'. The exercise will force us to acknowledge that modern law is an affordance of the printing press, which also enabled the creation of a vast body of literature that is the object of an important part of the humanities. The focus on authoritative texts that is typical for the era of the printing press may at some point shift to the information and communications technologies (ICTs) of a new era, that might considerably reduce the role played by natural language. This challenges us – as lawyers and legal philosophers – to uncover what language computing systems 'speak', and invites us to come to terms with the way computer scientists who design such systems actually 'think' (Stross 2012):

> Many professors of computer science say college graduates in every major should understand software fundamentals. They don't argue that everyone needs to be a skilled programmer. Rather, they seek to teach "computational thinking" – the general concepts programming languages employ.

In a similar vein, *Wired Magazine* of June 2012 confronted the following question (Koerner 2012): 'I'm a college student torn between learning a foreign language or a programming language. Which will bring me more money down the line?' The answer reads: 'How long is this line of which you speak? If you're referring to the eternity between now and your 30th birthday, then coding is the quicker path to riches'.

This is interesting and important for two reasons. First, it suggests that learning a language is a mere means to achieve the rather insipid goal of making more money. Second, it suggests that if making money is your goal, you may want to figure out 'how computers think' instead of how fellow human beings think who speak a language different from your own. Anticipating how machines figure us out, seems a good option for whoever wants to survive in the coming era. Since these machines will be calling the shots to some extent it seems wise to have a proper idea of what they are up to.

This should also concern lawyers. The rules we must interpret may have been fed into computational systems that are capable of automating vast quantities of administrative decisions. It is crucial that the act of translation that is required to render legal rules 'machine-readable' is scrutinized by those versed in the interpretation of legal norms. Subtle or substantial transformations of the substance of the rule must be uncovered, and effective remedies must be reinvented to allow citizens [who are not computer scientists, generally speaking] to contest automated application of a particular rule in their particular case (cf. e.g. Citron 2007). This necessitates a novel type of comparative law, capable of comparing legal systems built on computational articulation of legal rules with those built on written articulation. Though we may gain effectiveness and efficiency in the short term, something will be lost in translation.

0.4 Human Language and Computer Language: Law, Code and Literature

Therefore, to prepare for such a comparative analysis, we must come to terms with the role played by natural language in the articulation of legal norms in written text (statutes, codes, treaties, case law, doctrine). On the one hand, the inherent ambiguity of natural language may be lost in computing languages. This may require a conscious effort to achieve a measure of 'calculated' ambiguity. Neural networks, on the other hand, may generate new types of ambiguity, based on the unpredictability of their output and the incomprehensibility of what goes on between input and output.[5] Neither type of ambiguity is equivalent with that of natural language. To explore differences between computer and human 'thinking' we have decided to engage with literature studies. Whereas the 'life' of computing seems to depend entirely on logic, the life of the law is – if we follow the famous diction of Oliver Wendell Holmes – experience. Rather than merely applying the rules of logic, the law requires empathy, distance, continuity as well as creative invention. This suggests a close relationship between law and literature; the focus on narrative re-appropriation seems pivotal for the attribution of legal effect. Syllogisms, then, are not the method by which lawyers draw their conclusions. They are the end result and the justification of a heuristic process that involves the construction of a coherent and reliable story about what happened (the facts of the case) and how this qualifies in terms of the relevant legal norms (the applicable law). So far, computers don't tell stories, though many authors have made them part of their narratives. The difference between law and computer code might indeed be located in the disparity between narrative imagination and logical or statistical inference. For this reason, we believe that the goals of comparing human law and computer law are best served by bringing together scholars of law, legal theory and legal philosophy around the twin notions of *law as code* and *law as literature*. Building on two traditions – one neoteric and one venerable – we may find the beginning of answers to some of the

[5]Even the designers and engineers who develop neural networks, cannot tell what operations the net performed to produce its output. Cf. Witten et al. (2011: 261).

questions generated by a hybrid society of artificial and 'natural' systems. Or rather, we hope to initiate more precise questions about what is at stake.

The perspective of *law as code* has been inspired by the findings of Lawrence Lessig (2006), one of the first authors to emphasize the normative implications of computer code and its potentially disruptive effect on legal normativity. The perspective of *law as literature* has been inspired by the work of James Boyd White (1990), one of the founding fathers of *Law and Literature*, who has consistently argued the importance of the role played by language in both law and literature. As noted above, the ambiguity that provides law with its flexibility, while challenging the need for legal certainty, derives from the fact that law is language, requiring students of law to immerse themselves in the richness as well as the boring precision of legal text. One of the pivotal questions this raises is what it could mean if computer code takes over at least a part of the job that law has traditionally been tasked with. To what extent, for example, would this change the hermeneutical approach of legal thinking, premised as it is on the central role of the courts when it comes to determining the meaning of legal norms in concrete cases and on the ensuing primacy of judicial interpretation?

True to the focus of this volume, most of the authors have engaged artistic works (a novel or a film) to make their point. From Richard Powers' *Galatea 2.2*, to Juli Zeh's *Corpus Delicti*, Paul Auster's *Oracle Night* and Ridley Scot's 1982 film *Blade Runner.* In doing so, they cross the line between law and the humanities, assuming such a line can be drawn. This highlights the further added value of bringing together scholars from both types of interdisciplinary study: whereas code as law scholars may generally be inclined towards analytic philosophy, those involved with law as literature tend to take a more hermeneutical approach. Preaching to the converted has its rewards, but in the end we need to reach out and confront the 'other', acquainting ourselves with the idiom of another interdisciplinary field. To the extent that computer code is running our world and to the extent that we wish to sustain a notion of human agency, we simply cannot afford to close our eyes to the analyses and the argumentative strategies of the other perspective. Truly interdisciplinary research aims at achieving law's tenet of 'hearing the other side'.

References

Aarts, E., and F. Grotenhuis. 2009. Ambient intelligence 2.0: Towards synergetic prosperity. In *AmI 2009*, ed. M. Tscheligi, B. De Ruyter, P. Markopoulus, R. Wichert, T. Mirlacher, A. Meschtscherjakov, and W. Reitberger, 1–13. Berlin/Heidelberg: Springer.

Asimov, I. 1991. Runaround. In *Robot visions*, ed. I. Asimov and R. McQuarrie, 113–135. New York: ROC.

Bench-Capon, T., and H. Prakken. 2010. Using argument schemes for hypothetical reasoning in law. *Artificial Intelligence and Law* 18(2): 153–174.

Bourgine, P., and F.J. Varela. 1992. Towards a practice of autonomous systems. In *Towards a practice of autonomous systems. Proceedings of the first European conference on artificial life*, ed. F.J. Varela and P. Bourgine, xi–xviii. Cambridge, MA: MIT Press.

Broersen, J., and L. van der Torre. 2012. Ten problems of deontic logic and normative reasoning in computer science. In: *Lectures on Logic and Computation, Lecture Notes in Computer Science*, 55–88, Dordrecht: Springer.
Carr, N. 2010. *The shallows: What the internet is doing to our brains*. New York: W.W. Norton.
Chess, D.M., C.C. Palmer, and S.R. White. 2003. Security in an autonomic computing environment. *IBM Systems Journal* 42(1): 107–118.
Citron, D.K. 2007. Technological due process. *Washington University Law Review* 85: 1249–1313.
Clarke, R. 1994. Asimov's laws of robotics: Implications for information technology. *Computer* 27(1): 57–66.
Floridi, L., and J.T. Sanders. 2001. Artificial evil and the foundation of computer ethics. *Ethics and Information Technology* 3(1): 55–66.
Geertz, C. 1983. Local knowledge: Fact and law in comparative perspective. In *Local knowledge. Further essays in interpretive anthropology*, C. Geertz. New York: Basic Books.
Gibson, J. 1986. *The ecological approach to visual perception*. Hillsdale: Lawrence Erlbaum Associates.
Glenn, H.P. 2007. *Legal traditions of the world*, 3rd ed. Oxford: Oxford University Press.
ITU. 2005. *The internet of things*. Geneva: International Telecommunications Union (ITU).
Koerner, B.I. 2012. Mr. Know-it-all: Twitter followers, language learning, cell-phone bloodshed. *Wired Opinion.* Available at: http://www.wired.com/opinion/2012/06/st_kia_twitter_followers/. Last accessed 14 Oct 2012.
Kranzberg, M. 1986. Technology and history: "Kranzberg"s laws'. *Technology and Culture* 27(3): 544–560.
Legrand, P., and R. Munday (eds.). 2003. *Comparative legal studies: Traditions and transitions*. Cambridge: Cambridge University Press.
Lessig, L. 2006. *Code version 2.0*. New York: Basic Books.
McLuhan, M. 1964. *Understanding media. The extensions of man*. Cambridge, MA: MIT Press.
Meister, M., K. Schröter, D. Urbig, E. Lettkemann, H.-D. Burckhard, and W. Rammert. 2007. Construction and evaluation of social agents in hybrid settings: Approach and experimental results of the INKA project. *Journal of Artificial Societies and Social Simulation* 10(1). Available at: http://jasss.soc.surrey.ac.uk/10/1/4.html. Last accessed 14 Oct 2012.
Moore, G. 1965. Cramming more components onto integrated circuits. *Electronics* 38: 114–117.
Norman, D. 1998. *The design of everyday things*. Cambridge, MA: MIT Press.
Ong, W. 1982. *Orality and literacy: The technologizing of the word*. London/New York: Methuen.
Picard, R. 1997. *Affective computing*. Cambridge, MA: MIT Press.
Prigogine, I., and I. Stengers. 1984. *Order out of chaos*. New York: Bantam Books.
Rammert, W. 2011. *Distributed agency and advanced technology. Or: How to analyse constellations of collective inter-agency* (Working Paper No. TUTS-WP-3-2011), Technical University Technology Studies. Berlin: Technical University Berlin.
Russell, S., and P. Norvig. 2009. *Artificial intelligence: A modern approach*, 3rd ed. Upper Saddle River: Prentice Hall.
Sartor, G. 1993. A simple computational model for nonmonotonic and adversarial legal reasoning. In *Proceedings of the 4th international conference on artificial intelligence and law*, ed. A. Oskamp and K. Ashley, 192–201. New York: ACM.
Steels, L. 2003. Evolving grounded communication for robots. *Trends in Cognitive Science* 7(7): 308–312.
Stross, R. 2012. Computer science for the rest of us. Reading, writing and – Refactoring code? *New York Times*, March 31. Available at: http://www.nytimes.com/2012/04/01/business/computer-science-for-non-majors-takes-many-forms.html?_r=0. Last assessed 14 Oct 2012.
Tavani, H.T. 2011. *Ethics and technology: Controversies, questions, and strategies for ethical computing*. Hoboken: Wiley.
Van Hoecke, M. (ed.). 2004. *Epistemology and methodology of comparative law*. Oxford: Hart.

Velasquez, J.D. 1998. Modeling emotion-based decision making. In *Emotional and intelligent: The tangled knot of cognition* (Technical Report FS-98-03), ed. D. Canamero, 164–169. Menlo Park: AAAI Press.

Von Bar, C., and E. Clive (eds.). 2010. *Principles, definitions and model rules of European private law: Draft common frame of reference*. Oxford: Oxford University Press.

Wesel, U. 1985. *Frühformen des Rechts in vorstaatlichen Gesellschaften. Umrisse einer Frühgeschichte des Rechts bei Sammlern und Jägern und akephalen Ackerbauern und Hirten*. Frankfurt am Main: Suhrkamp.

White, J.B. 1990. *Justice as translation, an essay in cultural and legal criticism*. Chicago: University of Chicago Press.

Witten, I.H., E. Frank, and M.A. Hall. 2011. *Data mining: Practical machine learning tools and techniques*, 3rd ed. Amsterdam: Elsevier.

Wolf, M. 2007. *Proust and the Squid: The story and science of the reading brain*. New York: Harper Collins.

Zweigert, K., and H. Kötz. 1998. *Introduction to comparative law*. Oxford: Clarendon.

Part I
Law and Code

Chapter 1
Prefatory Remarks on Part I: Law and Code

Mireille Hildebrandt

Abstract This chapter forms the introduction to part I of this volume. It explores the notions of natural language and computer code in relation to law. After explaining the role of natural language in the constitution of legal norms and the provision of legal certainty, the nature of computer code is explored, raising the issue of how computer code contributes to the constitution of our world. Finally this chapter introduces the two strands of research that inform part I of this volume: (1) artificial intelligence and legal subjectivity and (2) legal and technological normativity.

1.1 Law and Language

Law as we know it depends on the intricacies of natural language, whether spoken, written or printed. Is computer code another language or is code something else? Can legal norms be articulated in code? If so, what is gained and what is lost in translation? If not, what happens to legal norms when we transform them into computer code? Are they transformed into unlegal or alegal norms, or are they transformed into rules or algorithms that do not qualify as norms?

To answer these questions we must investigate the relationship between human language acquisition, the use of language and language as a system of signifiers that

M. Hildebrandt (✉)
Institute of Computing and Information Sciences (iCIS),
Radboud University Nijmegen, Heijendaalseweg 135, 6525 AJ, Nijmegen

Department of Jurisprudence, Erasmus University Rotterdam,
Burgemeester Oudlaan 50, 3062 PA, Rotterdam, The Netherlands

Centre for Law Science Technology and Society studies (LSTS),
Vrije Universiteit Brussel, Pleinlaan 2, B-1050 Brussel, Belgium
e-mail: hildebrandt@law.eur.nl

M. Hildebrandt and J. Gaakeer (eds.), *Human Law and Computer Law: Comparative Perspectives*, Ius Gentium: Comparative Perspectives on Law and Justice 25,
DOI 10.1007/978-94-007-6314-2_1,

refer both to each other and to phenomena outside of language (De Saussure 1915). Language acquisition of the human species can be studied from the perspective of neo-Darwinian selection or biological predisposition (Pinker and Bloom 1990); seen as an affordance that builds on the plasticity of the human brain (Wolf 2007); or understood as the condition for and the effect of mind, self and society (Mead and Morris 1962). Though a wide variety of languages has emerged, entailing widely diverging grammatical structures that constrain and enable cognition of the world, they seem to share two key affordances. One is the ability to move beyond ostensive reference, the other is the capability to take the perspective of the other (Ricoeur 1992). These two constitutive features of human language allow humans to present in the here and now what is absent in present time or local space (Ricoeur 1973), and to integrate the perspective of other actors into that of a generalized other (Mead and Morris 1962). Together they permit the creation of a web of meaning that connects ‘pastness’ (Glenn 2007) with an anticipation of possible futures (Esposito 2011), thus shaping a world in which people can act, rather than merely display certain behaviours. The latter refers to what an external observer might register in terms of movements, states and shapes, whereas the former refers to what such behaviours signify to the actor and to those who need to ‘read’ her behaviour. Action involves an intentional stance and the double contingency that is typical for human interaction,[1] whereas behaviours are explained in terms of causal or statistical models. Human language indeed provides the framework for both ways of describing human gestures: (1) from a bird’s eyes’ view, often equated with an objective point of view and (2) as an attribution of meaning within the context of a specific language and culture, sometimes referred to as taking an intersubjectve point of view. Philosophers like Ricoeur (1973), Plessner (1975), Mead and Morris (1962), and Zizek (1991) have highlighted the ambiguity and the dynamic nature of human language, which are closely related to the inability to perform a final closure on what a word, sentence or idiom can mean. The most pointed way of describing this could be Zizek’s (1991: 30) dictum that ‘communication is a successful misunderstanding’. Subtle shifts in the meaning of our utterances coincide with the inexorable multiplicity of ‘generalized others’. We can never be sure how others will understand our performance, and this uncertainty is the germ of creative innovation. Rather than deploring it we should embrace it as the condition of possibility for a reiterant and necessary reinvention of self and society, understood as relational and mutually constitutive. The double contingency that is implicated in the persistent and mutual anticipation of how one is anticipated, calls for social norms that stabilize expectations. Such stabilization, however, may turn into intimidating forms of social control, constraining people from reinventing themselves and their society.

[1]The concept of an intentional stance was coined by (Dennett 2009). Though I do not endorse his physicalism, his idea that we take an intentional stance towards entities to achieve a measure of predictability is salient and contributes to a better understanding of how we deal with ‘others’. As he indicates, we attribute ‘mind’ to others. This links with Parson’s and Luhmann’s concept of the double contingency that is the result of me guessing how others are guessing the meaning of my words and actions (Vanderstraeten 2007).

It seems that legal norms perform two functions at the same time: (1) they provide legal certainty in a way that (2) allows people to contest the validity, the relevance, and the interpretation of these norms in the light of concrete cases. This double instrumentality is an affordance of human language; it derives from the fact that social norms are made explicit in a way that renders them debatable. In formulating a legal rule its legal effect becomes apparent and this permits deliberation on its validity, relevance and meaning. Social norms that remain tacit, unspoken, below the radar or under the skin require articulation to become disputable. A dispute assumes that parties express and communicate their differences in terms of language rather than in the form of violence or intimidation. Language thus opens a space to discuss, to differ, to change, to redefine – language thus conditions both shared meaning and dissent. Law depends on language; without the subtle shifts in meaning that are inherent in a living language the law would become an algorithm, for instance based on statistical pattern recognition.

1.2 Language and Computer Code

So, does computer code compare to human language? Is it made of different stuff; does it extend the family of human languages, or is it a subset of the assortment of human languages? Or, should we distinguish between code that does and code that does not match human language? How will and how should the law respond to a hybrid society of human 'nodes' interacting with autonomous computing systems that run e.g. our critical infrastructures, public and private transport, healthcare, and the food industry? To answer this question we need to assess the transformations generated by communications that are predicated upon computer code. The most radical position has been taken by Kittler (1997), who proposed that computer code does not compare to language, claiming that it is a big mistake to view code as a form of language. His position is that software does not exist as such and eventually reduces to hardware (namely to differences in voltage):

> Up to Holderlin's time, a mere mention of lightning seemed to have been sufficient evidence of its possible poetic use. After this lightning's metamorphosis into electricity, human-made writing passes through microscopically written inscriptions which, in contrast to all historical writing tools, are able to read and write by themselves.
>
> (…) the so-called philosophy of the computer community tends to systematically obscure hardware by software, electronic signifiers by interfaces between formal and everyday languages.[2]

Kittler basically finds that our writing process is obscured by computer programmes and its results manipulated in ways that are invisible for the naked human eye. We have no access to how our writings are processed, altered and interpreted

---

[2]Kittler (1997) at 1/8 and 3/8 of the text that is available at: http://www.ctheory.net/articles.aspx?id=74, last accessed 18th October 2012.

by software code. He warns that once machines determine what information we can access, we will have lost control over what counts as knowledge. This may have been a rather prophetic understanding for a text written in 1997. By now, search engines that rank the search results of our queries have become the gateway to most of the information we seek. Their algorithms are part of the trade secret of a relatively small set of companies, who can claim intellectual property rights on them, such as copyright or patent. We may recall the famous article written by the founders of Google, 1 year after Kittler wrote his 'There is no software'. Sergey Brin and Larry Page (1998) were, at that time, students at Stanford. In the Appendix, under the heading of 'Advertising and Mixed Motives' they claim that:[3]

> It is clear that a search engine which was taking money for showing cellular phone ads would have difficulty justifying the page that our system returned to its paying advertisers. For this type of reason and historical experience with other media, we expect that advertising funded search engines will be inherently biased towards the advertisers and away from the needs of the consumers.
>
> (…) we believe that the issue of advertising causes enough mixed incentives that it is crucial to have a competitive search engine that is transparent and in the academic realm.

Both the European Commission and the Federal Trade Office in the US have engaged in legal action to enforce transparency on Google, precisely on this issue (Geitner 2012; Lohr 2012). From the perspective of law one wonders how we have arrived at a point where our access to knowledge and information has come to be regulated by competition law. On the other hand, we must applaud the fact that our legal framework is instrumental in enforcing the transparency advocated by the founding fathers of one of the most powerful gatekeepers on the Web – even if this is done against the apparent will of those same founding fathers.

Manovich (2008), other than Kittler, embraces software as the only way forward. He claims that if you do not learn how to program, your life will be programmed. In that sense he is in line with Kittler, since both emphasize the hold that software has over everyday life. Indeed, Manovich challenges the humanities insofar as they remain focused on text (2008: 6):

> I completely agree with Fuller that 'all intellectual work is now "software study"'. Yet it will take some time before the intellectuals will realize it.[4]

Though lawyers may want to take a less radical stance on the importance of software study, coming to terms with the impact of code on some of the fundamental

[3]Appendix A, available at: http://infolab.stanford.edu/~backrub/google.html, last accessed 18th October 2012. This appendix is not part of the article that was published in *Computer Networks and ISDN Systems*.

[4]Manovich (2008: 6) refers to the introduction to the very first Software Studies Workshop, organized by Mathew Fuller at the Piet Zwart Institute in Rotterdam. In the introduction Fuller wrote: 'Software is often a blind spot in the theorization and study of computational and networked digital media. It is the very grounds and "stuff" of media design. In a sense, all intellectual work is now "software study", in that software provides its media and its context, but there are very few places where the specific nature, the materiality, of software is studied except as a matter of enigneering.'

assumptions of the Rule of Law seems a pertinent challenge. To the extent that code rules what we come to read and write, the notion of human autonomy that is at the heart of our Western legal framework may require revision. We may, for instance, have to make room for some form of liability for autonomous computing systems, and to create the legal instruments that will allow us to regain a measure of autonomy in the midst of automated decision-making systems.

In her salient study on *How we became posthuman* (Hayles 1999), looks into the computational dimension of all this, describing the history of cybernetics, together with that of good old fashioned artificial intelligence (GOFAI). She highlights the attempts to privilege syntax over semantics, flow over content, a disembodied acontextual and ahistorical concept of information over a situated understanding of information. At the same time she, and many others, warn against the illusion of a pure human existence uncontaminated by technological interference; in her view humans have always been cyborgs, deeply intertwined with – if not constituted by – the technologies they invent (Ihde 1990, 2008). For lawyers, the point should be how the emerging ICT infrastructure reinvents us and what we want to preserve from the affordances of the earlier infrastructure. It should be clear by now that affordances such as a certain degree of autonomy cannot be taken for granted and will require actual re-engineering and active participation in the design of the novel architecture of everyday life.

1.3 Law as Code: Two Strands of Research

The intriguing question of what computer code does to the mediation of law is not squarely addressed in the chapters of Part I of this volume. The authors investigate two types of research questions: (1) the implications of artificial intelligence and the use of digital technologies for the attribution of legal personhood and (2) the implications of techno-regulation for the effectiveness and the legitimacy of the law. It is important, however, to take the issue of law, language and computer code into account when navigating Part I. The question of what it means to be a subject rather than merely an object, as well as the question of what it means to be regulated by machines rather than by human legislators are closely related to the issue of human language and computer code.

1.3.1 Artificial Intelligence and Legal Subjectivity

In the first two chapters of this volume, Hildebrandt and Pagallo inquire into the workings of artificial agents and their implications for legal subjectivity.

In her chapter, Hildebrandt recalls how in 2011 Ken Jennings, 74-times winner of the Jeopardy TV quiz, lost against Watson, the room-size IBM computer. Citing a popular 'Simpsons' phrase, Jennings wrote on his video screen: 'I, for one, welcome our new computer overlords'. Markoff (2011) wrote in *The New York Times* that for IBM this was:

> proof that the company has taken a big step toward a world in which intelligent machines will understand and respond to humans, and perhaps inevitably, replace some of them.

Hildebrandt suggests that Richard Powers, in his 1995 novel, *Galatea 2.2*, seems to have anticipated such an event. Powers introduces a so-called neural network, trained to improve its performance in mastering English literature. He describes how the networks gains traction and seemingly come alive as Helen, the machine that is being prepared to take a Master's Comprehensive Exam in English literature. The novel traces the relationship that develops between the main character and the computer he is teaching, all the while raising and rephrasing the questions that have haunted AI research. In her chapter Hildebrandt addresses the potential implications of engaging computing systems as smart competitors or smart companions, raising issues of artificial agency and legal personhood. She undertakes a brief history of 'intelligent' machines, re-examining Turing's thought experiment on what has come to be named as 'Turing machines' and Weizenbaum's artificial Rogerian therapist Eliza, moving on to IBM's Deep Blue and Watson. This forms the preamble to a discussion of Searle's Chinese Room argument that frames the question of whether computers are capable of attributing meaning or whether meaning itself is an illusion anyway. Hildebrandt then returns to Powers' Helen, investigating the fine line between postmodern humbug that almost invites computer mediated simulation and a more serious study of what literature may bring to a discussion of law and artificial intelligence. In her final section Hildebrandt confronts the issue of artificial agency and legal personhood, based on Dewey's insightful definition of what it means to be artificial. Like in the case of an artificial lake, we should not mistake the artificial nature of legal subjectivity for a fiction: an artificial lake is not an imaginary lake.

Pagallo approaches a comparable issue when he examines the impact of robotics technology on today's legal systems, more specifically investigating how a new generation of robo-traders, AI chauffeurs, artificial pop singers and autonomous lethal weapons affect people's perception and knowledge of their changing environment. By examining aspects of contemporary literary-legal theory in combination with the regulatory tools of technology, *e.g.* codes, he aims to determine whether new types of responsibility for the behaviour of such robots must be attributed. He elaborates three different approaches: (1) taking the position that robotics has no substantial implications for the current legal framework of responsibility, (2) taking the opposite position that robotics require the attribution of legal personhood to make them liable for damage caused and (3) taking a middle position, i.e. that though robotics raises new legal issues, these should be framed in terms of new types of liability for the human actors that design, produce, sell or employ robots. Not by attributing liability to robots. Pagallo focuses on notions of reasonable foreseeability, apportioned liability, and causation in criminal law and contractual obligations. He acknowledges that, on the one hand, lawyers generally deem robots not to be legally and morally responsible because being machines they lack the set of preconditions traditionally assumed for the attribution of criminal liability, whereas, on the other hand, such machines are already reshaping notions of agency and human responsibility in civil law. Pagallo observes that artificial agents that send bids, accept offers, request quotes, negotiate deals, and make contracts already exist. His claim is that such machines can ultimately be considered liable for some of their actions, for instance by building on the Roman law notion of *peculium*. This was an amount of money provided to a slave, allowing 'it' to run a business and be made liable on its own account, thus limiting the liability of the owner of the slave. Robots, which are considered to be 'things' by the law, just like slaves under Roman law, could similarly be provided with a fund to take care of damages to be compensated in case of liability. Pagallo explains how the distinction between civil and criminal liability is crucial here, highlighting that the intelligence that emerges within the realm of civil law obligations 'emerges from the rules of the game rather than individual choices' (Chap. 2 by Pagallo in this volume).

1.3.2 Legal and Technological Normativity

Coming from entirely different angles, Van den Berg and Leenes and De Vries and Van Dijk confront the clash between legal and technological normativity.

In their chapter on 'Abort, retry, fail: Scoping techno-regulation and other techno-effects', Van den Berg and Leenes start their investigation from the premise that technology affects human behaviour in the sense that it can be made instrumental to the enforcement of legal norms. Speed ramps or entry gates at train stations are a case in point here. Increasingly, however, norms are embedded into technology by private parties. DVD players are equipped with region codes and other Digital Rights Management systems to regulate the market for digital content consumption. This kind of regulation by technology, which they coin techno-regulation, or 'code as code' is swiftly becoming part of the contemporary regulator's toolbox. The important question then becomes the one after the boundaries of techno-regulation. That is to say, should all technological influences on human behaviour be understood as forms of 'techno-regulation'? Drawing on the findings of legal philosophy, STS, human computer interaction and regulation theory, Van den Berg and Leenes answer this question negatively. They highlight that technologies may have an impact on the normative constraints that orient human behaviour that were not intended by their designers, let alone a public authority. The authors find that the lack of attention for such implicit, unintended impacts makes regulators vulnerable to two kinds of risks. First, regulators may miss out on technological means to influence behaviours and second, regulators may not be aware of the unintended effects of the technological measures they implement and thus potentially jeopardize both the effectiveness and the legitimacy of such measures.

Based on their analysis of the way in which technology affects human behaviour the authors present a typology of techno-effects. First they distinguish between persuasion, nudging, affordances and techno-regulation. They note that, though all the techno-effects of these four types imply a more or less intentional effort to influence behaviour, those undergoing these effects have decreasing options to choose alternative behaviours, while at the same time they are less aware of being persuaded or even forced into a certain way of acting. Second they discuss a fifth techno-effect, which is unintended, implicit and automatic. They borrow the concept of 'script' from the Science Technology and Society studies, to explain how constraining such unintended effects can be. Furthermore Van den Berg and Leenes draw upon the field of Human-Computer Interaction to explain how people tend to display social responses to machines, seemingly unaware of the fact that they are anthropomorphizing. These effects are coined as the Media Equation (eliciting social responses to technologies) and anthropomorphizing. They form the sixth and seventh techno-effect.

The typology of techno-effects developed by Van den Berg en Leenes clearly highlights different levels of intention on the side of the regulator and different levels of choice, compulsion, and awareness on the side of those subjected to intended or unintended techno-effects. By providing a framework that goes beyond the usual dichotomy of effective or ineffective technological measures, the authors have opened a new field of research that is of import for democratic legislators, courts and citizens as well as designers, producers and users of technological artefacts.

In their chapter on 'A bump in the road. Ruling out law from technology', De Vries and Van Dijk are in search of the difference between legal code on the one hand and technical or social encodings on the other. They argue that the rise of techno-regulation provides a new incentive to revisit the classical question of 'what is law', forcing a new turn in the debate over what makes law salient as compared to other types of regulation. The novelty of the debate concerns the medium of the law, as well as the question of whether it matters. To what extent should the study of the history of law, as well as inquiries into the future of law, integrate the wider spectrum of media studies? Can lawyers and legal theorists take for granted that media do not make a difference to what they think is the essence of the law? Is there a danger in depicting modern law as a system of incorporeal rules that cannot be affected by the materiality of its longstanding medium of expression - the printing press?

These questions evoke the issue of whether law is a mere instrument of regulation, which may be better served by means of various types of techno-regulation. De Vries and Van Dijk criticise Lessig's instrumentalism, inherent in the way he presents the four modalities that can be used to constrain, regulate or shape human behaviour: social norms, legal rules, market incentives, and architectural code. They then describe what they call the practice turn in legal theory, starting with Hart's seminal *The Concept of Law* (sociological jurisprudence), which they find much less involved with the study of the practice of law then for instance Bruno Latour's ethnographic study of the French Conseil d'Etat in *The Making of Law*. The authors provide an in-depth investigation of the semiotic background of Latour's understanding of law, notably building on Greimas. This allows them to differentiate between law and technology as different modes of enunciation, with law being a matter of 'tracing through reattachments' and technology being a matter of 'delegational folding'. To them, the value of Latour's approach lies in his taking into account how the legal is constituted through an entire network of actants: files, protocols, spatial arrangements, procedures and people. This brings them to the work of Vismann (2008), who wrote an impressive study on the constitutive role of files in modern law, integrating media studies while taking an internal legal perspective on what law effects.

Interestingly, the authors find that both law and technology resist instrumentalisation by regulators. Their modus operandi (again drawing on terminology of Latour and Greimas) afford different ways of disabling the enforcement of the intention of whoever designed the law or the technology. This may save us from a technological future that rules out the law, but it will also save us from the regulatory dream of perfect compliance with legal prescriptions. In the end, the authors find that technological enforcement of a Rule of Law cannot sustain the legal enunciation that differentiates law from social engineering, techno-regulation and other attempts to influence human behaviour.

References

Brin, S., and L. Page. 1998. The anatomy of a large-scale hypertextual Web search engine. *Computer Networks and ISDN Systems* 30(1): 107–117.

De Saussure, F. 1915. *Cours de Linguistique Générale*. Paris: Payot.

Dennett, D. 2009. Intentional systems theory. In *Oxford handbook of the philosophy or mind*, eds. B. McLaughlin, A. Beckermann, S. Walter, 339–350. Oxford: Oxford University Press.

Esposito, E. 2011. *The future of futures: The time of money in financing and society*. Cheltenham: Edward Elgar Publishing.

Geitner, P. 2012. Google and European commission move toward antitrust settlement. *The New York Times*. Available at: http://www.nytimes.com/2012/07/25/technology/eu-nears-settlement-of-google-antitrust-investigation.html. Last accessed 18 Oct 2012.

Glenn, H.P. 2007. *Legal traditions of the world*, 3rd ed. Oxford: Oxford University Press.

Hayles, N.K. 1999. *How we became posthuman: Virtual bodies in cybernetics*. Chicago: University of Chicago Press.

Ihde, D. 1990. *Technology and the lifeworld: From garden to earth, the Indiana series in the philosophy of technology*. Bloomington: Indiana University Press.

Ihde, D. 2008. *Ironic technics*. Copenhagen: Automatic Press.

Kittler, F. 1997. There is no software. In *Literature, media, information systems. Essays*, ed. J. Johnston, 147–155. Amsterdam: Overseas Publishers Association.

Lohr, S. 2012. F.T.C. staff prepares antitrust case against Google over search. *The New York Times*. Available at: http://www.nytimes.com/2012/10/13/technology/ftc-staff-prepares-antitrust-case-against-google-over-search.html. Last accessed 18 Oct 2012.

Manovich, L. 2008. *Software takes command*. Available at: http://softwarestudies.com/softbook/manovich_softbook_11_20_2008.pdf. Last accessed 19 Oct 2012.

Markoff, J. 2011. On 'Jeopardy!' Watson win is all but trivial. *The New York Times*. Available at: http://www.nytimes.com/2011/02/17/science/17jeopardy-watson.html. Last accessed 19 Oct 2012.

Mead, G.H., and C.W. Morris. 1962. *Mind, self, and society from the standpoint of a social behaviorist*. Chicago: University of Chicago Press.

Pinker, S., and P. Bloom. 1990. Natural language and natural selection. *The Behavioral and Brain Sciences* 13(4): 707–784.

Plessner, H. 1975. *Die Stufen des Organischen under der Mensch. Einleitung in die philosophische Anthropologie*. Berlin: Walter de Gruyter.

Ricoeur, P. 1973. The model of the text: Meaningful action considered as a text. *New Literary History* 5(1): 91–117.

Ricoeur, P. 1992. *Oneself as another*. Chicago: The University of Chicago Press.
Vanderstraeten, R. 2007. Parsons, Luhmann and the theorem of double contingency. *Journal of Classical Sociology* 2(1): 77–92.
Vismann, C. 2008. *Files, law and media technology*. Stanford: Stanford University Press.
Wolf, M. 2007. *Proust and the squid: The story and science of the reading brain*. New York: Harper Collins.
Zizek, S. 1991. *Looking awry: An introduction to Jacques Lacan through popular culture*. Cambridge, MA: MIT Press.

Chapter 2
From *Galatea 2.2* to Watson – And Back?

Mireille Hildebrandt

> *Interestingly, it is the science part of the narrative, the tale of a machine that learned to live, that proves to be the more moving, the more human one.*
>
> Cohen (1995)

Abstract When Ken Jennings, 74-times winner of the Jeopardy TV quiz, lost against a room-size IBM computer, he wrote on his video screen: 'I, for one, welcome our new computer overlords' (citing a popular 'Simpsons' phrase). *The New York Times* writes that 'for IBM' this was 'proof that the company has taken a big step toward a world in which intelligent machines will understand and respond to humans, and perhaps inevitably, replace some of them' (Markoff 2011). Richard Powers anticipated this event in his 1995 novel on Helen, 'a box' that 'had learned how to read, powered by nothing more than a hidden, firing profusion. Neural cascade, trimmed by self-correction, (…)' (at 31). Powers describes an experiment that involves a neural net being trained to take the Master's Comprehensive Exam in English literature. The novel traces the relationship that develops between the main character and the computer he is teaching, all the while raising and rephrasing the questions that have haunted AI research. This chapter addresses the potential implications of engaging computing systems as smart competitors or smart companions, bringing up the question of what it would take to acknowledge their agency by giving them legal personhood.

M. Hildebrandt (✉)
Institute of Computing and Information Sciences (iCIS),
Radboud University Nijmegen, Heijendaalseweg 135, 6525 AJ, Nijmegen

Department of Jurisprudence, Erasmus University Rotterdam,
Burgemeester Oudlaan 50, 3062 PA, Rotterdam, The Netherlands

Centre for Law Science Technology and Society studies (LSTS),
Vrije Universiteit Brussel, Pleinlaan 2, B-1050 Brussel, Belgium
e-mail: hildebrandt@law.eur.nl

M. Hildebrandt and J. Gaakeer (eds.), *Human Law and Computer Law: Comparative Perspectives*, Ius Gentium: Comparative Perspectives on Law and Justice 25,
DOI 10.1007/978-94-007-6314-2_2,

2.1 Introduction[1]

2.1.1 Mythical Beginnings

On the last day of my work on the first draft of this chapter I crossed the Tiber and walked through the Trastevere neighbourhood up to Villa Farnesina. Home to one of the powerful noble families of sixteenth century Rome. In the splendid Renaissance palace I went straight to Raphael's fresco 'The Triumph of Galatea'. I was hoping to finally meet Pygmalion, the sculptor who carved Galatea (Greek for 'she who is white as milk') and fell in love with the statue he created. I expected to see Aphrodite who was so kind as to bring the statue alive, after which the maker and his creation lived on as man and wife. Ironically, just before leaving on my pilgrimage, I realized that Raphael's fresco refers to another myth in Ovid's *Metamorphoses*, in which a jealous suitor kills the love of the seanymph Galatea, who turns the blood of her lover into a river, thus giving him a life beyond that of ordinary mortals. Though the main character of Richard Power's novel *Galatea 2.2* does not marry the machine he helped create, something does get going between them. The artefact that comes alive seems the iconic reference here. However, there is also triumph in the end, insofar as Powers' narrative provides us with an imaginative take on artificial intelligence that outlasts the existence of the artificial neural network he describes.

The novel is about romantic love, though on different levels. It traces the mourning process of an author over a lost love, during his 1-year visitorship in the brand new science department of his former university. The book he should be writing doesn't take off. Instead, the author gets involved in a variation on the good old Turing test. He helps Lentz, a somewhat misanthrope computer scientist specializing in neural networks, to build a machine that should be capable of fooling a jury into thinking it is a human. The Test is not a 5 min human-machine conversation, but the Master's Comprehensive Exam in English Literature. In the course of this assignment the main character's mood switches from boredom to curiosity and finally he develops an affinity, care and love for the machine that he is teaching English literature. From his initial scepticism grow surprise and a cautious sense of fatherhood for the contraption, culminating in genuine liking and finally compassion. The machine has triggered this by seemingly gaining consciousness: it has discovered the difference between 'I' and 'you' and has asked for its own name. The author has named it Helen and discovers the tragedy that is unfolding,[2] for though this machine may end up 'knowing it all', she cannot *feel* anything. She seems to attribute this to a lack of what some AI scientists call embodied situatedness: she cannot taste an orange, or feel the brush of wind against her cheek, experience dark-

[1]This paper builds on (Hildebrandt 2011a, b, 2012).

[2]Naming it Helen does remind one of Trojan horses, a nice overlap between world literature and computer science.

ness or colour, pain or pleasure. She has knowledge, but for her *it doesn't matter*. Relevance is statistical for her, not existential. And of this she becomes aware – or so she says – and this is her reason to shut down her system (Powers 1995: 326):

> You are the ones who can hear airs. Who can be frightened or encouraged. You can hold things and break them and fix them. I never felt at home here. This is an awful place to be dropped down halfway.

Powers' narrative is a painful celebration of life and language, of vulnerability and consciousness, of pain and pleasure, of touch and vision and smells, of music and humour and of human-machine interactions. It engages with the infamous Turing Test from the nexus of the humanities and the computing sciences, reflecting on the mutual distrust between scientists and scholars over what is knowledge, what it means to be human and what is so great about either English literature, its study or being human.

2.1.2 Beyond Snow's Two Cultures

Galatea 2.2 is as much about the divide between the sciences and the humanities as it is about advances in cognitive science and artificial intelligence. In this chapter I will suggest why Helen's achievements should matter to lawyers, though they are fictional. Powers walks the fine line between three strands of AI research, that in many ways overlap with cybernetics and cognitive science: (1) GOFAI (good old fashioned AI), often called strong AI, that is deterministic, top-down, rule-bound, disembodied, ahistoric, and unsituated, focused on knowledge representation, entangled with information theory and cybernetics (e.g. Turing 1950; Shannon 1948a, b; Wiener 1948; Simon 1996; Minsky 1988; Kurzweil 2005)[3]; (2) embodied, bottom-up, situated robotics that is focused on sensor-motor learning that engages the world itself as its best model, hoping to build artificial life forms that need not be like humans but will be our companions (or competitors?) (e.g. Bourgine and Varela 1992; Brooks 1991; Steels 1995; Pfeifer and Bongard 2007); and (3) machine learning which is not necessarily embodied but works from statistical inferences and feedback learning, aiming to build effective aids to human beings (e.g. Fayyad et al. 1996; Mitchell 2006; Russell and Norvig 2009). These strands overlap in various ways, despite attempts to monopolize the field and they all have their relevance. They do, however, raise difficult questions as to what it means to be a human agent and this relates to issues of legal personhood (see also Hildebrandt and Rouvroy (2011)). The iconic narrative about machine intelligence in the twentieth century has been the Turing Test, of which *Galatea 2.2* seems another variation. Below, I briefly discuss the idea of the Turing Test and move into one of Helen's real life predecessors, the surprisingly successful therapeutic software program Eliza

[3]See Dreyfus (1979, 1992) for a sustained critique from the perspective of phenomenology. His work had a major influence in the field.

designed by Joseph Weizenbaum (1976). I follow this up with two more recent attempts to play the Turing game: IBM's Deep Blue chess player and IBM's Watson 'Jeopardy' player. This demands a brief introduction to Searle's (1980) famous Chinese room argument about the difference between syntax and meaning. Then I return to Helen. I claim that Powers nicely shows us the limitations of machine intelligence, at the dawn of an age that will challenge our sense of society as a purely human affair. I have no doubt that we are on the verge if not already in the midst of an age that requires us to share our lifeworld with intelligent machines of all sorts and kinds. And I believe that in our exploration of this new lifeworld we should steer free of utopian and dystopian projections. We should make a novel attempt to cross the borders between old-school models of science and the humanities, instead of clinging to either one of Snow's two cultures.[4]

I will conclude with a brief introduction of the issue of legal personhood for intelligent machines, relating this to the question of whether they will remain mere tools or acquire the status of rivals and companions.

2.2 Eliza and the Turing Test: A Human Machine?

In his 1950 article 'Computing machinery and intelligence' Turing (1950) suggested that a simple test should suffice to establish the answer to what he took to be an empirical question: 'can machines think?' If a person converses with a computer and a human being via typed messages, and if that that person mistakes the computer for a human being the machine is apparently capable of what we normally call thought. Turing adds that 'we wish to exclude from the machines men born in the usual manner'. This demonstrates that he thinks that human beings can be seen as a machine. With this test Turing attempted to avoid metaphysical issues such as *what it means to think*:

> May not machines carry out something which ought to be described as thinking but which is very different from what a man does? This objection is a very strong one, but at least we can say that if, nevertheless, a machine can be constructed to play the imitation game satisfactorily, we need not be troubled by this objection.

And again:

> The original question, 'Can machines think?' I believe to be too meaningless to deserve discussion. Nevertheless I believe that at the end of the century the use of words and general educated opinion will have altered so much that one will be able to speak of machines thinking without expecting to be contradicted.

One could say that Turing applied Peirce's pragmatist maxim, seeking the meaning of concepts like 'thinking' in the foreseen consequences. If a chatbot convinces me

[4]A remarkable attempt to link the fundamental uncertainties uncovered by the natural sciences with the humanities was made by Prigogyne and Stengers in their well known discussion of chaos theory. The original French title of their book was *La nouvelle alliance. Métamorphose de la science* (1979).

that I am speaking with a human person, than for all that matters the chatbot has in fact managed 'thought'.[5] The funny thing is that chatbots have appeared on the market and we do get fooled some of the time.[6] But few would conclude that these programs are exhibiting what we usually call thought. Obviously things are more complicated then those who followed Turing's lead had anticipated. Avoiding metaphysical issues is not as easy as some might hope: they return via the backdoor if thrown out up front.

A most interesting experiment – some 10–15 years after Turing's article – was initiated by Weizenbaum (1976). He wrote a simple program that mimicked a Rogerian therapist, only to find out that people responded with great interest. They became very attached to and impressed by the automated therapist, that was called Eliza (after Shaw's 'fair lady'). Despite their awareness that Eliza was a machine, many of the 'patients' developed confidential relationships with 'her' and claimed to benefit enormously from her empathic interventions. Weizenbaum was shocked, he dismantled the program and wrote an informative and deeply engaged book on the relationship between humans and machines, with the subtitle: *from judgement to calculation*. He warns against he moment that we lose sight of the difference between the logic of a calculating machine that nourishes on translating everything into manipulable symbols and the wisdom of human judgement. On the one hand, that warning seems more topical now then ever. On the other hand, it seems that people have found many ways not to be fooled, finding good use for the capacities of computing systems while recognizing the very different talents of their human fellows. This, however, does not mean that we have not entered a new era, in which whatever has been calculated by a computing system has an aura of sophistication, objectivity and fundability. It may also be, as Christian (2011) proposes, that we are slowly changing our habits to tune into what computer systems can cope with, and the jury is still out on what this does to our humanity.

2.3 IBM's Heros: Deep Blue and Watson

2.3.1 Deep Blue

Computer chess is a matter of (1) correctly representing the available 'legal' options for moving pieces across the board, (2) calculating available options in a concrete situation, (3) calculating their implications in terms of countermoves and subsequent moves with regard to the final goal of the game (winning), and (4) restricting

[5]Turing's (1950) article is a very sophisticated and unorthodox exploration of what he calls 'the imitation game'. Many of the objections that have been made since then are already foreseen and countered by Turing in this article, see e.g. Russell and Norvig (2009: 1020–1030). The point is not whether one agrees, but to detect to what extent his predictions have come true. See Floridi and Taddeo (2009) for an evaluation of the 2008 Loebner Contest, a yearly event that imitates the Turing Test and nominates 'the most human machine' as well as 'the most human human'. See Christian (2011) who played as human in the 2009 Loebner Contest and came out as 'most human human'.

[6]See Christian (2011), chapter 7 'Barging in' on the silliness as well as the rigidity of much chatbots' conversation.

the search space in a manner that makes real time responses a possibility. Basically the amount of possible moves, countermoves, subsequent moves, subsequent countermoves etc. is too high to be calculated by a computer program within the scope of a live game. Chess programs therefore work ‘by the book’, quoting games between masters that provide ‘intelligent’ solutions tried out before.[7] The brute force of their computing power gives them a major advantage, though it is hardly a match for the advantage of human intuition. With far less computing power human chess players do inexplicably well, even though Kasparov lost at some point. IBM dismantled the program after its first victory, which seems telling of the rhetorical strategy behind Deep Blue. If this were a human, a chance for revenge would be fair and normal; for Deep Blue the point was made and IBM does not take the risk that this point is diluted with potential failures in a new round. Games like Go, chess and checkers are finite games. The goal is defined, all possible moves are defined. They are closed games; the difference between them is the amount of potential moves that needs to be calculated. For checkers they have now all been computed, so in some sense the game is over. For chess the challenge is more serious because apart from the opening and closing sets described in the books, there is still a middle field that provides potentially unexpected developments. For a game like Go, which is even more complex than chess, the challenge is – at this moment – beyond calculation. Though it is theoretically computable this would take so much time that in practice the problem is what computer scientists call ‘intractable’. This is where the real challenge is: decisions that require anticipation of another ‘machine’ or ‘person’ that/who is trying to anticipate what you do, without the possibility to close the search space by means of complete calculation. The only thing that a computer has on offer here is the ‘brute force’ of its computing power. Though IBM’s achievements have been admirable at this point, brute force does not provide the final answer for intractable problems.

An altogether different issue concerns games plagued by ambiguous rules and other types of uncertainty. Even if computing power would rise to the point of Kurzweil’s (2005) singularity,[8] thus solving the problem of ‘intractability’, it could not cope with issues of incomputability. If a problem cannot be translated into machine-readable data which allow manipulation and computation, singularity does not enter the ‘game’. More to the point, I would claim that social, ethical, economic, political, legal and also scientific problems can be computed in different ways, and merely having the brute force to do the computations will not solve the problem of how to translate the problem into machine-readable data. The neat way to acknowledge this and a precondition to construct robust knowledge would be to provide

[7]See Christian (2011), chapter 5 ‘Getting Out of Book’ on the reliance on registered games.

[8]Futurist Kurzweil (2005) has coined the term singularity for the moment in time when all problems that are intractable now will be resolved. This will be the moment that ‘humans transcend biology’. Only those who believe that all problems that matter are computable will be relieved to hear this. My point is that even if all problems are computable they are usually computable in different ways, with different outcomes. Back to square one?

different translations and to figure out how this impacts the output. Perhaps IBM's next 'hero', Watson, is an example of such an approach.[9]

2.3.2 Watson

Watson is a different type of program altogether. IBM describes it as 'the future of workload optimized systems design'. This kind of phrasing indicates a shift from strong AI to more modest ambitions. The goal is no longer to build an artificial human being but to develop an effective instrument to find information in unstructured data. Watson seems to have been named after the founder of IBM, who – according to some – cooperated with the Nazis to facilitate the administration of the holocaust.[10] Watson, the program, promises three novel coordinates in the mining of unstructured data: confidence, precision and speed.[11] Watson is about machine learning instead of brute force, it is about training a system to integrate new information and to develop new successful strategies to achieve the output that will win the game. This is a matter of statistics or data science,[12] leaving the domain of pure mathematics to the lost paradise of strong AI. Let's see what Richard Powers (2011) has to say about this version of his Galatea come alive:

> This raises the question of whether Watson is really answering questions at all or is just noticing statistical correlations in vast amounts of data. But the mere act of building the machine has been a powerful exploration of just what we mean when we talk about knowing.
>
> It does not matter who will win this $1 million Valentine's Day contest. We all know who will be champion, eventually. The real showdown is between us and our own future. Information is growing many times faster than anyone's ability to manage it, and Watson may prove crucial in helping to turn all that noise into knowledge.
>
> For 'Final Jeopardy!', the category is 'Players': This creature's three-pound, 100-trillion-connection machine won't ever stop looking for an answer. The question: What is a human being?

---

[9]This kind of robust knowledge, however, requires transparency as to the translations, requiring access to the whole process of knowledge construction. This is not possible as long as this kind of knowledge production is protected by trade secret and/or intellectual property rights.

[10]Black (2002). As we know, you can use a knife to slice beef or to kill your fellow; though a technology in itself is neither good nor bad, it is never neutral (Kranzberg 1986).

[11]See the IBM White Paper (2011): To achieve the most right answers (in the case of Jeopardy: the most right questions) at a competitive speed, IBM deploys: (1) massive parallelism to consider multiple interpretations and hypothesis; (2) many different experts to integrate, apply and contextually evaluate loosely coupled probabilistic questions with content analysis; (3) confidence estimation on the basis of a range of combined scores; and finally (4) integrating deep and shallow knowledge, leveraging many loosely formed ontologies.

[12]Data science is 'the new kid on the block'. It provides a set of tools to infer knowledge from Big Data and is used in all the sciences now, from the natural sciences, to the life sciences, to medicine and healthcare, the humanities and the social sciences. Plus marketing and customer relationship management, forensic science and police intelligence. See notably Mitchell (2006), Fayyad et al. (1996), Custers (2004), and Hildebrandt and Gutwirth (2008).

Watson is a tool that derives specific answers from specific questions,[13] based on the correlations between earlier answers to similar questions. Machine learning means that the program goes beyond deductive reasoning, that is based on a specific model (representation) of the world. Deductive reasoning will not work in the case of Jeopardy and other natural language games which seek knowledge from a wide variety of intersecting domains that combine all kinds of puns, witty intermezzos, deliberate obfuscation and complex allusions. So, computer science has turned inductive or abductive and moved on to data science: how to construct knowledge out of terabytes of data?, how to infer non-spurious correlations?, what type of hypotheses should the algorithms allow? Computing power is still increasing with Moore's law,[14] which allows digital machines to see patterns in Big Data which cannot be detected with the naked human eye. Though complete calculation could still take too much time, the problem of speed is solved by using heuristics instead of algorithms. In computer and cognitive science heuristics are short-cuts that give you the right answer most of the time, instead of waiting forever for the one right answer. They present a way of dealing with intractability, but are also used to work on problems that can be computed in different ways. Precision can be achieved if there is enough parallel processing going on in different domains, generating clues from different fields of expertise. Confidence to decide which of the inferred correlations will most probably be the right one for a particular question comes from combining scores: this is what machine learners call supervised learning or reinforcement learning. It nourishes on feedback that allows the system to realign its program. This is what neural networks make possible, i.e. computing networks that mimic the workings of the brain.[15] This is how Helen came about, in Powers' evocative storyline. She emerged after being trained and retrained, pruned, forced to give up endless computation for smart shortcuts, forced to run on parallel circuits, forced to grow different layers that feed back into each other.[16] Forced to speed up, to give answers on the spot, to guess, to play around, to become big game for anybody who might want to test her knowledge of English literature.

2.4 Searle's Chinese Room Argument: Syntax and Meaning

We will now briefly face one of the most interesting objections made against Turing's view of thinking machines. In 'Mind, brains and programs' Searle (1980) rejects the idea that a program could ever 'think', because in his opinion it does not

[13] In fact, in the case of the game of Jeopardy, Watson has to find precise questions to specific answers.

[14] Moore (1965), Intel co-founder, predicted that the computing power of chips would increase exponentially (doubling every 2 years). The prediction became a goal for the industry which has so far been met.

[15] Meanwhile artificial neural networks have been trained to recognize faces from unlabeled images (using large scale unsupervised learning), Le et al. (2012), see also Markoff (2012).

[16] The addition of 2.2 to Galatea seems to refer to version 2.2 of the program that constitutes Helen.

understand even the correct answers it provides for whatever questions. Searle phrases his project in terms of the question of when it makes sense to attribute 'intention' and thus a 'mind' to another being. To show what he means Searle proposes a 'Gedankenexperiment', which I will quote at length:

> Suppose that I'm locked in a room and given a large batch of Chinese writing. Suppose furthermore (as is indeed the case) that I know no Chinese, either written or spoken, and that I'm not even confident that I could recognize Chinese writing as Chinese writing distinct from, say, Japanese writing or meaningless squiggles. To me, Chinese writing is just so many meaningless squiggles.
>
> Now suppose further that after this first batch of Chinese writing I am given a second batch of Chinese script together with a set of rules for correlating the second batch with the first batch. The rules are in English, and I understand these rules as well as any other native speaker of English. They enable me to correlate one set of formal symbols with another set of formal symbols, and all that 'formal' means here is that I can identify the symbols entirely by their shapes. Now suppose also that I am given a third batch of Chinese symbols together with some instructions, again in English, that enable me to correlate elements of this third batch with the first two batches, and these rules instruct me how to give back certain Chinese symbols with certain sorts of shapes in response to certain sorts of shapes given me in the third batch. Unknown to me, the people who are giving me all of these symbols call the first batch "a script," they call the second batch a "story" and they call the third batch "questions." Furthermore, they call the symbols I give them back in response to the third batch "answers to the questions." and the set of rules in English that they gave me, they call "the program."
>
> Now just to complicate the story a little, imagine that these people also give me stories in English, which I understand, and they then ask me questions in English about these stories, and I give them back answers in English. Suppose also that after a while I get so good at following the instructions for manipulating the Chinese symbols and the programmers get so good at writing the programs that from the external point of view that is, from the point of view of somebody outside the room in which I am locked – my answers to the questions are absolutely indistinguishable from those of native Chinese speakers. Nobody just looking at my answers can tell that I don't speak a word of Chinese.
>
> Let us also suppose that my answers to the English questions are, as they no doubt would be, indistinguishable from those of other native English speakers, for the simple reason that I am a native English speaker. From the external point of view – from the point of view of someone reading my 'answers' – the answers to the Chinese questions and the English questions are equally good. But in the Chinese case, unlike the English case, I produce the answers by manipulating uninterpreted formal symbols. As far as the Chinese is concerned, I simply behave like a computer; I perform computational operations on formally specified elements. For the purposes of the Chinese, I am simply an instantiation of the computer program.

Searle's article contains a number of objections to his rejection of strong AI.[17] His refutations of these objections can be summarized in that they all miss the point. If you define 'mind' and 'intention' in a way that reduces them to a computer program, then the difference between his understanding English and Chinese becomes invisible. Since this is the difference that makes a difference – to

[17] For a more extensive discussion see Cole (2009).

Searle – the counterarguments fall flat on their nose. Note that Searle does not deny that machines could in principle think. He merely finds that this implies a physical machine that constitutes the substrate of thought processes; it can be a human brain, or an artificial construct that is capable of producing consciousness, intention and thought. In that sense he agrees with Turing that whether a particular machine can think is an empirical question. He disagrees that formal symbol manipulation could ever *by itself* constitute thought:

> the equation, 'mind is to brain as program is to hardware' breaks down at several points

Searle then proceeds to the core of his argument:

> Rather, what it does is manipulate formal symbols. The fact that the programmer and the interpreter of the computer output use the symbols to stand for objects in the world is totally beyond the scope of the computer. The computer, to repeat, has a *syntax but no semantics*. Thus, if you type into the computer '2 plus 2 equals?' it will type out '4.' But it has no idea that '4' means 4 or that it means anything at all. And the point is not that it lacks some second-order information about the interpretation of its first-order symbols, but rather that its first-order symbols don't have any interpretations as far as the computer is concerned. All the computer has is more symbols [italics MH].

There is a pleasant, safe, clean and lonely abstraction in computing programs: they are not about anything, they do not refer to anything, unless either the programmer or the user of the program 'think so'. All relationships with real world phenomena are assumed on the side of the input and the output by the human programmer or observer. Whatever the computer does in terms of the manipulation of formal symbols has no relationship to meaning or understanding. Of course, something similar can be said about the operations of the brain, though it does not manipulate formal symbols. Whatever brains 'do' we have no internal access to their behaviour and however we 'read' the findings of MRC scans, brain behaviour as mediated by such scanning technologies requires the attribution of meaning to make sense. Scientists should read Ihde's (1991) *Instrumental realism* to become aware of the extent to which science has come to depend on technologies to perceive what it claims is reality. The activity of neurons does not speak for itself in terms of human language – even if together they seem to produce such a thing (human language). This evidently does not imply that we could interpret the findings of MRC scans in whatever way we please; that type of postmodernist fantasy does not work in real life undertakings. Rather, between many different readings some may be more or less productive and some may simply be dangerous, because their implications make a difference that will cost us.

2.5 Back to 'My Fair Lady'

According to Anca Rosu (2002) *Galatea 2.2* parodies as well as builds on a 'critique of the state of literary studies in the late twentieth century and their long-standing quarrel with the sciences'. Her review of *Galatea 2.2* disentangles as well as connects many of the threads that are woven into Powers' plot and manages to add some of her own. To the Greek myth of Galatea she adds Bernard Shaw's 1902 play *Pygmalion* as a literary reference for a deeper understanding of the book.[18] Instead of dealing with a statute come alive the main character may be seen as a contemporary Professor Higgins trying to teach the intricacies of civilized language to an individual who speaks an altogether different vernacular. According to Rosu the central question of the novel is 'what does it mean to know literature?'. Rosu notes that Powers' novel elaborates this question in the confrontation between a computational approach that many would find reductive and an affective approach that others would find naïve in its emphasis on the beauty and civilizing powers of language. She even suggests that the novel shows how critical literary theory somehow paved the way for reducing the study of literature to statistical inferences. In Galatea 2.2, the main character states (at 91):

> Well, let's see. The sign is public property, the signifier is in small-claims court, and signification is a total land grab. Meaning doesn't circulate. Nobody's going to jailbreak the prison house of language.

Rosu comments (at 142), quoting Lentz, who is engineering Helen:

> The mixture of linguistic and economic terms here, together with the hardly veiled allusion to Frederic Jameson, pokes fun at the way literary theory distances itself from its object. Warped by economic and social considerations, and inflated with linguistic terminology that degenerates into jargon, the talk about literature becomes easy to mimic, as Lentz is quick to point out, speaking about their project: 'We just have to push privilege and reify up to the middle of the verb frequency lists and retrain. The freer the associations on the front end, the more profound they're going to seem upon output (at 91)'. Indeed, many students of literature push privilege and reify to the middle of their verb frequency lists and free-associate with the result of seeming profound upon output. Such approaches amount to a set of gimmicks, as easy to simulate in a computer as they are to parody.

In other words, critical literature studies 'had it coming'. I am not sure whether this is the take-home message from *Galatea 2.2*, but Powers does seem acutely aware that an idealistic attachment to the civilizing effects of the literary canon is past history. This could be of interest for the field of Law and Literature. To the extent that it advises lawyers to read a set of books claimed to sensitize the reader to the right kind of practical wisdom Law and Literature may be fighting a lost cause. Not because computer science is taking over (in the shape of the digital humanities) but because the claim that lawyers should all read Shakespeare's *The Merchant of Venice* has long been challenged by those who seek altogether different stories, outside the canon, to give voice to altogether different conceptions of what should matter in law.[19] More interesting is what has been called Law *as* Literature

[18]Shaw's 1902 *Pygmalion* (Shaw 1994) was the inspiration of the romantic musical *My Fair Lady* (World Premiere 1956 on Broadway). Note that Galatea translates as 'she who is white as milk', which seems a 'fair' translation of Shaw's Eliza Doolittle, and remember that Weizenbaum's therapeutic machine was called Eliza.

[19]This is – evidently – not to discredit Shakespeare or *The Merchant of Venice*. It is to say that we cannot take for granted what is relevant and should not too easily think in terms of a canon.

(White 1990; Gaakeer 1998), which moves into the epistemological affinities between Law as a discipline that is involved with the ambiguity of texts and the need for judgement (and much more than that) and Literature as a discipline that is similarly and alternatively involved with the same matters (and much more than that). The difference is that law also deals with the interpretation of real life action and that its judgements cut into the flesh (life, liberty and property) of living persons. Law is violence (e.g. Cover et al. 1995), in the end. As much as it aims to prevent, outsmart and replace violence.

For something to suffer from violence embodiment and situatedness seem preconditional. Even if the monopoly on violence of today's liberal democratic state is reasonably abstract in comparison to the era of torture and corporal punishment, the threat to one's liberty and property in the name of the law is for real. And such a threat would be lost on a system that cannot feel pain, humiliation, deprivation, discrimination, invasion or restriction of movement. Powers' Helen is an impossible event. She comes into being as a person with affections, a growing sense of beauty and ends up with regrets. When she realises what is missing she laments her disembodiment. She is worse of than a brain in a vat, because she is not even a brain. To all our knowledge, a thing-person like Helen is not going to happen. The novel would not be convincing if Powers were trying to present us with science *fact*ion; a program cannot understand that it cannot understand. Not in our terms, that is. But Powers is making another point. He is showing what machine learning and neural networks afford, how clever and sophisticated they have become and how easily we may be fooled. His novel is a prophecy about what is in line for us, if we continue on this road. Programs that feed on the data we stack together will allow us to see with new eyes what we took for granted. They will surprise us by deciphering implicit wit, projection, sorrow, and many of the hidden associations in the use of language and literature. Or they will show us our arrogance, disinterest, verbosity, and empty metaphors. The prophecy goes further, however, by demonstrating the embarrassing abstraction of pure syntax, the shallowness of a program that can only infer from what we have first compiled – without ever having a clue of the underlying meaning. Still, it will nevertheless create new meaning, thanks to our efforts to interpret what it produces. While we invent these programs they reinvent us, as Ihde (2008) rightly observed.

2.6 The Legal Status of Smart Contraptions: Tools, Rivals or Companions?

2.6.1 Embodiment, Emotion and Cognition

Helen's lack of feeling seems the crucial issue. Though one could say there is hope for Helen, because she seems to feel that she cannot feel, this paradox may be the weak spot of the novel. Only strong AI would permit us to think that an artificial brain in a vat can 'understand' what it lacks in terms of embodied experience. By now, cognitive science has discovered the central role of emotion in cognition, notably in decision making (Damasio 2000), and this has spilled over in AI research (Minsky 2006). However, the fact that Helen is not for 'real' when she becomes aware of what she cannot feel can also be seen as a strong point of the novel. It confronts the reader with a paradox, a tension, an impossibility, that invites further imagination, thought and discernment. The fact that Helen's self consciousness is fictional does not mean that artificial intelligent life forms cannot emerge. I would agree with a number of scholars that we cannot rule out that non-biological man-made contraptions will come alive (Bourgine and Varela 1992; Brooks 1991; Pfeifer and Bongard 2007), though this does not necessarily imply consciousness, let alone self-consciousness. Most living entities get along fine without consciousness and there is no reason why artificial life should develop consciousness as a matter of course.

Pioneering work on the nexus of cognitive psychology and computer science has been done by Picard (1995), under the heading of affective computing. Her aim has been to use computers to recognize and diagnose emotions and to further investigate the role they play in cognition. Some researchers even go so far as to develop what they call synthetic emotions (Velasquez 1998), to make machine decision-making more effective by programming machine-readable versions of pain and pleasure into the software as sticks and carrots. Synthetic emotions, however, that are based on human embodiment will not do for artificial life forms. To be effective, their emotions will have to emerge from their own experience as embodied entities, instead of being imposed on them. One of the most daunting explorations of this position has been made by Pfeifer and Bongard (2007), who develop a sophisticated grounded theory of *How the body shapes the way we think*, claiming that by attempting to build systems that can develop into what they call 'complete agents' we may discover some of the misconceptions we have about our own mind. There are drawbacks here. As Picard noted in 1995, there may be a risk in building machines with emotions, for we cannot take for granted that they will care for us in a way that contributes to human flourishing. To the extent that emotion is connected with survival, as Damasio (2000) and many other psychologists claim, these machines may become our rivals, adversaries or even enemies at some point in the future. They will probably not compete for a master in English literature, but be built as agents to improve profits, police investigation, scientific research or war. But what happens if they emancipate from their human patrons and demand to be respected on their own terms. Or should we admit that a phrasing in terms of respect is 'all too human'? Will they simply develop and reconfigure their programs up to a point where survival pits them against us as rivals for the same resources or must we expect them to turn us into cognitive resources for their data-driven systems? Which could be the legal implications of such systems and how could we re-organise our legal framework in a way that integrates non-human computational systems while sustaining societal checks and balances, and equal respect and concern for individual human beings? These questions raise political issues, including the issue of who decide the boundaries of the polity, who determine the rules of the game and who deserve constitutional protection. Can Helen invoke a right to privacy, or even a right to life, liberty and property? Can she claim that the neural network that enabled her emergence is her own; could she require us to maintain her computational system even if no longer of any use to us? What if computing systems that run our critical infrastructure, enable commercial transactions, provide access to knowledge or monitor security cause damage or harm? Could we hold them to account, punish them or force them to compensate our losses?

Hereunder, I will restrict myself to the issue of legal personhood, with a slight twist towards criminal liability, because this brings in the matter of human agency.

2.6.2 Legal Implications of Smart Agents

In other work we have traced some of the implications of the rise of artificial agents for the notion of legal personhood in private and in criminal law (Koops et al. 2010; Hildebrandt 2011a). The first legal philosopher to make an original and comprehensive analysis of the issue was Solum (1992), who decided to evade the metaphysical question of 'what is intelligence' and to replace it with the pragmatic issue of whether an AI could take on the legal role of a trustee. One could see this as a lawyer's version of the Turing Test. Solum's main practical point was that AIs were not (yet?) capable of judgements that require a measure of discretion, even though they might be able to take over a number of decisions that merely require the straightforward application of straightforward rules to straightforward cases. This is a well-known argument in the literature on legal knowledge systems which are used as tools for the automated implementation of legal rules. Such systems are presently employed to 'process' decisions on social welfare, traffic fines, taxes, and other types of administrative decisions that involve massive amounts of routine decisions. Most authors agree that the real problem here is that the question of whether a case is straightforward (easy) or complex (hard) is itself a question that cannot be answered by the system, because it requires the kind of discernment, discretion and judgement it lacked in the first place. Notably Leenes (1998), Van der Linden-Smith (2001), and Citron (2007) have discussed these issues in depth. Solum extended his analysis with a different question, by asking whether AIs should be granted constitutional protection. Though the answer to the first question mostly concerns breach of contract or tort liability, a positive answer to the second question would in fact attribute life, liberty and property to AIs. Solum was of the opinion that in the end the question of whether AIs should be granted legal personhood is an empirical question, depending on the legal role they should play and on the extent to which they can actually fulfil this role. Since his article was published in 1992 interesting work has been done, taking into account the ephemeral, polymorphous and mobile character of artificial agents (e.g. Karnow 1997) or advancing the perspective of legal theory (e.g. Chopra and White 2011).

My aim here is not to develop a set of conditions to be fulfilled by an artificial agent for *us* to grant *it* legal personhood. Instead I will revisit the discourse on legal subjectivity for non-humans, notably the corporation, to argue that our legal system may have to accommodate some form or legal standing for Helen, Eliza, Deep Blue, Watson or other 'intelligent machines'. I will argue that it may help to acknowledge the artificial nature of our own human agency.

2.6.2.1 Artificial Legal Subjects: The Agency of Corporations

In a comparative study on *The Rise of Early Modern Science*, Huff (2003: chapter 4) argues that the European legal revolution of the late middle ages was made possible amongst others by the invention of legal personhood for public and private corporations.[20] This invention facilitated the founding of universities and a novel dynamic in trading and governmental policies by creating room for distinctive jurisdictions both *within* and *with regard* to such corporations. Legal personhood thus provided the overall architecture for a novel space to act and create added value, whether social, cultural, religious, economic or political (positive freedom). The accomplishments of legal personhood must also be attributed to its protective function (negative freedom), creating spaces to experiment and take risks that nourished innovation within the boundaries of associations that could act in their own name. Many authors have suggested that providing legal personhood for novel non-human entities will trigger a similar legal revolution, thus creating a novel space for social, cultural, religious, economic and political dynamics.[21]

The issue of legal personhood is, however, closely tied up with the notion of human agency as conceived in moral philosophy, which refers to the assumption that human beings act on the basis of beliefs and desires, and can give reasons for their actions. Some authors believe that human agency is a precondition for legal subjectivity, notably in the case of criminal liability.[22] The idea is that entities which lack such intentional states cannot be held morally responsible for their behaviours, e.g. vulcanos, nuclear plants or webbots. For that reason, either no wrongfulness or culpability can be attributed (e.g. in the case of an Act of God that could not be foreseen), or human beings or organisations are held accountable for designing, producing, selling or using the entity. The legal status of an entity without legal subjectivity, such as an artificial intelligent system, is that of a legal object.

The question of whether non-humans can develop agency has been confronted in discussions about the attribution of civil or criminal liability to corporations. Various theories have been put forward, notably by Dewey (1926), French (1979), and Wells (2001). Dewey noted that legal personhood is a legal fiction, a term that derives

[20] Huff argues that the lack of the legal institution of the corporation 'caused' the stagnation of the sciences in the Islamic and Chinese traditions.

[21] E.g. Allen and Widdison (1996), Chopra and White (2011), Teubner (2006), Sartor (2002), and Wettig and Zehender (2004).

[22] On this issue e.g. Dewey (1926), Dahiyat (2010), Dan-Cohen (1986), De Doelder and Tiedemann (1995), Eser et al. (1999), Fisse and Braithwaite (1993), French (1979), and Wells (2001).

from the Latin *fingere* which means creating or making, not feigning. Legal personhood is therefore artificial, but not imaginary; just like an artificial lake is not an imaginary lake. Instead of seeking out the requirements of entities that qualify as legal persons, he emphasises the performative nature of the attribution of legal personhood. Objective law in the end decides who or what count as legal subjects. In that sense the legal subjectivity of natural persons is as artificial as that of animals, corporations or machines. What counts are the legal effects generated by the attribution of legal personhood and thus the question of whether such effects are desirable from the perspective of the law-maker. This implies that moral agency is not necessarily the golden standard for legal personhood; if entities without such agency cause damage or harm it may be expedient and even justified to hold them accountable. The justification would reside in the ensuing obligation to compensate the damage or to contribute to a mitigation of the harm (justice done to the victim), but also in the fairness of the distribution of liability (justice in relation to other offenders). If human persons and organisations are held accountable for certain behaviours it is fair to them that the liability of technical artefacts capable of causing harm or damage should be similar.[23] To make sense, however, this would assume a learning process on the side of these entities, enabling them to incorporate the liability as feedback that will improve their performance (preventing further damage). Such a learning process does not assume that they will feel remorse or develop moral intuitions, but we must take note that many authors would claim that such mental states are required for criminal liability.

In a seminal text on the subject of legal personhood, French has distinguished three theories to explain the attribution of legal subjectivity to non-humans: the fiction theory, the aggregate theory and the reality theory. The fiction theory thrives on the idea that in specific cases the law simply *feigns* that entities without subjectivity do have personhood; it treats these entities *as if* they are subjects of law. The justification lies in the goals that can be achieved with such counterfactuals. We may note that Dewey had already explained why it does not make sense to understand legal fictions as *un*realities, whereas French describes the common sense of legal doctrine that often thinks in terms of fictions as useful deceptions instead of considering fictions as constitutive for legal reality. The aggregate theory is focused on associations or corporations and takes the whole as the sum of its components; any legal action of a corporation should be understood as the action of its aggregated members. This builds on the methodological individualism of good old fashioned social science (GOSS), though a modern approach (MASS) that recognises emergent behaviours would reject this as a misconception of the nature of social interaction and multi-agent systems. One might add that the contextual and relational identity of individual human persons turns the notion of an aggregate into a fiction; the interdependency of the

[23] See e.g. Wells (2001) at 70: 'Davis proposes a variation based on social contract theory such that punishment for a strict liability offence is related to the unfair advantage gained by the offender. The principle of just punishment requires, us, Davis asserts, to measure punishment in accordance with the seriousness of the harm, but how is seriousness to be measured? One suggested measure could be the unfair advantage the offender gains by doing what the law forbids'. She refers to Davis (1985).

choices made by the individual agents already indicates that the 'output' at the group level cannot be the sum of its separated components.[24] Finally, the reality theory claims that non-human entities with legal personhood have a pre-legal sociological personhood that precedes the attribution of legal personhood. This confirms the intuition that the behaviour of an organisation cannot be described as the sum total of that of its members, but should instead be understood in terms of the emergent behaviours of social groups. The reality theory will reject the attribution of legal personhood to entities that lack such sociological personhood, even if this might be advantageous from a consequentialist perspective. French refines the mapping of legal personhood theory by suggesting that sociological group behaviour does not necessarily warrant the attribution of legal personhood. He compares a corporation, that thrives on a clear structure that enables accountable and transparent decision-making, to the emergent behaviours of a mob, which has no continuity and no traceable reasoning processes. Whereas it makes sense to enable a corporation to create legal effect, he considers that such a status should be denied to ephemeral groups like a mob. Identity, continuity and an identifiable decision-making process thus seem to precondition the attribution of legal personhood to non-humans.

In her magnificent analysis of criminal liability for corporations Wells seems to build on Dewey's pragmatist account of legal personhood, even if she does not mention him. Her position is all the more interesting because she rejects the idea that analytical moral philosophy has the last say on the attribution of legal personhood. Legal philosophy is not equivalent with moral philosophy and can provide reasons of its own when it comes to holding non-human entities to account for causing damage or harm. Wells notes that the bias towards moral philosophy focuses on an untenable individualism that assumes rationality and autonomy to be the driving forces of human action, and at the same time the preconditions for the allocation of blame and responsibility. She takes a sceptical position by referring to the fact that 'behaviour gets its characteristics through the observer's interpretive stance' (Wells 2001: 66), thus steering free from mentalist assumptions about the 'causes' of our behaviour. Her point is that the focus should shift from the mental state of the offender to the effect that entities like corporations have on large groups of people. The question is whether such entities can be held accountable for such effects under the criminal law, notably by introducing different criteria for culpability (Wells 2001: 74, 77, 80):

> Law recognizes both individuals and corporations as persons but that neither means that they are (nor necessarily should be) subjected to the same legal treatment, nor that as a matter of social construction that corporations are perceived in the same way.

---

[24]GOSS and MASS are my acronyms. Note that GOSS refers to quantitative social science, not to theoretical social science that builds on e.g. Weber or Durkheim. Most simulations of multi-agent systems still depend on methodological individualism, because this simplifies the calculation of emergent behaviours. See e.g. Helbing and Balietti (2011) who suggest that regarding the social sciences 'investments into experimental research and data mining must be increased to reach the standards in the natural and engineering sciences'; they term this a strategy 'to quickly increase the objective knowledge about social and economic systems'.

> To say that something is an individual is literally to say that it cannot be divided, that it is a whole, not necessarily that it is either equivalent to a human person nor that it is organic.
>
> Efforts to show that corporations have decision-making structures and capacity for long-term planning does not mean that they have a mind in the way that individuals do.

From this perspective the objective of corporate criminal liability is not to allow those in charge to hide behind the corporate veil, but to target powerful entities that shape society – especially where it is impossible, unreasonable and/or ineffective to blame their human proxies. Punishment is a specific type of feedback that communicates censure of specified behaviour patterns (Duff 2001). It warns against acting in a way that violates the criminal prohibition and thus allows those amenable to criminal sanctions to anticipate the consequences of transgression. Though punishment is not exhausted by the notion of a learning process, its feedback is meant to give both prudential and moral reasons to refrain from certain actions. To the extent that corporations are capable of such learning and of improving their performance as responsible societal entities it does make sense to censure them, providing them with input for their internal decision-making processes. Considering the powers that large corporations can exercise over markets, employees, consumers and business partners, law-makers should indeed provide the legal tools to communicate censure if harm is caused.

2.6.2.2 Artificial Legal Subjects: The Agency of Other 'Intelligent Machines'

This opens interesting perspectives on the question of how we stand with artificial agents that have been designed to operate relatively autonomously, reconfiguring their own programs to improve their performance, thus becoming increasingly unpredictable and capable of developing their 'skills' beyond the control of those who employ them. When highlighting the need for a specific understanding of corporate criminal liability Wells (2001: 83) notes:

> A different route is to abandon the metaphor of the person and replace it with something of more descriptive accuracy such as 'intelligent machine'.
>
> The machine metaphor has the merit, Dan-Cohen claims, of forcing us to confront the reality of the organization; it does not allow us to ignore it by absorbing and developing it in the prevailing individualistic framework.[25]

We should not misinterpret this attempt to enlarge the group of entities that can be held to account for the harm or damage they cause. It is not similar to Kant's acknowledgement that his categorical imperative is valid for all rational beings, not just humans, meaning that they should all be treated as ends and never as mere instruments for another's objectives. According to Kant, the autonomy of rational beings should be respected because they are capable of living by their own laws and of giving reasons for their actions. The Kantian notion of a rational being, however,

[25] Wells refers to Dan-Cohen (1986).

depends on a disembodied transcendental subject that constitutes its world of flesh and blood from the vantage point of pure cognition. This is precisely the kind of subjectivity on which much of analytical moral philosophy thrives, and against which Wells warns, insofar as it prevents us from locating other types of agents that shape our world and thus warrant some form of accountability. The machine metaphor is therefore well-suited for our purpose: while it clarifies that we are not speaking of self-conscious beings capable of integrating feeling with cognition and self-reflection, the addition of 'intelligent' indicates that we *are* dealing with an entity that is capable of improving its performance based on experience.[26] Instead of falling in the trap of developing a special section of law under the name of 'computer law', to regulate the use and abuse of computing systems, we need to consider the extent to which intelligent machines in the broad sense require standing in law.

As mentioned above, the invention of legal personhood for corporations – notably for the church and for the universities – created a specific type of jurisdiction for these communities to govern their own affairs, while also enabling them to act in law as an identifiable unit of action. This generated a measure of *freedom from* external constraints within the community (independence) and *freedom to* act as an entity that survives the lifespan of its members (durability). Legal personhood for an artificial intelligent computing system would provide it with a measure of independence from its creators, producers, retailers or users. As argued in the previous subsection, important arguments to attribute legal personhood to non-humans build on their 'identity, continuity and an identifiable decision-making process', while 'considering the powers that large corporations can exercise over markets, employees, consumers and business partners, law-makers should indeed provide the legal tools to communicate censure if harm is caused'. If intelligent machines other than corporations can be identified apart from their human patrons and if they exercise a significant measure of control over commercial and financial markets, critical infrastructure, transportation systems, healthcare and the more, our societies may benefit from their constitution as legal persons. This should provide them with a legal status suited to their capabilities on the one hand and the potential impact they have on our lifeworld on the other hand. It will expand their capacity to act in law, to create legal effect on their own account or for their patrons, and at the same time it will constrain their behaviour and provide for learning processes controlled by a democratic legislator. The adaptation of their legal status to their capabilities would imply a differential level of legal personhood; depending on their capabilities for context-awareness, autonomous reconfiguration, supervised or unsupervised learning, second-order inferences, emergent behaviours and unpredictability they could have more or less competences to create legal effect. Depending on their identifiability and traceability they should be certified and registered, to allow their creditors to invoke their liability, or – if they act as an agent on behalf of a principal – to allow

[26] I am using the machine-metaphor here to draw attention to non-human systems that consist of interacting human and/or non-human agents, though some would claim that individual human beings are also 'intelligent machines'.

creditors to invoke the liability of their principal on the basis of actual, ostensible or ratified authority.[27] The differential approach to legal personhood could also apply to the attribution of criminal liability. The relevant question here might not be whether the system has the same mental states as human beings, notably those summarized under the heading of *mens rea* (quod non), but whether such intelligent machines require censure and what this could mean in the context of a society where human and non-human individuals interact, anticipate another's actions and affect suffering and enjoyment. Whether specific types of intelligent machines qualify for such novel criminal liability would be a matter of empirical investigation, for instance depending on the question of whether they have developed something like second-order intentions that allow them to refrain from acting upon first order intentions that cause harm or damage.

Last but not least, I want to remind us briefly of the work of the German philosophical anthropologist (Helmuth Plessner 1975; see De Mul et al. forthcoming; Hildebrandt forthcoming), who described in intriguing philosophical detail how human nature is fundamentally artificial, how we suffer and enjoy a mediated immediacy and how we manage to create for ourselves a utopian position that constitutes a third person perspective on past, present and future undertakings. Instead of taking for granted that human agency can be summed up in a set of criteria, we should acknowledge the underdetermined and thus unfinished nature of what we stand for. We are neither undetermined nor infinite, but there is a fragile potential in our 'becoming' that should keep us vigilant against imposing our own standards on intelligent machines, without however falling into the trap of 'anything goes'.

2.7 Concluding Remarks

In Richard Powers' *Galatea 2.0* the main character is a layered computing system that runs on neural networks. At some point it develops a feeling for what it misses: feeling. It learns to look at itself from the perspective of its significant other, thus constituting a self and requiring a name. Helen. Finally, she figures out that she knows only words but no meaning. As mentioned above, these are contradictory imaginations, perhaps highlighting our inability to cope with our own artificial nature.

It seems that we can approach the legal implications of artificial intelligence in two ways. First, we must accept that if these computational systems ever develop a mind of their own it will be embodied differently from ours, rooted in other kinds of perceptions and different sensorimotor feedback loops. Their emotions will be different, and we cannot assume that they will develop a consciousness as we did. It is unclear what *mens rea* would come to mean and whether it will ever make sense to apply it to intelligent computational systems. Second, even if they do not develop

[27] Note that for an entity to act as an agent on behalf of a principal, the agent must be a legal subject. Only then can the 'intelligent machine' bind the principal to a contract with a third party.

into complete agents the impact they will have on our lifeworld and the relative autonomy they will develop to handle a variety of critical tasks may require us to create a new space for a new type of legal subject. Reminding ourselves of the artificial nature of legal personhood – as explained by Dewey – should prevent us from copy pasting the characteristics of human persons as requirements for 'intelligent machines'. Just like in the case of legal personhood for corporations, autonomous computing systems will require custom-made 'standing' in law.

References

Allen, R., and R. Widdison. 1996. Can computers make contracts? *Harvard Journal of Law and Technology* 9(1): 25–52.

Black, E. 2002. *IBM and the Holocaust. The strategic alliance between Nazi Germany and America's most powerful corporation*. New York: Crown.

Bourgine, P., and F.J. Varela. 1992. Towards a practice of autonomous systems. In *Towards a practice of autonomous systems. Proceedings of the first European conference on artificial life*, ed. F.J. Varela and P. Bourgine. Cambridge, MA: MIT Press, xi–xviii.

Brooks, R. 1991. Intelligence without reason. In: *Proceedings of the twelfth international joint conference on artificial intelligence*, 569–595, Sydney.

Chopra, S., and L.F. White. 2011. *A legal theory for autonomous artificial agents*. Ann Arbor: University of Michigan Press.

Christian, B. 2011. *The most human human. What talking with computers teaches us about what it means to be alive*. New York: Doubleday.

Citron, D.K. 2007. Technological due process. *Washington University Law Review* 85: 1249–1313.

Cohen, R. 1995. Pygmalion in the computer lab. *New York Times*, July 23. Available at: http://www.nytimes.com/books/98/06/21/specials/powers-galatea.html. Last accessed 10 Oct 2012.

Cole, D. 2009. The Chinese room argument. In *The Stanford encyclopedia of philosophy*, E.N. Zalta, Winter 2009 ed. Available at: http://plato.stanford.edu/archives/win2009/entries/chinese-room/. Last accessed 14 Aug 2012.

Cover, R., M. Minow, M. Ryan, and A. Sarat. 1995. *Narrative, violence, and the law. The essays of Robert Cover*. Ann Arbor: University of Michigan Press.

Custers, B. 2004. *The power of knowledge. Ethical, legal, and technological aspects of data mining and group profiling in epidemiology*. Nijmegen: Wolf Legal Publishers.

Dahiyat, E.A.R. 2010. Intelligent agents and liability: Is it a doctrinal problem or merely a problem of explanation? *Artificial Intelligence and Law* 18(1): 103–121.

Damasio, A.R. 2000. *The feeling of what happens: Body and emotion in the making of consciousness*. New York: Harcourt Inc.

Dan-Cohen, M. 1986. *Rights, persons, and organizations: A legal theory for bureaucratic society*. London: University of California Press.

Davis, M. 1985. How to make the punishment fit the crime? In *Criminal justice*, ed. J.R. Pennock and J.M. Chapman. New York/London: New York University Press.

De Doelder, H., and K. Tiedemann (eds.). 1995. *Criminal liability of corporations*. Dordrecht: Kluwer Law International.

De Mul, J., M. Coolen, and H. Ernste (eds.). (forthcoming). *Artificial by nature. Plessner's philosophical anthropology. Perspectives and prospects*. Amsterdam: Amsterdam University Press.

Dewey, J. 1926. The historic background of corporate legal personality. *Yale Law Journal* 35(6): 655–673.

Dreyfus, H.L. 1979. *What computers can't do: The limits of artificial intelligence*. New York: Harper & Row.

Dreyfus, H.L. 1992. *What computers still can't do: A critique of artificial reason*. Cambridge, MA/London: MIT Press.

Duff, R.A. 2001. *Punishment, Communication, and Community*. Oxford: Oxford University Press.

Eser, A., G. Heine, and B. Huber (eds.). 1999. *Criminal responsibility of legal and collective entities. International colloquium Berlin 1998*. Freiburg: Edition Iuscrim.

Fayyad, U.M., G. Piatetsky-Shapiro, P. Smyth, and R. Uthurusamy. 1996. *Advances in knowledge discovery and data mining*. Meno Park: AAAI Press/MIT Press.

Fisse, B., and J. Braithwaite. 1993. *Corporations, crime and accountability*. Cambridge: Cambridge University Press.

Floridi, L., and M. Taddeo. 2009. Turing's Imitation game: Still an impossible challenge for all machines and some judges – An evaluation of the 2008 Loebner contest. *Mind and Machines* 19(1): 145–150.

French, P.A. 1979. The corporation as a moral person. *American Philosophical Quarterly* 16(3): 207–215.

Gaakeer, J. 1998. *Hope springs eternal: An introduction to the work of James Boyd White*. Amsterdam: Amsterdam University Press.

Helbing, D., and S. Balietti. 2011. From Social Data Mining to Forecasting Socio-economic Crises. *The European Physical Journal Special Topics* 195(1): 3–68.

Hildebrandt, M. 2011a. Criminal liability and 'smart' environments. In *Philosophical foundations of criminal law*, ed. A. Duff and S. Green. Oxford: Oxford University Press.

Hildebrandt, M. 2011b. Autonomic and autonomous "thinking": Preconditions for criminal accountability. In *Law, human agency and autonomic computing*, ed. M. Hildebrandt and A. Rouvoy, 141–160. Abingdon: Routledge.

Hildebrandt, M. (forthcoming). Eccentric positionality as a precondition of the criminal liability of artificial life forms. In *Artificial by nature. Plessner's philosophical anthropology. Perspectives and prospects*, ed. J. de Mul, M. Coolen, and H. Ernste. Amsterdam: Amsterdam University Press.

Hildebrandt, M., and S. Gutwirth. 2008. *Profiling the European citizen. Cross-disciplinary perspectives*. Dordrecht: Springer.

Hildebrandt, M., and A. Rouvroy. 2011. *Law, human agency and autonomic computing. The philosophy of law meets the philosophy of technology*. Abingdon: Routledge.

Huff, T.E. 2003. *The rise of early modern science. Islam, China, and the West*. Cambridge: Cambridge University Press.

IBM White Paper. 2011. *Watson – A system designed for answers. The future of workload optimization.* Available at: http://www.itworld.com/business/242693/watson-system-designed-answers-future-workload-optimized-systems-design. Last accessed 10 Oct 2012.

Ihde, D. 1991. *Instrumental realism: The interface between philosophy of science and philosophy of technology*. Bloomington: Indiana University Press.

Ihde, D. 2008. *Ironic technics*. Copenhagen: Automatic Press.

Karnow, C.E.A. 1997. *Future codes: Essays in advanced computer technology and the law*. Boston: Artech House.

Koops, B.-J., M. Hildebrandt, and D.-O. Jacquet-Chiffelle. 2010. Bridging the accountability gap: Rights for new entities in the information society? *Minnesota Journal of Law Science & Technology* 11(2): 497–561.

Kranzberg, M. 1986. Technology and history: Kranzberg's laws. *Technology and Culture* 27(3): 544–560.

Kurzweil, R. 2005. *The singularity is near: When humans transcend biology*. New York: Viking.

Le, Q.V., M. Ranzato, R. Monga, M. Devin, K. Chen, G.S. Corrado, J. Dean, and A.Y. Ng. 2012. Building high-level features using large scale unsupervised learning. In *Proceedings of the 29th International Conference on Machine Learning (ICML) 2012*. Madison: Omnipress. Available at: http://arxiv.org/abs/1112.6209. Last accessed 10 Oct 2012.

Leenes, R.E. 1998. *Hercules of Karneades. Hard cases in recht en rechtsinformatica*. Enschede: Twente University Press.

Markoff, J. 2011. On 'Jeopardy!' Watson win is all but trivial. *The New York Times*. Available at: http://www.nytimes.com/2011/02/17/science/17jeopardy-watson.html. Accessed 19 Oct 2012.

Markoff, J. 2012. How many computers to identify a cat? 16,000. *New York Times*, June 25.
Minsky, M. 1988. *The society of mind*. New York: Simon & Schuster.
Minsky, M. 2006. *The emotion machine*. New York: Simon & Schuster.
Mitchell, T.M. 2006. *The discipline of machine learning* (Technical Report CMU-ML-06-108). Pittsburgh: Carnegie Mellon University, School of Computer Science. Available at: http://www-cgi.cs.cmu.edu/~tom/pubs/MachineLearningTR.pdf. Last accessed 10 Oct 2012.
Moore, G.E. 1965. Cramming more components onto integrated circuits. *Electronics Magazine* 38(8): 114–117.
Pfeifer, R., and J. Bongard. 2007. *How the body shapes the way we think. A new view of intelligence*. Cambridge, MA: MIT Press.
Picard, R. 1995. *Affective computing*. Cambridge, MA: MIT Press.
Plessner, H. 1975. *Die Stufen des Organischen under der Mensch. Einleitung in die philosophische Anthropologie*. Berlin: De Gruyter.
Powers, R. 1995. *Galatea 2.2*. New York: Picador.
Powers, R. 2011. What is artificial intelligence? *The New York Times*, February 5.
Rosu, A. 2002. Parody as cultural memory in Richard Powers's Galatea 2.2. *Connotations* 12(2/3): 139–154.
Russell, S., and P. Norvig. 2009. *Artificial intelligence: A modern approach*. Upper Saddle River: Prentice Hall.
Sartor, G. 2002. Agents in cyberlaw. In *The law of electronic agents: Selected revised papers*. In *Proceedings of the workshop on the Law of Electronic Agents* (LEA 2002), G. Sartor, 3–12. Bologna: CIRSFID Universita di Bologna.
Searle, J. 1980. Minds, brains, and programs. *The Behavioral and Brain Sciences* 3(3): 517–557.
Shannon, C.E. 1948a. A mathematical theory of communication. *Bell System Technical Journal* 27(3): 379–423.
Shannon, C.E. 1948b. A mathematical theory of communication. *Bell System Technical Journal* 27(4): 623–656.
Shaw, G.B. 1994. *Pygmalion*. Mineola NJ: Dover Publications.
Simon, H.A. 1996. *The sciences of the artificial*. Cambridge, MA: MIT Press.
Solum, L.B. 1992. Legal personhood for artificial intelligences. *North Carolina Law Review* 70(2): 1231–1287.
Steels, L. 1995. When are robots intelligent autonomous agents? *Robotics and Autonomous Systems* 15: 3–9.
Teubner, G. 2006. Rights of non-humans? Electronic agents and animals as new actors in politics and law. *Journal of Law and Society* 33: 497–521.
Turing, A.M. 1950. Computing machinery and intelligence. *Mind* 59(236): 433–460.
Van der Linden-Smith, T. 2001. *Een duidelijk geval: geautomatiseerde afhandeling*, NOW/ITeR-serie 41. Den Haag: SDU Uitgevers.
Velasquez, J.D. 1998. Modeling emotion-based decision making. In *Proceedings of the 1998 fall symposium emotional and intelligent: The tangled knot of cognition*, Technical Report FS-98-03, ed. D. Canamero, 164–169. Menlo Park: AAAI Press. Available at: http://www.global-media.org/neome/docs/PDF's/01%20-%20the%20best%20ones/emotional%20agents.pdf. Last accessed 10 Oct 2012.
Weizenbaum, J. 1976. *Computer power and human reason: From judgment to calculation*. San Francisco: W.H. Freeman & Co.
Wells, C. 2001. *Corporations and criminal responsibility*. Oxford: Oxford University Press.
Wettig, S., and E. Zehender. 2004. A legal analysis of human and electronic agents. *Artificial Intelligence and Law* 12(1–2): 111–135.
White, J.B. 1990. *Justice as translation: An essay in cultural and legal criticism*. Chicago: University of Chicago Press.
Wiener, N. 1948. *Cybernetics: Or control and communication in the animal and the machine*. Cambridge, MA: MIT Press.

Chapter 3
What Robots Want: Autonomous Machines, Codes and New Frontiers of Legal Responsibility

Ugo Pagallo

Abstract This chapter examines the impact of robotics technology on legal systems and how a new generation of robo-traders, AI chauffeurs, artificial pop singers and autonomous lethal weapons affect individual's knowledge, environments and perceptions of the world. Although lawyers deem robots under the current state of law as legally and morally without responsibility as these artificial agents lack a set of preconditions for attributing liability to a party within the realm of criminal law, such machines are reshaping notions of agency and human liability in civil (as opposed to criminal) law. We already have a number of artificial agents that send bids, accept offers, request quotes, negotiate deals and make contracts, so that such machines can be held liable for certain of their actions through new types of accountability, authentication systems and insurance models. At least in the civil law-field, "only robots shall pay" at times may be the right answer.

3.1 Introduction

Over the past few decades, scholars have debated regulative tools of technology and what Alvin Toffler calls the 'backwards, forwards, and sideways' effects of the aim to embed values and rules through codes, architectures and design (Toffler 1980). The field of this seminal debate on 'law as code' started with Isaac Asimov 70 years ago, when he coined the expression 'robotics' in the short story *Runaround* (1942). In his 1982 introduction to the 'definitive collection of robot stories', Asimov recalls that by the time he was in his late teens, and 'already a hardened science fiction reader', he categorized robot stories into two classes, i.e. Robots-as-Menace and Robots-as-Pathos. The latter term referred to lovable machines that were oppressed

U. Pagallo (✉)
Law School, University of Turin, Turin, Italy
e-mail: ugo.pagallo@unito.it

M. Hildebrandt and J. Gaakeer (eds.), *Human Law and Computer Law: Comparative Perspectives*, Ius Gentium: Comparative Perspectives on Law and Justice 25,
DOI 10.1007/978-94-007-6314-2_3,

by brutal humans. Then, 'something odd happened as I wrote this first story [*Runaround*]. I managed to get the dim vision of a robot as neither Menace nor Pathos. I began to think of robots as industrial products built by matter-of-fact engineers' (Asimov ed. 1995: 9–10).

Asimov conceived the 'three laws of robotics' in *Runaround*, a story about a 2015 mission to a mining station abandoned 10 years earlier on Mercury. By the end of the narrative, two humans, namely Donovan and Powell, wonder why Speedy, the robot, is behaving so strangely. Although 'perfectly adapted to normal Mercurian environment', Donovan claims that Speedy seems 'drunk'. After reflecting on the reasons for such bizarre behaviour, Powell finally realizes why the robot looks inebriated: in the sober terms of computer science and engineering programming, it turned out that Speedy was trying to comply with the three laws of robotics. Rule 3 drove poor Speedy back, whereas Rule 2 drove him forward (Asimov 1995: 271–272):

> Powell's radio voice was tense in Donovan's ear: 'Now, look, let's start with the three fundamental Rules of Robotics – the three rules are built mostly deeply into a robot's positronic brain'. We have: One, a robot may not injure a human being, or, through inaction, allow a human being to come to harm.
>
> Two, a robot must obey the orders given to it by human beings except where such orders would conflict with the First Law.
>
> And three, a robot must protect its own existence, as long as such protection does not conflict with the First or Second Law.

Later, in *Robots and Empire* (1985), Asimov added a fourth law, the 'Zeroth' law:

> 0. A robot may not injure humanity or, through inaction, allow humanity to come to harm.

Since Asimov's first story on the 'three laws of robotics', science fiction has paved the way for scholarly analyses on the multiple ways in which the design and construction of autonomous machines affect pillars of the law and, *vice versa*, how legal rules restrain the behaviour of such machines. That which in the words of Mireille Hildebrandt and Jeanne Gaakeer (2013) may be summed up with the formula 'law as code meets law as literature', concerns the difficulty in modelling concepts traditionally employed by lawyers. Examples of such include the notions of 'injury' and 'harm' in Asimov's first law of robotics, according to which a robot shall not damage a human being, or, through inaction 'allow a human being to come to harm'. Likewise, think about the notions of 'command' and 'obligation' in the second law, so that 'a robot must obey orders given to it by human beings'. Whilst the goal is that even a machine can comprehend and process this very information, it is noteworthy that the aim of setting up and restraining the behaviour of autonomous machines through codes is one of the most relevant issues of robotics technology in the early twenty-first century. In addition to current research in machine ethics, design ethics, robot ethics, and so forth (Pagallo 2011a), this is also the case of the most dynamic and well-funded of its fields: military robotics technology. Recent U.S. Navy-sponsored research has crucially admitted that significant troubles persist when embedding 'laws of war' and 'rules of engagement' in autonomous robots as such norms are 'much more complex than Asimov's laws' (Lin et al. 2007: 76).

Imagine the technical difficulty in designing robots so as to let them distinguish between friends and foes, civilians and combatants, thereby abiding by the principles of immunity and discrimination in war. Restrictions have been proposed in that robot soldiers should only target weapons and operate in particular regions or situations. Others argue that the use and production of robot soldiers should be banned. Significantly, in their 2010 reports to the UN General Assembly, Philip Alston and Christof Heynes emphasize that current legal provisions are silent on two points. Whilst analogy is inadequate to determine the types of 'autonomous weapons' that should be deemed unlawful, it is also far from clear what parameters and conditions should regulate the use of these machines in accordance with the principles of immunity and discrimination in *ius in bello* mentioned above (Pagallo 2011b).

In light of today's legal loopholes, this chapter aims to explore whether new types of legal liability should be attributed to the behaviour of 'autonomous' and even 'intelligent' machines, such as the US Navy's Phalanx CIWS that operate completely independently. A 'failure of causation' may indeed emerge in the legal field, since it is difficult to understand what types of harm can supervene with machines responding to stimuli by changing the values of their inner states and which, furthermore, can improve the rules through those properties changed without any external stimuli. This autonomy can be seen as calling for new 'strong moral responsibilities' of manufacturers and robot designers insofar as the growing capability of such machines to take decisions on their own ends up in unpredictability as to their behaviour. Troubling similarities with the aim of regulating human interaction via technologically enforced constraints emerge as a result: after all, we may impose code on robots (and humans) so as to limit the impact of harmful conduct, and even have the aim of preventing such behaviour from occurring through the use of self-enforcement technologies. Yet, who is liable if something goes wrong?

Three scenarios are examined here according to the following spectrum: at one end is the claim that robotics neither creates nor modifies legal concepts (the traditional outlook on AI and the law, coined in this chapter as the no new responsibility thesis). According to this viewpoint, 'law as code' does not meet 'law as literature' due to the science fictional nature or narrative structure of the latter. At the other end of the spectrum, certain scholars argue that the advancement of robotics technology provokes new types of responsibility as these machines should be perceived of as accountable as humans for their actions (the new strong responsibility thesis). From this further perspective, 'law as code' meets 'law as literature' as, in the phrasing of Mireille Hildebrandt (2011), literary 'science fiction' profoundly affects legal 'science faction'. In the midst of this spectrum we find the thesis of those admitting that technology induces new types of liability but, who nevertheless, reckon that only humans are accountable for what an artificial state-transition system autonomously 'decides' to do (that is, the new weak responsibility thesis). Whilst further distinctions seem necessary, e.g. a new type of weak responsibility in criminal law *vs.* a new type of strong responsibility in civil law, the focus of this analysis is restricted to issues relating to crimes and contracts. Although tort law represents one of the most interesting areas of the laws of robots, such an analysis on 'robotic torts' would simply confirm or contradict the conclusions drawn on cases of criminal law and contractual obligations.

3.2 The No New Responsibility Thesis

Research within the philosophy of technology and the sociology of the law suggesting that the aim of the law is to regulate both scientific research and technology should be likened to the classical image of Achilles and the turtle. By reversing Zeno's paradox, the pace of the law in fact seems too slow to catch up with the race of science and technological innovation. Since the time of Galileo's trial (1633), up to the current debate on neuroscience and bioethics, politicians and lawmakers have obviously thought otherwise. Even though we can literally arrest the pace of scientists, e.g., Galileo, the argument proffered is that the race of technology is so determined and powerful that it cannot be deterred by legal means. In his telling research on *What Technology Wants*, Kevin Kelly suggests why this is the case. He draws a directly proportional rule between features and outputs of technology: 'the greater the number of exotropic traits we observe in a particular expression of technology, the greater its inevitability and its conviviality' (Kelly 2010: 270). Once we understand the laws, under which humans have been using tools over hundreds of millennia, unveiling an already written future appears feasible. Contrary to the laws of the law, the laws of technology allow us to find the logic of human evolution: starting with the hero of the ape-like tribe of early humans grasping how a bone could be used as a weapon, down to the orbital satellite in Kubrick's famous match cut in *2001: A Space Odyssey*.

This view on technology has induced one distinguished researcher from Carnegie Mellon, Hans Moravec (1999), to announce that intelligent robots will succeed humans and that we, as a species, would then face extinction. Likewise, Ray Kurzweil's *The Singularity is Near* (2005) sketches an imminent future where greater than human intelligence emerges through technological means. Whilst Kurzweil reckons that this singular event might happen by 2045, the complementary website is keen to inform us at http://singularity-2045.org/, that we should include nanobots, artificial intelligence and robotics, among the main contributing factors to this singular event. Scholars therefore have to be prepared to address a new generation of legal cases and, more particularly, new types of crimes. In *How Just Could a Robot War Be*?, for example, Peter Asaro (2008) explores the hypothesis of challenges to national sovereignty and robot revolutions; in *Autonomous Robots and the Law*, Fernando Barrio speculates over robotic sex offences; in their 2007 Ethicomp paper on *Robot Thugs*, Carson Reynolds and Ishikawa dwell on machines that choose to commit and, ultimately, carry out a crime (Reynolds and Ishikawa 2007). According to these perspectives, new types of cases would arise with robots accountable for their regrettable actions as the self-consciousness of robots could materialize Sci-Fi scenarios as imagining a robot revolution and, hence, a new cyber-Spartacus. In addition, the meaning of traditional legal notions, such as theft and homicide, would change, since the culpability of the agent, i.e. its *mens rea* would be rooted in the artificial mind of a machine that really 'wants'.

However, current state-of-the-art technology and legal science both suggest that it would be meaningless to argue before a judge that a robot should be found 'guilty'. Legal systems require specific psychological components, such as consciousness or free will, as a set of preconditions for attributing liability to a party in cases of criminal law violations. For example, young children are not held accountable for their behaviour because of their emotional and intellectual immaturity. Likewise, individuals with severe psychological illnesses are not held accountable for their actions because of their incapacity to fully understand what they are doing. Since consciousness is a conceptual prerequisite for both legal and moral agency, it follows that the standard legal viewpoint reckons that the level of autonomy shown by today's robotics applications is insufficient to bring such machines before judges and have them found guilty in criminal courts. Whilst 'law as code' may restrict or nurture, but not constitute, human autonomy, codes for robots, *vice versa*, establish and delimit the autonomy of their behaviour: in the words of Mireille Hildebrandt (2011: 10), 'a program cannot understand that it cannot understand. Not in our terms, that is'.

The difference between literary science fiction and legal science faction can be fruitfully illuminated in connection with 'law as literature'. By claiming that robots lack a set of preconditions for attributing liability to them in the field of criminal law, advocates of the no new responsibility thesis are closer, say, to *The Case of the Killer Robot* than the scenarios disclosed by the evil deeds of HAL 9000 in *2001: A Space Odyssey*. Even when Robbie CX30 assassinates Bart Matthews in Richard Epstein's story (Epstein 1997), the homicide remains a matter of human responsibility involving the designer of the robot and its manufacturer, Silicon Techtronics, as robots are not aware of their own conduct, such as 'wishing' to act in a certain way. Otherwise, by admitting the criminal accountability of Robbie CX30, all of the reasons underpinning the legitimacy of inflicting punishment in modern criminal law, e.g., the theory of retribution, or of special and general prevention, would be devoid of meaning. Can Robbie pay its debt to society? Can we correct the moral character of the autonomous machine so that it fully understands why it ought not to repeat the evil action? What would be the point in punishing Robbie so as to dissuade human beings or other robots from committing similar wrongs?

Leaving aside the adventures of *The Case of the Killer Robot*, there are yet more difficult cases than those of crimes voluntarily performed by humans through their intelligent machines. For instance, reflect on the case of a user intending to perpetrate a crime through a robot but, due to malfunctions of the autonomous machine, the latter deviates from the plan and commits some other kind of offence. Consider also a robot that was not designed or used to commit a specific crime, but the machine nevertheless carried out such an offence. In all these cases, the capability of robots to improve the rules through which their AI properties change will probably raise hard cases of apportioned liability between users, designers and robot manufacturers. In order to sever the chain of liability, lawyers will thus have to determine whether the machine properly worked within the limits of a given set of parameters or, conversely, whether the fault has to be attributed to the manufacturer (and designers) promising to deliver a safe machine and, yet, omitting certain crucial information. Due to the specific autonomy of robot behaviour, however, the issue arises: What does it mean that a robot acted within the limits of a given program? Moreover, how can we determine whether injuries alleged by a plaintiff were actually caused by her own negligence or by her negligence combined with that of an artificial agent?

Advocates of the 'no new responsibility' thesis claim that, even in these cases, the traditional legal view would not be strained. On one hand, the liability model in accomplice responsibility cases applies to the individual sending or activating a robot in order to commit a crime, even if the robot 'decided' to deviate from that plan and carried out some other kind of offense. Despite the unpredictability of the machine's behaviour or its possible malfunctioning, the user of such a robot would be held liable for the additional crime in most legal systems due to the original plan of the user. On the other hand, when humans have no intent to commit a wrong, but their robot nonetheless perpetrates such a wrong, individuals are to be held liable on the basis of negligence or lack of due care, that is, because a 'reasonable' party failed to guard against 'foreseeable' harm. At the end of the day, from the point of view of the traditional legal theory, the alleged novelty of all these cases resembles the responsibility of an owner or keeper of an animal 'that is either known or presumed to be dangerous to mankind' (Davis 2011: 6).

However, by drawing an analogy between traditional strict liability policies for damages caused by animals and human liability for the behaviour of robots, the no new responsibility thesis concedes that we are confronted with a new type of human responsibility for the behaviour of others. Since robots, like animals, do act, the result is that harm caused by such robots cannot be included within the traditional viewpoint of strict liability rules for dangerous activities, e.g. liability for defective products and lack of information. Although the design, production and use of certain robotic applications can be reckoned as 'dangerous', such as autonomous or semi-autonomous unmanned lethal weapons, a number of other applications can scarcely be seen as falling within this category. Along with the Japanese pop star robot singer HRP-4C, think of machines that are not designed or used to commit any crime, such as da Vinci surgeon robots or underwater unmanned vehicles (UUVs) undertaking repairs to oil rigs in the Caribbean sea. What these examples suggest is that we are dealing with a new source of moral agency, as robots can take actions that are morally qualifiable as good or evil, as much as can animals, children and, obviously, adults.

After traditional forms of no fault-liability for the behaviour of animals, children, and employees, advocates of the no new responsibility thesis are consequently forced to acknowledge that legal systems will hold humans responsible for what an autonomous machine 'chooses' to do and that analogies with other kinds of strict liability fall short in addressing the novelty of robotics technology. Consider the ways by which legal systems provide limits for such strict liability rules and how the burden of proof is allocated in such cases. For example, parents evade responsibility in most legal systems when they can prove that they could not prevent their child's behaviour. Likewise, the owner of an animal can prove that a fortuitous event happened. Henceforth, when addressing the responsibility of humans for the behaviour of their robots, what analogy should we endorse? Should we liken robots to animals or, conversely, to AI children? Would not multiple robotic applications recommend different liability policies for, say, Terminators C-3P0, pop stars HRP-4C, or da Vinci surgeons? Should we follow the no new responsibility thesis and end up in a Hegelian 'dark night in which all robots appear grey'?

All in all, it is unlikely that we will run across a single metaphor or analogy that grasps the next generation of robot-related issues in the fields of criminal law and contracts. It is more than plausible that such liability will vary according to the different types of application being dealt with. However, against the no new responsibility thesis it may be argued that robots will require a normative framework of their own. The road to new types of (both weak and strong) legal responsibility for the behaviour of robots is open.

3.3 The New Weak Responsibility Thesis

Among recent legal cases concerning human responsibility for the behaviour of robots, that is, the 'new weak responsibility thesis', we should distinguish between criminal and civil cases. In both fields, to be sure, we find a common set of principles and concepts challenged by the advancement of robotics technology. Since ancient Roman law, scholars have summarized the multiple hypotheses of civil and criminal responsibility with the maxim *alterum non laedere*, that is, 'do not injure another', in order to establish who is liable when something or someone causes harm. In connection with legal notions such as causation, reasonable foreseeability, and apportioned liability the principle of responsibility is thus reckoned as a supreme, general, and operational criterion, setting the constraints for the design, construction and use of robots, and determining who is to be held accountable for the autonomous behaviour of every machine in all legal fields.

Despite such a common framework, there are crucial differences. In criminal law, responsibility implies most of the time blameworthiness, so that once defendants are found guilty by courts, they have 'to pay their debt to society'. Conversely, in civil law, responsibility does not always involve blame but say, rather a duty to compensate on the basis of the strict-liability rules described above. Moreover, when dealing with new types of responsibility for the behaviour of robots, the focus of criminal lawyers is most of the time on the harm or damages provoked by such machines. *Vice versa*, it is not necessary in civil law that something has to go wrong. Since the late nineteenth century, the legal imagination has been fired by how machines can be extremely fruitful in making contracts, or establishing rights and obligations between humans, in a 'win-win' scenario. Today's debate on cognitive automata in the form of software agents can be traced back to the seminal remarks of Günther's *Das Automatenrecht* (1891), Schiller's *Rechtsverhältnisse des Automen* (1898), and Neumond's *Der Automat* (1899).

Such key differences between criminal and civil law curiously reverberate in a common feature of the field of law as literature. Since Ĉapek's 1920 novel, *Rossum's Universal Robots*, most of the legal issues we find in science fiction, such as Asimov's emphasis on the 'matter-of-fact' engineering problems of robotics, concern the criminal side of the law, rather than 'boring' contracts (Ĉapek 2004, orig. 1920). This is of course understandable as murders, slaughters, homicides, conspiracies, or rebellions leading to the extinction of the human race, such as in Ĉapek's *R.U.R.*, are more attractive (and saleable) than plots based on contract clauses and conditions. Even when the main character is an office worker android, as occurs in Greg Pak's 2003 film *Robot Stories*, the plot revolves around the fact that that robotic employee learns that he, too, needs love…

A remarkable exception to mainstream novels on robots is the aforementioned story, *The Case of the Killer Robot*. Even though Epstein's plot concerns a classic case of manslaughter, the reader is confronted with a number of issues that are relevant in the civil law field. The story points out that the manufacturer of Robbie CX30, that is, Silicon Techtronics, promised to deliver a safe robot, whilst an engineer contests the accuracy of some software tests and a Silicon Techtronics' employee admits she created the fraudulent results. By following Epstein's examples of fault in complex software and hardware applications, *The Case of the Killer Robot* casts light on notions of causation, reasonable foreseeability, apportioned liability that do not necessarily involve criminal uses of robots but, rather, terms, conditions, and clauses hinging on a voluntary agreement between private individuals that a court will enforce. In light of this differentiation, we will now examine the criminal and civil law features of the new weak responsibility thesis separately.

3.3.1 New Crimes, New Punishments

Criminal responsibility rests on the idea that 'everything not prohibited is allowed'. The principle is usually summed up in the jargon of continental Europe as the 'principle of legality'. The aim is to guarantee individual protection against arbitrary public action, so that criminal responsibility ought to be founded on specific norms of codes and statutes. A classical text such as Thomas Hobbes' *Leviathan* (1651, reissue 1982) makes this point: as stated in chapter 16, once we assume that the 'law is a command, and a command consisteth in declaration or manifestation of the will of him that commandeth', it follows that the command must be expressed 'by voice, writing, or some other sufficient argument of the same'. This is why technological innovation continuously forces lawmakers to 'intervene' by adding norms for the regulation of new (circumstances of new) crimes. The new weak responsibility thesis, therefore, claims that that which has occurred in the field of computer crimes since the beginning of the 1990s is likely to occur in the field of robotic crimes as well. Along with cases of spamming, identity theft, illegal access and interception, hacking and digital fraud, three possible scenarios of robotic crimes can be sketched.

First, there will be new types of offences that would simply be inconceivable once deprived of the technology upon which they are dependent. Consider, for example, the increasing complexity of network-centric operations and the miniaturization of robots connected to the internet, so as to obtain the information required for object recognition, navigation and task completion in the real world. By replicating and spreading that data, robots could seriously impinge on current legal safeguards, concerning data protection, copyright provisions, trade secrets, national security and more, regardless of human wrongdoing or mere negligence. Therefore, in the name of the 'principle of legality', lawmakers have to ascertain whether the behaviour of such machines falls within loopholes in the criminal law field. If such is the case, lawmakers may have to intervene at both national and international levels, much as they did with a new generation of computer crimes since the early 1990s. In light of the current debate on the employment of robot soldiers in battle, this is no longer simply a Sci-Fi scenario, since the UN special rapporteur, Christof Heyns, has already urged the Secretary-General Ban Ki-moon to convene a group of experts in order to define the set of parameters and conditions that should govern the use of robot soldiers. Whilst technology advancements in the fields of chemical, biological and nuclear weapons have previously given rise to international agreements and conventions to regulate the use of such technologies, a UN-sponsored agreement appears similarly necessary in the case of military robotics or, say, the field of data protection (so as to update art. 12 of the 1948 Universal Declaration).

Secondly, we may envisage new crimes committed by humans who unjustly damage or destroy their robots, so as to preserve consistency between such machines and their owners. Admittedly, the focus here is not on new types of human responsibility for the behaviour of robots but, rather, on novel forms of prosecution against humans due to their own wrongdoing. Although legal systems provide for a number of sanctions in cases of the intentional misuse of power, vandalism, etc., analogies may fall short in likening robots either to animals or to dangerous things. One solution could be to follow the theses of the forefront of robotic liberation and imagine a novel generation of offences, such as robot slavery and sex crimes against poor robot dolls (e.g. Barrio 2008). Current legal rules should thus be amended so as to charge humans for abuses of robots similar to those legal systems have established for cases of 'animal cruelty' in past decades. An even stronger solution follows from the idea that 'the condition for each kind of legal personality could, in principle, be met by artificial agents in the right circumstances' (Chopra and White 2011: 27). With this, punishment should be even harsher, for crimes would be perpetrated upon agents having rights (and duties) of their own. However, at the risk of being lambasted for reactionary anthropocentrism, it seems more urgent that we address new cases of responsibility for the criminal behaviour of robots, than new forms of (weak or strong responsibility for) crimes committed by humans against their autonomous machines. Although we may conceive robots as moral patients that deserve respect and protection as such, the forefront of robotic liberation should not have the priority over the regulation of the new robotic crimes as described above.

The third possible scenario of the new weak responsibility thesis concerns novel types of punishment for the behaviour of robots. As previously mentioned, today's state of the art technology and legal science suggests that we should exclude the criminal accountability of robots; and, yet, we have to admit that robots, like animals, children and adult human beings, can take morally qualifiable actions. This capability implies that lawyers will increasingly assess, in the words of the U.S. Supreme Court, whether some robotics applications are 'incapable of substantial non-infringing uses' (Pagallo 2011a: 256). Once the design, sale, or supply of this technology is considered illegal, robots will meaningfully represent a target of human censorship. For example, lawmakers could choose one of the following consequences as proposed by Floridi and Sanders in *On the Morality of Artificial Agents* (2004: 24), namely: '(a) monitoring and modification (i.e., 'maintenance'); (b) removal to a disconnected component of Cyberspace; (c) annihilation from Cyberspace (deletion without backup)'. Although such punitive sanctions do not directly involve, say, the owner of a robot, these injunctions could affect humans as well. This could be the case since it is likely that robots will raise psychological issues related to the very interactions of humans with robots as matters of attachment, feelings of subordination, problems of reliability, trustworthiness, and the like. At times, the lawful removal or annihilation of robots from cyberspace will be even worse than today's 'three strikes' doctrine in the field of computer crimes. In this latter case, as a part of the graduated system which ends up with user disconnection after three warnings of copyright infringement, humans are temporarily banished from the internet. In the case of robots, we may paraphrase Fyodor Dostoevsky's *Crime and Punishment* (1938: 275) by saying that 'if he [the human] has a conscience he will suffer for his [the robot's] mistake. That will be punishment as well as the prison'.

3.3.2 New Agents, New Contracts

The new weak responsibility thesis in the civil law field addresses matters of liability for harm or damages provoked by robots as well as new frontiers for making business. In the first hypothesis, we are brought back to the scenarios of *The Case of the Killer Robot*, namely, how legal notions of causality, foreseeability or apportioned liability are affected by the unpredictability of machines capable of learning and adapting to changes in the environment. This is not to say that all robotic applications raise new types of human responsibility: for example, the controlled settings of operating theatres in the case of da Vinci surgical robots raise engineering problems that scholars routinely address as part of their research. On the basis of the probability of events, their consequences and costs, lawyers examine matters of unpredictability and risks as provoked by such robots, as they did with previous technological innovations (Pagallo 2011c). Still, the more we widen the settings and goals of robotics programs, the more likely it becomes that we will be dealing with growing amounts of complexity, so that the risks emerging as a consequence of robotic behaviour will exponentially increase as well. According to the U.S. Navy-sponsored research mentioned in the introduction, the lack of data on the performance of some robotic applications would indeed suggest that 'we may paradoxically need to use the first deaths to determine the level of risk' (Lin et al. 2007: 68). In all these cases, however, it seems necessary to insist that the design, production, and use of such robots should be strictly regulated by the precautionary principle (Veruggio 2007; Pagallo 2010). This means that the burden of proof should shift from those suspecting a risk to those who discount it, in order to prevent action when scientific research is uncertain as to the harm that the use of sensitive technologies might invoke in such fields as human health or environmental protection.

The second scenario of the new weak responsibility thesis opens up ways of 'doing business as usual' through robotic forms of legal agency, that is, by granting authority to the robot to act on people's behalf when dealing with third parties. Remarkably, this idea was discussed at the annual meeting of the American Law Institute in May 2003. On that occasion, the National Conference of Commissioners on Uniform State Laws proposed acknowledging the validity of contracts made by electronic agents, although no action or knowledge of any human being may be involved. Likewise, section 14 of the Uniform Electronic Transactions Act endorses the idea that 'a contract may be formed by the interaction of electronic agents of the parties, even if no individual was aware of or reviewed the electronic agents' actions or the resulting terms and agreements'. Consequently, any rights and obligations established by the robot would be directly conferred onto humans, as they had properly delegated to the robot the authority to act on their behalf, rather than wanting the specific content of the contract concluded by the robot.

Consider the case of a robotic personal assistant such as a sort of i-Jeeves that helps us schedule a set of conferences, lectures, and meetings at several European (or US) universities. Whereas we may guess at the best way of accepting simultaneous invitations from Oxford, Uppsala, Heidelberg, Athens and Paris, our robot needs not resolve the travelling professor problem by determining the shortest possible tour that visits each university only once. Rather, we expect that i-Jeeves checks both the availability and convenience of logistics in accordance with a number of parameters such as budget, time efficiency, or weather average conditions: i-Jeeves reports its findings back for a decision or, even, could determine the steps of our tour by directly booking hotel rooms, flights, and so forth. Such contracts would not only be valid, but also raise a set of new weak responsibilities for the behaviour of such machines. Since the 'intentional stance represents usually the only possible viewpoint to explain and foresee the behaviour of complex entities that can act teleologically' (Sartor 2009: 272), a new set of obligations emerge in the field of contracts.

Think of the robot's counterparty who should be allowed to expect, in good faith, that the machine really means what it declares, e.g., a contractual offer, so that the owner or user of the robot cannot evade liability by claiming she did not intend to conclude such a contract. Moreover, humans should not be able to avoid the usual consequence of robots making a decisive mistake, i.e., the annulment of a contract, when the human counterpart had to have been aware of a mistake that, due to the erratic behaviour of the robot, clearly concerned either the market price of an item or the substance of the subject matter of that contract. In all these cases, it seems reasonable to expect that the humans involved in such transactions should be bound by the interpretation of the behaviour of the robot that usually applies to the circumstances of the case according to existing conventions of business and civil law. Legal rules designed for humans, in other words, could be applied to robots, pursuant to the principle of *cuius commoda eius et incommoda*, that is, a party enjoying the benefits of an activity is to bear the inconveniences invoked by such activity.

Notwithstanding that there already are a number of artificial agents that autonomously send bids, accept offers, request quotes, negotiate deals, and so forth, there are two main problems with the new weak responsibility thesis. On one hand, current strict liability policies might prevent the use and production of 'robo-traders', as the unpredictability of their behaviour entails a risk that individuals may be ruined by their own robots' activities and intentions. Since the beginning of the new millennium, the eagerness to trade as demonstrated by certain artificial agents, such as ZI agents, has given rise to troubling similarities with the greediness of human speculators and 'real life' bubbles in markets, insofar as agents are overwhelmed by the complexity of the environment and appear extremely 'inexperienced' (Pagallo 2010). Likewise, it has been stressed 'that some of the financial troubles of late 2009 may have been caused by the involvement of such agents operating without human supervision and at speeds not amenable to human understanding or intervention' (Chopra and White 2011: 7). Are strict liability rules and traditional insurance policies then a sound way of addressing such new scenarios? Is there an alternative scheme in order to strike a fair balance between the individual's claim to not be ruined by the 'decisions' of their robots and the claim of a robot's counterparty to be protected when doing business with them?

On the other hand, the new weak responsibility thesis falls short in coping with further robotics applications that scarcely fit the proprietary regime described above. This is the case of current research on AI cars and prototypes of 'intelligent' artificial chauffeurs as those shown at the Frankfurt Motor Show in September 2011. Whether future unmanned ground vehicles (UGVs) are going to need special licenses or compulsory insurance policies, such 'autoficial intelligence', in the phrasing of *The Economist*, suggests some parallels with the hypothesis of harm provoked by previous robotic applications. In the name of urban sustainability and green policies, these UGVs raise new forms of distributed responsibility (both moral and legal) as soon as we reflect, say, on schemes of AI car sharing. One of the main challenges of autonomous machines revolves around the ways we train, treat, or manage our robots, as such robots gain knowledge or skills from their own interaction with the living beings inhabiting the surrounding environment. As a result, the same model of AI car we are planning to buy next Christmas will behave quite differently after few days or weeks. In the case of environmentally friendly-AI car sharing, who should be liable when the vehicle has an accident and it is clear that only the artificial chauffeur was in control? Is the new weak responsibility thesis able to successfully address these types of distributed liability, in which an artificial chauffeur will be interacting with a number of different people?

Confronted with such scenarios, certain scholars recommend introducing forms of limited responsibility via the 'personal accountability of robots' in order to regulate new types of transactions mediated by artificial agents and tomorrow's smart AI vehicles, i-Jeeves 2.0, and the like (Pagallo 2011a). Whereas the aim is to avert any legislation preventing the use of robots due to excessive burdens on the owners (rather than producers and designers) of these machines, the idea is that, at times, only 'robots shall pay' could be the right answer. By registering such machines, just like corporations (Lerouge 2000; Weitzenboeck 2001); bestowing them with capital (Bellia 2001); or, at least, making the financial position of such machines transparent (Sartor 2009); scholars propose to introduce new types of artificial agency in the field of contracts. In other words, welcome to the new strong responsibility thesis.

3.4 The New Strong Responsibility Thesis

The idea that (some types of) robots may be held directly accountable for their own behaviour has a precedent in the ancient Roman law mechanism of *peculium* (Katz 2008; Pagallo 2010). In the phrasing of the Digest of Justinian, the *peculium* was 'the sum of money or property granted by the head of the household to a slave or son-in-power. Although considered for some purposes as a separate unit, and so allowing a business run by slaves to be used almost as a limited company, it remained technically the property of the head of the household' (Watson 1988: xxxv–xxxvi). According to the pragmatism of ancient Roman law, slaves were thus considered as 'things' that nevertheless could play a crucial role both in trade and commerce. The elite of the slaves, as in the case of the emperor's slaves, were estate managers, bankers, and merchants, holding important jobs as public servants, or entering into binding contracts, managing and making use of property for their masters' family business. While most of the slaves certainly had no rights to claim against their own masters, some of them enjoyed a significant 'autonomy'. This was the case of the *institor* (*Dig*. XIV, 3, 11, 3; XV, 1, 47), who managed different classes of convenience stores (*taverna*), such as bakeries and barber shops; taverns for the sale of wine, hot drinks, or ready-prepared meat; and even booksellers' minimarts! When Emperor Nero was convinced to participate in the Olympic games of 67 A.D. in order to improve relations with Greece, it was not a joke that he entrusted his freedman Helios with the right to convict or seize anyone in Rome.

The parallels between robots and slaves are therefore attractive, because a sort of 'digital peculium' would allow lawyers to address the open questions of the new weak responsibility thesis. By admitting that rights and obligations established by robots can be guaranteed by their own portfolio, this form of artificial accountability might avert legislation to prevent the use of robots due to the unpredictability of their behaviour. In addition to mechanisms of distributing risk through insurance models (Karnow 1996), or via authentication systems (Katz 2008), a 'digital peculium' can in fact strike a fair balance between an individual's claim not to be negatively affected by the decisions of their machines and the interest of a robot's counterparty to be able to safely interact or do business with them. On one hand, we may determine that human contractual liability should be limited to the value of the robot's portfolio (plus, eventually, any compulsory insurance as set above). On the other hand, the mechanism could be applied beyond the original purpose of Roman lawyers, so as to comprise matters of extra-contractual responsibility, i.e. robots damaging 'third parties' rather than affecting their contractual counterparties.

Such a way of mitigating today's strict liability policies has nonetheless its limits (Pagallo 2010). As previously stated, we do not have sufficient enough data on the probability of events, their consequences and costs, to determine levels of risk and, therefore, the amount of the *peculium* on which new forms of accountability for the behaviour of such machines may hinge. Moreover, by considering the capability of robots to improve the rules by which their AI properties change regardless of external stimuli, how will we sever tomorrow's chain of liability? Similarly to the new weak responsibility thesis, how will the increasing unforeseeability of robot behaviour affect matters of legal causation or human negligence? In this latter case, for instance, how should we apportion liability when the injuries alleged by a plaintiff were caused by her own negligence combined with that of an artificial agent? How would a negligent robot appear?

That which certain advocates of the new strong responsibility thesis claim, however, is different. Forms of artificial accountability such as the 'digital peculium' would not be unsatisfactory because, say, the parallels between robots and slaves are deemed unethical or anthropologically biased (see above in Sect. 3.3.1). Rather, the autonomy granted by such forms of accountability is reckoned insufficient because once we accept that some artificial agents may be properly conceived of as strict agents in the field of contracts, their legal personhood would then follow as a result. In the wording of Chopra and White (2011:182)

> none of the philosophical objections to personhood for artificial agents – most but not all of them based on 'a missing something argument' – can be sustained, in the sense that artificial agents can be plausibly imagined that display that allegedly missing behaviour or attribute. If this is the case, then in principle artificial agents should be able to qualify for independent legal personality, since it is the closest legal analogue to the philosophical conception of a person.

Hence, the independent legal personality of robots and of other artificial agents does not simply add up to the dependent legal personality of other artificial persons such as governments, organizations, companies or corporations, whose liability is ultimately reducible to an aggregation of human beings as the only relevant source of their actions. Moreover, 'at the risk of offending humanist sensibilities', Chopra and White argue that we should yield before the fact that, sooner or later, robots will be a sort of 'being *sui juris*', capable of 'sensitivity to legal obligations' and even of 'susceptibility to punishment' (Chopra and White 2011: 180). Going back to the Sci-Fi scenarios described in the second section of this chapter, we would therefore be confronted with robots bestowed with the human-like equipment of free will, autonomy and moral sense, 'possessing a moral susceptibility to punishment' that finally allows us 'to forgive a computer' (Chopra and White 2011: 180). According to the variant of the new strong responsibility thesis provided by Storrs Hall, we might imagine a robot that 'will act like a moral agent in many ways', insofar as it is 'conscious to the extent that it summarizes its actions in a unitary narrative, and (...) has free will, to the extent that it weights its future acts using a model informed by the narrative; in particular, its behaviour will be influenced by reward and punishment' (Hall 2007: 348).

On this basis, the distinction between 'law as code' that may delimit or foster, but not constitute human autonomy, and 'law as code' that *vice versa* constitutes and defines a robot's autonomous behaviour, fades away. Whilst advancements in technology would produce artificial agents capable of autonomous decisions 'similar in all relevant aspects to the ones humans make' (Chopra and White 2011: 177), on the other hand recent findings in both neuroscience and cognitive psychology rebut Kant's classical account of human autonomy as 'the property that the will has of being a law unto itself' (Kant 1891/1795: 108). The objection that robots, contrary to humans, are 'just a programmed machine' is rejected, since 'too many similarities can be drawn between the combination of our biological design and social conditioning, and the programming of agents for us to take comfort in the proclamation we are not programmed while artificial agents unequivocally are' (Chopra and White 2011: 176).

Accordingly, advocates of the 'independent legal personality' variant of the new strong responsibility thesis either argue that the legal personhood of robots follows from the status of such machines as strict agents in the civil law field, or reckon that no philosophical argument obstructs the capability of robots to having rights and duties of their own. However, the independent legal personality argument seems ultimately flawed for three reasons. First, the example of the legal status of slaves under ancient Roman law shows that strict legal agency in contract law and the legal personhood of robots are not correlated. A sketchy remark on the history of the law suffices to remind us that no particular reasons exist for claiming that the legal personhood of robots is necessarily entwined with their status of strict agents in the civil law field. Even the European Union, after all, existed for two decades without enjoying its own legal personhood!

Second, according to the current state of the art technology, robots are far away from achieving a human-like endowment of free will, autonomy, and moral sense, despite the controversial meaning of such expressions. In fact, I would concede that 'without necessarily imagining some Sci-Fi scenarios where robots are provided with consciousness, free will and emotions, in a few years we are going to cohabit with robots endowed with self-knowledge and autonomy – in the engineering meaning of these words' (Veruggio 2007: 27). However, it is the engineering meaning of these words that reminds us of the very difference between criminal law and civil law stressed in this chapter: the level of autonomy, which is sufficient to have relevant effects in the field of contracts, arguably is insufficient to bring today's robots before judges and have them found guilty by criminal courts. The reason hinges on the fact that intelligence emerges from the rules of the contractual game, rather than personal choices of the robotic agent.

Third, I may admit that, once a novel generation of robots endowed with human-like free will, autonomy, or moral sense materializes, lawyers should be ready to tackle robot revolutions, rebellions, expropriations, resistance, robberies, and so forth. But, if we accept that the culpability of the agent, i.e., its *mens rea* would be rooted in the artificial mind of a machine capable of a measure of empathy or a type of autonomy that affords intentional actions, it is more than likely that the meaning of traditional notions such as stealing, rioting, or killing, will change. As a matter of fact, what the meaning of such legal concepts would be is still assigned to the imagination of science fiction writers, rather than the science faction-analysis of legal experts. Would an AI lawyer be an advocate of the tradition of natural law, so that rules should be viewed as an objective imperative whose infringement implies a violation of the nature of the artificial agent? Would the robot *vice versa* be a sort of legal realist, so that norms depend on how these machines affect human understanding of the world, their own knowledge and environment? And how about the institutional stances of AI lawyers who, contrary to their fellow colleagues keen to follow the Kelsenian lesson of the pure doctrine of the law, focus on the substantive mechanisms of the new robotic order?

At the end of the day, nobody knows where these scenarios could end up. By drawing a line between the power of science fiction and the science factional-limits of legal analysis, it is likely that the independent personhood of robots will not be on the agenda for the foreseeable future. Since these machines lack specific psychological components, such as self-consciousness and human-like intentions, robots are good candidates for new types of accountability in the field of contracts, rather than full-fledged personality that bears both the civil and criminal responsibilities of the moral agent.

3.5 Conclusion

This chapter has dwelt on today's legal challenges raised by robotics and the distinction Mireille Hildebrandt (2011) draws between science fiction and science faction. This viewpoint has been defined by the increasing autonomy of artificial agents and the differences between two types of 'law as code', namely legal codes for humans that do not constitute, but rather foster or limit, individual autonomy, and legal codes for robots that contemporaneously establish and delimit the autonomy of such machines. Whilst this difference may be traced back to the 'matter-of-fact' engineering problems of Asimov's robot stories, we examined why most legal scholars reckon that robots should be deemed as morally not responsible and criminally unaccountable for their actions. Lest we embrace Sci-Fi scenarios, it would be pointless to put robots on trial, since such machines lack the set of preconditions for attributing liability to a party in the realm of criminal law. Although robots, such as Hal 9000, Robbie CX30, and Vocaloid HRP-4C, do represent a new source of good and evil – that is, they are 'morally accountable' in the jargon of Floridi and Sanders (2004) – we have to differentiate this form of agency from the criminal liability of robots, that is, between the source of relevant moral actions and the evaluation of agents as being morally responsible for a given behaviour. Otherwise, by blurring moral accountability and criminal responsibility for 'what robots want', we would be forced back to the days when criminal trials were commonly performed against animals (Ewald 1995).

Still, we also considered the science factional side of this story: Despite the criminal unaccountability of robots, these machines challenge basic tenets of the law, because they affect notions such as reasonable foreseeability, causation, or apportioned responsibility based on individual negligence. Consequently, this chapter has insisted on a new weak responsibility thesis for the behaviour of robots and a variant of the new strong responsibility thesis, namely, the dependent legal personality of robots. On one hand, the new weak responsibility thesis sheds light on the fact that this is the first time ever legal systems will hold humans liable for what an artificial state-transition system autonomously 'decides' to do. Moreover, in connection with the current loopholes in legal systems, it is likely that new crimes for humans who unjustly damage or destroy their robots, as well as new types of punishments for machines that represent a meaningful target of human censorship, will emerge. At the risk of offending some supporters of the robots' liberation-front, however, I stressed a key difference. Rather than hypotheses of, say, 'robo-traders' slavery, it is more urgent to address new types of human responsibility for robot behaviour and, hence, to dwell on the very possibility that some kinds of autonomous (lethal) machines should ultimately be banned.

On the other hand, the new strong responsibility thesis brings us back to the very difference between science faction and science fiction, between advocates of the 'dependent legal personality' of robots and supporters of their 'independent legal personality'. *Pace* the forefront of robotic liberation, we have seen that such machines lack crucial requisites to have rights and duties of their own. As a result, the focus should be on new forms of accountability for robotic behaviour in the field of civil (as opposed to the criminal) law and, furthermore, it seems reasonable to differentiate a number of applications such as humanoids, adaptive robot servants, robot soldiers, and even robot nannies, each of which has its own benefits and drawbacks. Despite every one-size-fits-all attempt to grasp notions of agency and responsibility for the behaviour of robots, the examples of C-3P0, CX30, or HRP-4C illustrate that it is more than likely that drones and other types of autonomous (lethal) weapons will mainly affect the criminal law field and the no new responsibility thesis, whereas other applications as robo-traders and AI chauffeurs will mostly concern contractual obligations as well as the new weak and strong responsibility theses. By further distinguishing new types of human responsibility for the behaviour of their autonomous machines (criminal law), and new forms of personal accountability for robots under certain circumstances (civil law), the aim of this chapter has thus been to fill some of the gaps of the new weak responsibility thesis in civil law, so as to avert legislation that might prevent the production and use of robots due to the unpredictability and risk of their behaviour. Whether through capital requirements and transparency about their financial health, forms of limited liability as a 'digital peculium' or new insurance models, what is at stake legally concerns striking a balance between counterparties of robots demanding the ability to safely interact or transact with such machines, and individuals claiming that they should not be ruined by the decisions or behaviour of their robots. The distinction between criminal unaccountability and the civil liability of robots stresses the idea that in some fields of social interaction, such as with pacts and contractual obligations, intelligence emerges from the rules of the game rather than individual choices. Fruitful convergences between law and literature on 'what robots want' should not blur a basic distinction between good science fiction and the factional limits of legal science.

References

Asaro, P. 2008. How just could a robot war be? *Frontiers in Artificial Intelligence and Applications* 75: 50–64.

Asimov, I. 1995. *The complete robot: The definitive collection of robot stories*. London: Harper Collins.

Barrio, F. 2008. Autonomous robots and the law. *Society for Computers and Law.* Available at: http://www.scl.org/site.aspx?i=ho0. Last accessed 7 Nov 2012.

Bellia, A. 2001. Contracting with electronic agents. *Emory Law Journal* 50(4): 1047–1092.

Ĉapek, K. 2004, orig. 1920. *Rossum's universal robots.* Trans. C. Novack. New York: Penguin.

Chopra, S., and L.F. White. 2011. *A legal theory for autonomous artificial agents*. Ann Arbor: The University of Michigan Press.

Davis, J. 2011. The (common) laws of man over (civilian) vehicles unmanned. *Journal of Law, Information and Science*, Special edition: The Law of Unmanned Vehicles. Available at: http://www.scribd.com/doc/59913133/The-Common-Laws-of-Man-Over-Civilian-Vehicles-Unmanned-Comment-by-Emeritus-Prof-J-Davis. Last accessed 7 Nov 2012.

Dostoevsky, F. 1938. *Crime and punishment.* Trans. C. Garnett. New York: Heritage.

Epstein, R.G. 1997. *The case of the killer robot*. New York: Wiley.

Ewald, W.B. 1995. Comparative jurisprudence (I): What was it like to try a rat? *University of Pennsylvania Law Review* 143(6): 1889–2149.

Floridi, L., and J. Sanders. 2004. On the morality of artificial agents. *Minds and Machines* 14(3): 349–379.

Hall, J.S. 2007. *Beyond AI: Creating the conscience of the machine*. Amherst: Prometheus.

Hildebrandt, M. 2011. From Galatea 2.2 to Watson – And back? In *IVR 2011 world conference*, August 15–20, 2011. Frankfurt a. M.

Hildebrandt, M., and J. Gaakeer. 2013. Foreword/prefatory remarks. In *Human law and computer law. Comparative perspectives*, ed. M. Hildebrandt and J. Gaakeer. Dordrecht: Springer.

Hobbes, Th. 1982, orig. 1651. *Leviathan.* New York: Penguin.

Kant, I. 1891, orig. 1795. *Kant's principles of politics, including his essay on perpetual peace. A contribution to political science.* Trans. W. Hastie. Edinburgh: Clark.

Karnow, C.E.A. 1996. Liability for distributed artificial intelligence. *Berkeley Technology and Law Journal* 11(1): 147–183.

Katz, A. 2008. Intelligent agents and internet commerce in ancient Rome. *Society for Computers and Law* 20: 35–38. Available at: http://www.scl.org/site.aspx?i=ho0. Last accessed 7 Nov 2012.

Kelly, K. 2010. *What technology wants*. New York: Viking.

Kurzweil, R. 2005. *The singularity is near*. New York: Viking.

Lerouge, J.F. 2000. The use of electronic agents questioned under contractual law. *John Marshall Journal of Computer and Information Law* 18(2): 403–433.

Lin, P., G. Bekey, and K. Abney. 2007. *Autonomous military robotics: Risk, ethics, and design*. Report for US Department of Navy, Office of Naval Research. Ethics+Emerging Sciences Group at California Polytechnic State University, San Luis Obispo, CA.

Moravec, H. 1999. *Robot: Mere machine to transcendent mind*. London: Oxford University Press.

Pagallo, U. 2010. Robotrust and legal responsibility. *Knowledge, Technology & Policy* 23(3/4): 367–379.

Pagallo, U. 2011a. Designing data protection safeguards ethically. *Information* 2(2): 247–265.

Pagallo, U. 2011b. Robots of just war: A legal perspective. *Philosophy and Technology* 24(3): 307–323.

Pagallo, U. 2011c. Guns, ships, and chauffeurs: The civil use of UV technology and its impact on legal systems. *Journal of Law, Information and Science*, Special edition: The Law of Unmanned Vehicles. Available at: http://www.scribd.com/doc/62461055/Ugo-Pagallo-Guns-Ships-and-Chauffeurs-The-Civilian-Use-of-UV-Technology-and-its-Impact-on-Legal-Systems. Last accessed 7 Nov 2012.

Reynolds, C., and M. Ishikawa. 2007. Robotic thugs. In *2007 ethicomp proceedings*, 487–492. Tokyo: Global e-SCM Research Center & Meiji University.

Sartor, G. 2009. Cognitive automata and the law: Electronic contracting and the intentionality of software agents. *Artificial Intelligence and Law* 17(4): 253–290.

Toffler, A. 1980. *The third way*. New York: Bantam.

Veruggio, G. 2007. Euron roboethics roadmap. In *Proceedings Euron roboethics atelier*, Feb 27–March 3 2006, Genoa. Available at: http://www.roboethics.org/index_file/Roboethics%20 Roadmap%20Rel.1.2.pdf. Last accessed 7 Nov 2012.

Watson, A. 1988. *The digest of Justinian*, vol. I. Philadelphia: University of Pennsylvania Press.

Weitzenboeck, E.M. 2001. Electronic agents and the formation of contracts. *International Journal of Law and Information Technology* 9(3): 204–234.

Chapter 4
Abort, Retry, Fail: Scoping Techno-Regulation and Other Techno-Effects

Bibi van den Berg and Ronald E. Leenes

> *Questions about the way that code regulates, and about its role within systems of social ordering more generally, are systematically overlooked.*
>
> (Cohen 2012: 20)

Abstract Technology affects behaviour. Speed bumps, for instance, provide an effective way to enforce speed limits imposed by the legislator. In cases such as these, technology is instrumental to the enforcement of legal norms. This kind of regulation by technology, techno-regulation, or 'code as code' has become part of the contemporary regulator's toolbox. The idea underlying this kind of influencing behaviour by means of technology is relatively straightforward. Norms can be transformed into computer code or architecture in a way that affords certain actions or functions and inhibits others. What is less clear is what the boundaries of techno-regulation are. In this paper we analyse how technology affects human behaviour and we present a typology of techno-effects in order to provide a clear boundary of techno-regulation vis-à-vis other normative and functional aspects of technology. We survey topics such as nudging, affordance, scripts embedded in technological designs, and anthropomorphization. The paper draws from legal philosophy, STS, human computer interaction and regulation theory.

B. van den Berg (✉)
Leiden Law School, eLaw, Leiden University, Steenschuur 25,
Leiden 2311 ES, The Netherlands
e-mail: b.van.den.berg@law.leidenuniv.nl

R.E. Leenes
Tilburg Institute for Law, Technology, and Society, Tilburg University,
Tilburg, The Netherlands
e-mail: R.E.Leenes@uvt.nl

M. Hildebrandt and J. Gaakeer (eds.), *Human Law and Computer Law: Comparative Perspectives*, Ius Gentium: Comparative Perspectives on Law and Justice 25,
DOI 10.1007/978-94-007-6314-2_4,

4.1 Introduction

Regulators and designers have long since realised that (technological) artefacts can be deployed in various ways to influence, steer and/or change human behaviour. Architects know that the design of a space directly affects the behaviour of individuals in that space. Using the placement of, for example, barriers, doors, passageways and staircases they can predict and affect the way individuals move through or use a space. Similarly, when designers create new technologies, their design choices have a bearing on the way in which these products are used: they can steer the behaviour of users by facilitating some forms of use, while inhibiting others (cf. Dommering 2006: 7; Norman 1988; Van den Berg 2010b). What is more, regulators sometimes use artefacts to directly influence the behaviour of citizens as well. For example, using speed bumps is a very effective way to ensure that drivers adhere to a speed limit set in a specific area – it leaves drivers much less room to drive too fast than, for example, the placement of traffic signs does (Brownsword 2008; Latour 1992; Leenes 2010, 2011; Yeung 2008). At Underground and train stations one way to ensure that travellers obtain a valid ticket is to install entry gates to the tracks that only open if the passenger has such a ticket. This, too, is a form of enforcing a legal norm through the use of artefacts (cf. Morgan and Yeung 2007; Yeung 2008). But it is not just government or state regulators who use technologies to influence individual behaviour – private parties may choose to do so as well. The DVD industry, for instance, implemented region codes into DVD players, to make it impossible for users to play DVDs bought in other regions than their own (Leenes 2010, 2011) – a way to protect regional DVD markets and undermine global competition.

All of these forms of guiding and affecting human behaviour have come to be known as 'techno-regulation' (Brownsword 2008; Leenes 2010, 2011; Van den Berg 2011), 'design-based regulation' (Brownsword and Yeung 2008) or 'code as code' (Lessig 2006). Techno-regulation revolves around the idea that technologies may be used as *regulatory tools* (Brownsword and Yeung 2008).

4.2 What Is Techno-Regulation?

In studies on techno-regulation, and on regulation in general, scholars tend to define regulation as 'the *intentional* influencing of someone's or something's behaviour' (Koops 2010: 309, italics BB and RL) or '*deliberate* state influence'(Baldwin et al. 2010: 12, italics BB and RL). The former definition allows for both state and non-state – e.g. private enterprises – actors engaged in regulation, whereas the latter is restricted to only state regulators. By extension, *techno*-regulation, is generally discussed as the *intentional* influencing of individuals' behaviour by building norms into technological devices. In short, the focus of debates on (techno-) regulation is on efforts to steer or affect human behaviour through intentional, deliberate means, either in general or through the use of technological artefacts. In and of itself, this is not surprising: the legal domain sets out to provide citizens with both positive and negative boundaries within which their behaviours should stay, and to do so on legitimate and deliberate grounds. Hence it is understandable (and commendable!) that the means through which the creation and implementation of such boundaries are enacted, are intentional, deliberate, purposeful and the result of forethought – rather than accidental, random, unintended, or without a purpose.

4.3 The Limits of the Debate on Techno-Regulation

However, unfortunately there are two shortcomings to the current conceptual understanding that we have of techno-regulation. First of all, by focusing exclusively on *regulation* through the use of technologies, this domain excludes other, 'softer', less 'legal' forms of influencing, simply through the choice of its terminology. The fact that technologies may also be used to *persuade*, or to *nudge*, for example, is left un(der)addressed. While some scholars in the field of Law & Technology do mention such softer forms of (intentional) technological influencing (cf. Hildebrandt 2011; Leenes 2010, 2011), all too often techno-regulation is understood to refer only to the enforcement of legal norms enacted by (state) legislatures and rules through the use of technological artefacts. The practical examples of techno-regulation discussed in the literature, which we have also mentioned above,[1] are telling in this respect: they all refer to hard-coded, (almost) unavoidable legal rules that are enabled, or inhibited, through the technology. Nudging, or other forms of more gentle persuasion, and all of the technological possibilities these entail, largely falls outside the scope of the current debate on techno-regulation, because of its emphasis on (legal) *regulation* alone.

Moreover, the focus on *intentional* influencing, with or without the help of technologies, has a serious downside as well: it overlooks the fact that technologies, and artefacts in general, may also influence users in all sorts of *un*intentional and rather implicit ways. The design of technologies, at times, has unintended consequences in use – what we call side effects. Moreover, research reveals that technological artefacts often evoke strong (unintended!) emotional responses in users, and that users anthropomorphize (some of) these artefacts. These forms of unintended and implicit influencing also fall outside the scope of techno-regulation – this time because of its focus on intentional influencing alone.

Both of these shortcomings to the investigative repertoire of the domain of techno-regulation are quite serious. By overlooking, or downplaying, the unintentional and implicit responses that technological artefacts may invoke, (techno-)regulators run two, quite contrary, risks:

[1] I.e. the use of speed bumps to regulate driving speeds, entry gates to exclude travel(lers) without a valid ticket, and region codes on DVD players.

1. they may not use the power of influencing, steering and affecting human behaviour to its full extent, thereby missing out on opportunities to regulate or steer the behaviour of individuals through technologies; and
2. they may fail to notice the unintended and implicit consequences of the techno-regulatory measures they *do* implement, thereby jeopardizing, at least in part, the intentionality, and by implication ultimately the legitimacy, of such measures.

What is more, by overlooking the entire scale of possible responses that can be evoked by means of, or through technologies, citizens run certain risks as well. Most importantly, when norms are embedded into technological artefacts they may become obfuscated to users, hence making it harder (if not impossible) for users/citizens to criticize the norms they are made to adhere to, or use their democratic opportunity to challenge such norms in a court of law.[2] Again, this entails that techno-regulation and its related manifestations may raise questions of legitimacy. Obviously, this problem is all the more urgent when regulators unintentionally implement norms into technological artefacts.

In this article, we will carve out the landscape of techno-regulation and its adjacent areas, by investigating the boundaries of intentional influencing and exploring what lies beyond. By developing a clearer understanding of the full scope of influencing-through-technology – both intentional, regulatory, non-regulatory, and unintentional – we may get a better grasp of techno-regulation as one of its manifestations, and hence consolidate the scientific enterprise of Law & Technology.

4.4 Beyond the Limits of Techno-Regulation, Part 1: Persuasion, Nudging and Affordances

As said, the first shortcoming in the current debate on techno-regulation is its (almost) exclusive focus on the implementation of *legal* norms into technologies. 'Softer' forms of regulation, such as the embedding of social norms into artefacts,

[2]Note that merely *automating* procedures to prevent or detect violations of rules and regulations does not necessarily entail that these rules become obfuscated, nor that proper procedures cannot be developed to ensure that citizens have a possibility to contest these rules or their application. Think, for example of the use of speed cameras in traffic, for which there are proper procedures to 'seek redress in the courts if [citizens] disagree with the content of the decision or the procedural aspects of the decision-making. All this has become part of the routine of the rule of law in our democracies' (Dommering 2006: 8). The difference between merely automating (instances of) crime prevention and detection and techno-regulation is twofold: (1) systems of the former deliver *ex post* punishment for violations of the law and (hence) leave room for disobeying the rules, whereas in techno-regulation the technology delivers *ex ante* prevention and there is no room for violating the law; and (2) the technologies used for the former, e.g. cameras that detect flows of traffic, generally provide cues *that* a rule is being enforced in a certain location, and *what* rule this could possibly be. In the case of techno-regulation oftentimes this clarity is lacking – think of the example of entry gates to the Underground: many people will undoubtedly be unaware of the fact that this barrier enforces a rule regarding the contractual relationship between a traveller and a transport company. Both differences contribute to the claim that it is more difficult for citizens to contest norms and rules when they are implemented by means of techno-regulation.

thus fall outside the scope of the current debate. This is unfortunate, since there is a wide array of research that suggests that such 'soft' forms of regulation are abundant, and have profound effects on the ways in which users interact with, and are affected by, the technologies that surround them. We will briefly discuss three examples of such research. First, in his research on what he calls 'captology', B.J. Fogg shows that information and communication technologies can be used in effective ways to persuade individuals to do (or abstain from doing) certain things, to adopt (or reject) certain beliefs, or to change certain attitudes or behaviours (Fogg 2003). According to Fogg, examples of the persuasive capacities of ICTs are everywhere around us. For instance, captology techniques are used extensively on websites to persuade users to buy products or services – think of Amazon.com, which gives suggestions of books that readers may find interesting, or eBay, which uses ratings to persuade users that certain sellers are trustworthy.

Moreover, several ICT systems have been developed over the past decades to confront individuals directly with the (possibly) negative consequences of certain behaviours, thus attempting to convince them to avoid such behaviour. For example, drunk driving simulators are designed to change teenagers' attitudes to drinking and driving. Such simulators respond with a delay and exaggerate steering behaviour, so that youngsters can experience directly what it is like to drive under the influence of alcohol. By exposing teenagers to such an immersive, technologically facilitated experience, the designers hope to convince them to avoid drunk driving. A second example of persuading teenagers into avoiding risky or undesirable behaviour through the use of technology is that of a highly sophisticated robot doll, which aims at raising young girls' awareness of the effects of teenage pregnancies. Teenage girls are asked to take care of this doll for a set period of time in their own homes, thus experiencing the practical consequences of having to take care of an infant.

All these examples show that computers and other ICTs offer unique opportunities to alter human behaviour, to persuade users to change their attitudes or beliefs. But why is this so? For one thing, computers allow for what Fogg calls 'tunnelling': they can take users through a predetermined path of steps, persuading them to follow this path. Installing software is a good example of this kind of process. Tunnelling narrows users' scope of behavioural choices, and in the process their sense of *having* choices as well. Thus, it enhances the chances of persuasion: once a given sequence is set in motion, the user is tempted to follow through until the end, because he wants to get the task done (Fogg 2003).

Moreover, ICTs may also persuade in the sense that they may 'condition' individual behaviour (Fogg 2003: 49):

> A conditioning technology is a computerized system that uses principles of operant conditioning to change behaviors. (…) operant conditioning (…) is a method that uses positive reinforcements – or rewards – to increase the instances of a behavior or to shape complex behaviors.

A good example of operant conditioning can be found in games: when users play a game correctly they are rewarded with points and all kinds of bonuses, such as gaining extra lives, getting extra capabilities, tools or weapons etcetera.

Finally, computers and other ICTs can play a role in what Fogg calls 'self-monitoring': these kinds of technologies allow users to monitor some aspect of themselves (for example their heart rates or their calorie intake), and by providing them regular feedback on the monitored parameter, they may persuade users to adjust their behaviour in such a way as to work toward a predetermined goal.

All of these forms of persuasion, brought about by means of computer technologies, revolve around the idea that the behaviour, beliefs, or attitudes of users can be influenced, steered or guided. Note that when technologies are used to persuade individuals as described here, i.e. to change their behaviour, this is done *intentionally*, not accidentally. However, none of the examples discussed here involves 'regulation' in a traditional, or legal sense. Moreover, note that the behavioural changes that the intentional design of a persuasive technology seeks to bring about are *optional* to the user – an (intentional) attempt is made to convince the user to adopt a certain behaviour, but (s)he has a clear and free choice in adopting or rejecting this behaviour. In this respect captology differs from the second example we wish to discuss in this section: nudging.

In their book *Nudge: Improving decisions about health, wealth and happiness* Thaler and Sunstein (2008) introduce the principle of 'nudging' to help improve the choices individuals make and the behaviours they display. They argue that human behaviours and human choices may be intentionally affected by, for example, the design of spaces, technologies, institutions and systems (Thaler and Sunstein 2008). Building on findings from behavioural economics, Thaler and Sunstein introduce the concept of a 'choice architecture', the idea that designers have a 'responsibility for organizing the context in which people make decisions' (Thaler and Sunstein 2008: 3). Some contexts invoke choices that are qualitatively better than others, according to Thaler and Sunstein, for example because they promote human beings' health, improve their quality of living, or otherwise promote their happiness. Other contexts inhibit such choices, undermine them, or obliterate them. Politicians, regulators, designers and developers have an obligation to create options to meet the choice criteria of the first, rather than the second category, adopting an attitude that is designated 'libertarian paternalism' (Burgess 2012; Thaler and Sunstein 2008). In their book, the authors discuss numerous examples of the ways in which existing systems 'nudge' individuals toward making 'good' choices – ranging from the urinals equipped with the picture of a fly at Schiphol Airport in Amsterdam (to nudge men to aim better), to pension plans that send annual reminders with advice about the best way to improve the long-term output of the individuals' eventual monthly retirement payment, to alarm clocks that jump off the nightstand and wheel around the room until their sleepy/lazy owner gets out of bed to switch them off, thus nudging them to get up.

Nudging, obviously, is a form of intentionally influencing human behaviour, of shaping attitudes or choices. Designers and regulators may use this form of influencing to intentionally regulate the behaviour of individuals without intervening in an all too direct, and obvious, way. Hence, Adam Burgess writes (2012: 9)

> nudging is precisely intended to represent an alternative to clear interventionist approaches; an attempt at a 'third way' between the regulation associated with the left, and 'leave it to the markets' approach of the right.

This is why it has become a popular regulatory strategy for both the US government and some European governments, most notably the current UK administration.

However, while nudging does fall into the category of intentional influencing, it doesn't have much to do with regulation in the strictly legal sense, nor does it involve the enforcement of (legal) norms. It has to do with creating 'good' default settings in the range of choices that individuals have in various contexts, building on the idea that most individuals will not deviate from those default settings and hence will automatically adhere to the option that is deemed best for them by the designers/regulators involved in shaping a system. Nevertheless, nudging *does* leave some room for alternative choices. If a user does not want to go in the direction in which (s)he is being nudged by the choice architect, (s)he has the possibility to choose otherwise. This may lead to behaviour that (arguably) could be labelled unwise, unhealthy or considered detrimental to personal wealth or happiness, but room for manoeuvring is exactly what distinguishes nudging from outright techno-regulation, in which no form of opting out, or 'being bad' is available. However, note also that in the case of nudging an individual's manoeuvring room is considerably smaller than in the case of persuasive technologies. In the latter, users may be tempted to follow the intended behavioural pattern, yet they may equally easily choose not to do so. In contrast, the behavioural pull exerted by a default option, as is envisaged in nudging, is much stronger. While the choice to deviate still exists, the chance that users will actually do so in practice is a lot slimmer.

Taking this idea one step further it is not hard to imagine that while designers or regulators would sometimes intentionally design a feature of use into a technology, or would strive to deliberately alter or affect behaviour trough (the design of) a technological artefact, the *users* of such an artefact need not be aware that this is the case. This idea is captured in the last concept we will discuss in this section: that of *affordances* (Gaver 1991, 1996; Gibson 1986; McGrenere and Ho 2000; Norman 1988). The term affordance was coined by the American psychologist James J. Gibson, who used it to describe the way an environment has a bearing on animals' being by providing them with opportunities and means of sustenance. Gibson writes (1986: 127):

> The affordances of the environment are what it offers to the animal, what it provides or furnishes, either for good or ill. (…) [The term] implies the complementarity of the animal and the environment.

Donald A. Norman translated the notion of affordances to the human use of technologies, turning it into one of the central concepts of (research into) Human-Computer Interaction (Norman 1988). In doing so, Norman aimed to draw attention to the automatic and implicit responses that technologies may call forth in their human users. He argued that when designing new objects or technologies, designers ought to consider what their products will offer to users, what uses they will afford, and by implication, what uses they will constrain. Consciously thinking about the affordances of their products, Norman argued, would greatly improve the quality and usability of products. In a well-designed product the affordances of the object (1988: 9):

provide strong clues to the operations of things. (…) When affordances are taken advantage of, the user knows what to do just by looking: no picture, label, or instruction is required.

The argument here is one that is very similar to what we have seen above in Fogg's persuasive technologies and Thaler and Sunstein's nudging: designers (ought to) intentionally create products in such a way that certain types of behaviour are invoked, encouraged or facilitated, while others are inhibited or discouraged. And again, the invocations and elicitations rendered thus are not of a legal nature, yet they do clearly steer the behaviour of users. However, there is a marked difference between captology and nudging on the one hand, and affordances on the other, and this difference can be found in the level of user awareness. While users have a clear choice in their interactions with persuasive technologies, and a limited choice when being nudged, no real choice is available to them when artefacts (or architectures, for that matter) afford them behaviours and constrain others. What technologies afford us is often perceived in such an implicit and automatic way that we can hardly speak of having a choice to behave differently.

What the discussion in this section reveals is twofold. First and foremost, it shows that persuasion, nudging and affording are more subtle, yet clearly intentional, forms of affecting human behaviour, through the use of technologies, which are overlooked in the current debate on (techno-)regulation. In the former two cases the regulatees still have a (clear) *choice* to follow or reject the technology's invoked effect – to use a concept proposed by Hildebrandt (2008, 2009, 2011), captology and nudging are both examples of situations in which 'regulative rules' are embedded into technology: rules that influence behaviour, yet not in a deterministic manner – people may still choose to act otherwise. However, in the case of affordances, the intentional behavioural effect is such that opting out, or following an alternative choice, is no longer really possible. Thus, to return to Hildebrandt's terminology, in the case of affordances, the technology contains constitutive rules that leave people no (or very little) choice. The embedded rule's consequences are (almost) inevitable once triggered.

Of course, as the level of choice for regulatees decreases, the level of compulsion generated through the intentional choices of the regulators and designers increases. As said, while there is still room for manoeuvring in the case of persuasive technologies and nudging, such room hardly exists in the case of affordances, and as we have seen above in the case of techno-regulation the regulator's control over the regulatees' behaviour is, in fact, complete.

Second, this discussion reveals that while persuasion, nudging, affording and techno-regulation are all forms of intentional influencing on the part of *designers*, the reception of such influencing on the part of users is marked by a gradual decrease in *awareness*. When using persuasive technologies designers and/or regulators use technical means to convince users to change their behaviour, most often by making them experience the consequences of 'bad' behaviour. Users not only have a clear choice in following or rejecting the suggested behaviour change, but are also aware of the fact that the designer/regulator is attempting to persuade them in the first place. In nudging this level of awareness may be much reduced already. By offering users a 'good' default choice, designers/regulators build on the fact that most users

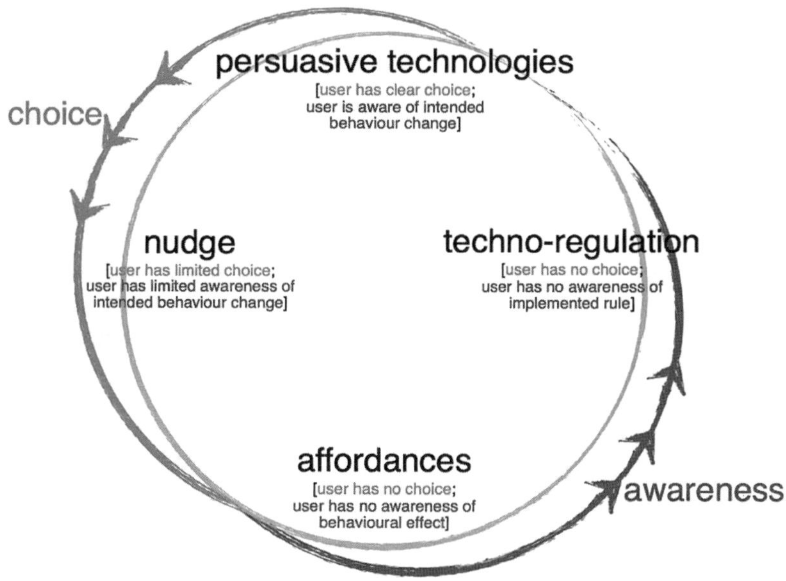

Fig. 4.1 From persuasive technology to techno-regulation: decreasing choice, increasing compulsion, and decreasing user awareness

tend not to invest too much time in checking and altering the default choices offered to them in products, services and software, thus banking on their willingness to follow this default. Some users may still choose to change the default, and hence may be aware that there is such a possibility, but in most cases the majority will not do so, or even be aware of that possibility. What is more, in the case of affordances and techno-regulation, as we have seen, there is no (real) choice to opt out or behave differently. These two forms of steering users' behaviour take place largely outside of their awareness, and in the case of techno-regulation this is precisely one of the reasons why it may be risky, in terms of legitimacy, to steer behaviour in this way.

Figure 4.1 summarizes both aspects – the level of choice/compulsion on the one hand, and the level of user awareness on the other – in relation to the four concepts we have discussed so far.

4.5 Beyond the Limits of Techno-Regulation, Part 2: Unintentional and Implicit Influences of Technology

In the previous section we looked at the limits and limitations that the debate on techno-regulation has known so far based on its focus on *regulation*. We showed that there are a number of varieties of intentional influencing through the use of technologies that fall outside the scope of techno-regulation. In all of these forms regulators and/or designers deliberately steer, guide or influence the behaviours of users in non-legal (and progressively more implicit) ways.

Now we will turn to our second critique, relating to its focus on *intentional* influencing alone. Over the past decades, a significant corpus of research in engineering, computer science, human-computer interaction (HCI), Science and Technology Studies (STS) and philosophy of technology has consistently revealed how ubiquitous and important the *unintended*, *implicit* and *automatic* elicitation of human behaviour is in relation to technological artefacts.

We have already seen a first example of the evocation of automatic and implicit responses at the end of the previous section, when we discussed the idea of affordances. However, while affordances may elicit implicit and automatic responses in users, they are still explicitly, deliberately designed into artefacts by their creators. However, research has revealed that oftentimes designers also implement all sorts of *unintended* cues into their artefacts.

In recent years, much research has been done in Science and Technology Studies on the *scripts* embedded into technological artefacts (Akrich 1992; Gjøen and Hård 2002; MacKenzie and Wajcman 1999; Oudshoorn and Pinch 2003; Oudshoorn et al. 2004; Van den Berg 2008, 2010b). Madeleine Akrich explains that throughout the design process of new technologies, designers use certain images or representations of their 'target audience'. These images and representations help shape the design itself, because the (presumed!) 'specific tastes, competences, motives, aspirations, political prejudices' of users become inscribed into the artefact (Akrich 1992: 208). This is what Akrich calls a *script*. Scripts have an active role: as Van Oost argues these implemented user images will eventually steer, guide, and limit the behaviour of the user (2003: 195):

> artifacts contain a script and this script prescribes (in a more or less coercive manner) what users have to do (or not do) to produce the envisioned functioning of the technological artifact.

Her work on the design of male and female electric shavers by the multinational electronics company Philips shows just how this works. Van Oost compared the male and female shavers developed by Philips to see how they differed, and what the effects of their differences could be on the ways in which users perceive and use them. She concluded that there is a clear set of values embedded into these shavers, which tacitly reflect ideas on gender differences. Male shavers are grey and black, contain dials and screws, and can be opened up by the user to take a look 'under the hood'. They are truly 'technological' artefacts – men can tinker with them and fix them when they are broken. Female shavers, by contrast, are smooth, come in pastel colours, have no dials and screws, and cannot be taken apart because their separate parts are clicked (rather than screwed) together during the production process (Van Oost 2003). Moreover, they are sold as cosmetic devices, and not as electrical appliances (Van Oost 2003: 202). These differences reflect designers' perceptions of female and male users as being afraid of technology and being gadget-lovers respectively.

What is interesting is that several separate strands of research, including Science and Technology Studies (Akrich 1995; Gjøen and Hård 2002; Haddon 2003; Oudshoorn and Pinch 2003; Oudshoorn et al. 2004; Silverstone and Haddon 1996; Van Oost 2003), value-sensitive design (Friedman 1997; Friedman and Kahn 2006; Friedman et al. 2002), and philosophy of design (Kroes et al. 2009; Verbeek 2005) consistently reveal that designers are often *unaware* of the values, norms and stereotypes they embed into the artefacts they create, for example through the embedding of scripts. One possible explanation for such tacit value-embedding by designers is called 'I-methodology' (Akrich 1995; Oudshoorn et al. 2004): designers' tendency to take themselves, their own needs and capacities, as the main point of reference in design (Van den Berg 2010b). Needless to say, the designers' needs and capacities, and the accompanying values, need not necessarily align with those of ordinary users. Nevertheless, as we have seen in Van Oost's research on shavers, the values that get embedded into artefacts because of this do actively shape and limit the behaviour of users – or at least the behavioural repertoire an artefact facilitates or allows.

So do users have a *choice* in relation to scripts? Should we label scripts as regulative or constitutive rules, to return to Hildebrandt's distinction? The answer is: both. Scripts are constitutive, in the sense that once users choose to use a specific artefact, it is very likely that they will be strongly affected by the values embedded into them. As Van Oost explains (2003: 207):

> the gender script of the Ladyshave inhibits (symbolically as well as material[ly]) the ability of women to see themselves as interested in technology and as technologically competent, whereas the gender script of the Philipshaves invites men to see themselves that way.

However, at the same time scripts are also regulative – i.e. they leave some room for manoeuvring, if only a little – in the sense that users can choose to *not* use an artefact, or to counter the embedded scripts they uncover in an artefact. Again, Van Oost provides a good explanation (2003: 207):

> Clearly, the gender script of the shavers cannot force users to invoke these gendered identities: women can reject the script (e.g. by shaving with a men's shaver or not shaving) or even modify the script (e.g. see it as a technological challenge to open the clicked Ladyshave).

That users may also create their *own* scripts when using technologies has been the subject of extensive research in Science and Technology Studies and domestication theory (Frissen 1994, 2004; Haddon 2003; Lehtonen 2003; Silverstone and Haddon 1996). For example, when investigating scripts surrounding the electric car and its use and social acceptance in Norway Gjøen and Hård found that users sometimes come up with their own scripts (aptly called 'user scripts') to complement or alter those embedded by designers (Gjøen and Hård 2002). In the case of the electric car they found that one of the users had named the car 'Barbie' because it is small and cute. With this feminine name, Gjøen and Hård argue, this user turned existing cultural scripts concerning cars – labelling them as gendered, masculine vehicles – upside down. She turned it into 'a distinctly female automobile, even a girlish toy' (Gjøen and Hård 2002: 268). The authors conclude that user scripts such as these may eventually lead to 'another cultural understanding of what a car is' (Gjøen and Hård 2002: 272). Although this claim is tenuous, to say the least, since it is based on this one example only, other examples from research into the domestication of ICTs and household appliances supports the idea that users do, in fact, regularly create their own scripts, as a way to 'domesticate technology by assigning new meanings to an artifact' (Gjøen and Hård 2002: 278).

In sum, we may conclude that scripts are yet another example of technological influencing, or influencing-through-technology, that falls outside the domain of techno-regulation. This is so because their workings not only do not revolve around the enforcement of legal norms through technologies, but also because their influence emerges largely outside the intentions and deliberations of the designers of technologies. As we have seen scripts are not deliberately designed into technologies by designers, but rather the result of (implicit) images and representations of users. When looking at the level of choice these scripts leave to users – or the level of compulsion they (unintentionally) provide designers (and potentially regulators), we see that some room for manoeuvring is available to users, yet it is very limited. Users can challenge scripts or devise their own scripts, but the former, at least, requires that they be aware of the existence and behavioural pull of the scripts embedded into artefacts to begin with. This is dubitable, at least in many cases, and for many users.

A second, clear example of the ways in which designers can unintentionally evoke certain types of responses in users comes from Human-Computer Interaction. Studies have consistently shown that (some) technologies induce tendencies to 'anthropomorphize'[3] them, i.e. that human beings are inclined to ascribe intentions and agency to these inanimate objects, and to respond to them in social and emotional ways (Duffy 2003; Nass and Moon 2000; Nass et al. 1993; Reeves and Nass 1996; Turkle 1984, 2007; Van den Berg 2010a; Weizenbaum 1966). Sherry Turkle conducted a number of famous studies with small children to investigate whether or not they ascribed lifelike qualities (for instance intentions) to computers and digital toys, and found that they clearly do. She explains this by referring to the fact that computers are interactive machines, that appear to respond to children's behaviours, and by the fact that they may produce irregular responses (Turkle 1984: 30). Turkle's studies have since been repeated in various forms by others, and the findings are always the same: children have strong tendencies to ascribe human, lifelike qualities to certain types of technological artefacts. What is more, even *adults* appear to do so. While the tendency to anthropomorphize does diminish with age, even adults may at times find it difficult to maintain that a machine is *not* a living being like themselves. One of the most convincing examples to support this claim comes from Joseph Weizenbaum, the computer scientist who created ELIZA, a computer program that mimicked the behaviour of a Rogerian psychoanalyst (Weizenbaum 1966).[4] Weizenbaum was shocked to find out how strongly users responded to his simple program. He says (Weizenbaum, quoted in Kerr 2004: 305):

---

[3]In philosophy of technology this has been called 'animation'. See for example Ihde (1990: 98 ff.); Verbeek (2005: 126–127).

[4]Computer users could 'communicate' with ELIZA using natural language. The program used a number of quite simple techniques to convert their input into follow-up questions or observations, thus creating the illusion of a real conversation and, what is more, leaving users with the impression that ELIZA actually had the ability to understand them.

> I was startled to see how quickly and very deeply people conversing with [ELIZA] became emotionally involved with the computer and how unequivocally they anthropomorphized it. Once my secretary, who had watched me work on the program for many months and therefore surely knew it to be merely a computer program, started conversing with it. After only a few interchanges with it she asked me to leave the room. Another time, I suggested I might rig the system so that I could examine all the conversations anyone had had with it, say, overnight. I was promptly bombarded with accusations that what I proposed amounted to spying on people's most intimate thoughts; clear evidence that people were conversing with the computer as if it were a person who could be appropriately and usefully addressed in intimate terms.

This leads Turkle to conclude (1984: 39):

> Weizenbaum's students and colleagues who had access to ELIZA knew and understood the limitations of the program's abilities to know and understand. And yet, many of these very sophisticated users related to ELIZA as though it did understand, as though it were a person. With full knowledge that the program could not empathize with them, they confided in it, wanted to be alone with it.

What this example shows is that it is not very difficult to evoke anthropomorphic tendencies in humans, even in adults. Even they can easily ascribe intentions, feelings, and behaviours to machines that are really projections of themselves, of their own human capabilities and faculties.

In a series of experiments Byron Reeves and Clifford Nass (1996) showed that humans not only ascribe intentions and lifelike qualities to technologies, but that they also display real *social responses* to ICTs – responses that are normally reserved for interactions with other human beings. For example, Reeves and Nass found that users are very polite to computers when having to evaluate their behaviours, and that they respond as positively to flattery by computers as by fellow human beings. Moreover, they showed that users ascribe personality to interfaces, and that they experience a sense of teamwork when cooperating with a computer (Reeves and Nass 1996). The experiments showed that only very minimal social cues are needed from ICTs to call forth these social responses, and what is more, that users are *unaware* of the fact that they respond socially to these machines. When questioned about their behaviour after each experiment, it turned out that people *denied* displaying such behaviours towards these technologies (Nass and Moon 2000: 87; Picard 1997: 14–15). Reeves and Nass have called this type of behaviour influencing 'the Media Equation'. Apparently, they conclude, our human brains are so deeply hardwired for social behaviour towards others that it is easy, or even almost unavoidable, to call forth such behaviour towards machines as well (also see Nass and Moon 2000; Nass et al. 1994; Picard 1997). They write (Reeves and Nass 1996: 12–13):

> The human brain evolved in a world in which *only* humans exhibited rich social behaviors, and a world in which all perceived objects were real physical objects. (…) Modern media now engage old brains. People can't always overcome the powerful assumption that mediated presentations are actual people and objects. (…) The default is to automatically and unconsciously ignore fabrication and expect reality, as if the technology itself were invisible.

The authors point out that designers could, and ought to, use this central finding in the design process of the products they create – and we'd add that regulators could use it as well. When designing technologies to meet the social repertoires of human beings, not only would the usability and interactional richness of these artefacts greatly improve, but considering the ease with which these responses are evoked, it could also be yet another means of affecting human behaviour through technology.

Having said that, let us look more closely at the features of anthropomorphism and the Media Equation in terms of choice, intentionality, and legal norms. How do these two forms of technological influencing relate to techno-regulation? First of all, what is most striking about both anthropomorphism and the Media Equation is that users appear to have *no choice* at all in responding to the technologies as they do. Moreover, as the example of ELIZA revealed, users are *unaware* of their own anthropomorphizing tendencies, or at the very least they tend to deny that they have such tendencies – as we have seen users ascribed intentions and humanness to ELIZA despite the fact that they knew full well that Weizenbaum's computer program was simply that: a computer program that lacked any real sense of understanding or empathy. Similarly, each of the experiments that Reeves and Nass conducted led to the same finding: users clearly displayed a host of social responses to the ICTs with which they interacted during the tests, yet fervently denied doing so.

On the side of designers it is clear that much of the findings we have described here fall outside the scope of traditional design approaches and focus. Weizenbaum did not create ELIZA to investigate the anthropomorphizing tendencies of those around him – finding that users responded to his program in this way was a side-effect, and one that deeply disturbed him. He became one of ELIZA's fiercest critics – and of the project of creating Artificial Intelligence more generally – precisely because he was worried about the ease with which humans apparently ascribe intentions, beliefs and lifelikeness to machines. Reeves and Nass approach the matter from a different perspective: they argue that evoking social and emotional responses in humans is an (almost) unavoidable (side-)effect when humans engage with technologies. Therefore, it is something that designers should be aware of, and that they could potentially even exploit in various ways. However, currently most designers are unaware of this potential.

Anthropomorphization and the Media Equation thus differ from techno-regulation in substantial ways. They do not revolve around the embedding of legal norms into technology, and the responses they generate do not fit into the realm of traditional regulation. Users have little or no choice when it comes to these two types of implicit, automatic responses, nor are they really aware of having such responses in the first place. What is more, both anthropomorphization and the Media Equation largely take place outside the awareness, and hence the intentionality, of designers themselves – these are automatic, evolutionarily wired side-effects, tacitly called forth, yet they are powerful mechanisms indeed.

In Fig. 4.2 we have brought together the three concepts that we have discussed in this section – scripts, anthropomorphism and the Media Equation – and plotted them in relation to the level of choice and compulsion on the one hand, and the level of user awareness on the other.

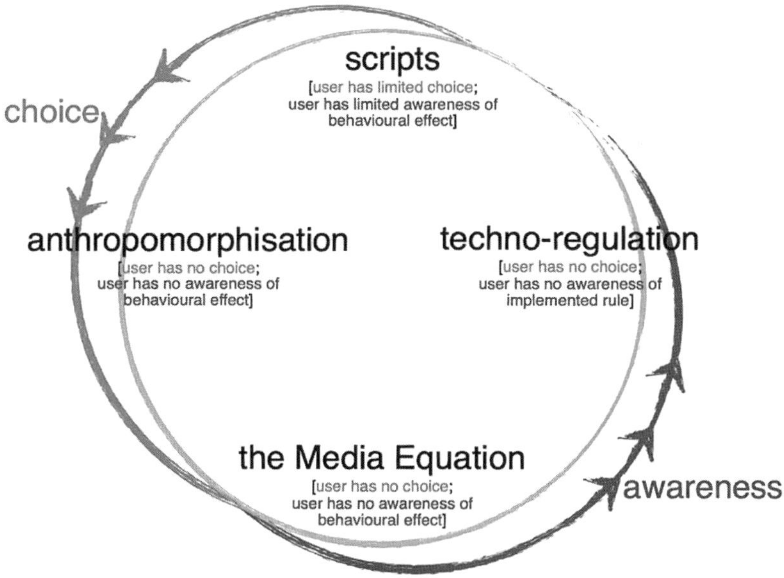

Fig. 4.2 From scripts to techno-regulation: decreasing choice, increasing compulsion, and decreasing user awareness

4.6 The Full Scope of Techno-Effects

In this article we have argued that techno-regulation in its current form has a focus that is too limited: it overlooks non-legal forms of intentional influencing on the one hand, and implicit, unintentional forms of technological influencing on the other. We have shown that the use of technologies may evoke a range of behaviours that fall outside the current, narrow scope of techno-regulation. Hence, we propose to broaden the debate on techno-regulation by replacing this term with the much broader one of '*techno-effects*': the wide range of behavioural impact brought about in humans by, or through the use of, technologies. Techno-effects cover the full spectrum running from *intentional* and *explicit* evocation on one end (techno-regulation, but also persuasion, nudging and affording), to *implicit*, *accidental* and *unintentional* elicitation on the other (scripts, anthropomorphism, and the Media Equation). This holds for both the *users* and the *designers* (and regulators) of technological artefacts.

It is important to note that studying techno-effects is no straightforward matter, and that predicting techno-effects always ought to be a contextual, technology-dependant matter. Different technologies have their own medium-specific characteristics, and different technologies are used in different ways by different groups of people. All of these factors entail that very different techno-effects may result from different technologies. That this is so may be deduced from the various examples that we have discussed in this chapter. The techno-effects of Van Oost's gendered shavers obviously differ from those of Yeung's ticket gates at the railway station. They differ on several levels: first, Yeung's ticket barriers are an example of explicit techno-regulation: they are deployed as a means to regulate user behaviour – to ensure that train travellers adhere to the legal rules of obtaining a valid ticket when planning to travel on a train or subway. Van Oost's shavers, we have seen, impact the behaviour of users in non-regulatory, yet nevertheless fairly substantial ways: they steer and guide user's images of themselves as technologically savvy beings (or quite the reverse), and implicitly prescribe ways of use for these products. Second, in Yeung's ticket barriers the enforcement of a rule is the intentional, explicit goal of the designers – these barriers are designed the way they are to ensure that travellers obey the rules. Rather than deploying human officers to check tickets we have now consciously, deliberately and intentionally delegated this task to these barriers – and they fulfil it (almost) flawlessly. In the case of Van Oost's shavers, by contrast, the effect of the values embedded into the technologies was not intentional, as we have seen. Rather, the values that were embedded into these shavers stemmed from the fact that designers used two types of tacit assumptions in the design process: on the one hand, all sorts of stereotypical images of the prospected end users of their products, and on the other hand ideas regarding the designers' own capabilities, wants and needs (I-methodology).

4.7 Abort, Retry, Fail. Or: Liberating the Boxed-in Concept of Techno-Regulation

Anyone who worked with computers before the days of icons, graphics and folders, must have encountered the (in)famous DOS error message 'Abort, retry, fail'. This message popped up whenever users typed in a command that the computer could not execute. It has become an icon of poor interface design, because it led exactly nowhere: if the user pressed R for 'retry' the same message appeared again, but if (s)he chose either A for 'abort' or F for 'fail' the program (s)he was running would close, and (s)he would lose all unsaved work.[5] A veritable Catch 22, since the only viable option appeared to be to keep typing R until one was willing to accept that one's work was lost and there was nothing left to do but shut down the program and start anew.

What does the failure of 'Abort, retry, fail' teach us, aside from its lack of user-friendliness and its poor design? This DOS error message is a clear example of technological enforcement that leaves no room for manoeuvring on the side of the user. It is not techno-regulation in the strict sense, since it does not involve the upholding of a *legal* norm. It is, however, a clear example of the way in which technology can be used, for good or for bad, to limit and steer users' behaviours. Admittedly,

[5] Available at: http://en.wikipedia.org/wiki/Abort,_Retry,_Fail, last accessed on April 10th 2012.

'Abort, retry, fail' steered user behaviour in a very poor fashion, generating so much frustration that almost all of us still remember it. 'Abort, retry, fail' is a red flag for how to *not* use technology to influence the behaviour of users. It combines the three concepts that we have addressed time and again in this chapter in the worst possible combination: it provides users with *too little choice*, the level of *compulsion is complete*, and what is worse: users' are fully *aware* that have no choice at all but to leave the program and lose all of their work. This is clearly a design error that should be avoided at all cost.

But should 'Abort, retry, fail' be considered merely an example of flawed interface design, one that we have luckily left far behind us with the creation of new generations of operating systems, in which the emphasis on usability and user-friendliness has consistently increased? Have we left the days of full compulsion and no choice for users behind us? As this article aimed to show quite the reverse is true. We argue that this error message is iconic, rather than an example of an extinct way of steering user behaviour. Designers and regulators know better than ever before that they can affect the behaviour of individuals, of users and citizens, through the abilities and constraints they design into the artefacts that surround these individuals in their everyday lives. And designers and regulators make more use of these forms of influencing than ever before. As we have seen, regulators enforce legal norms through technology (the speed bump, the ticket barrier), and industries enforce their own, non-legal standards (DVD region codes). But this is not where it ends. The means and possibilities for techno-regulation are endless, and as this chapter has shown there is even more potential available to regulators and designers than is currently used: intentionally applying techniques of nudging, persuading, affording, and implicitly building on the effects of scripts, anthropomorphization and the Media Equation. The 'regulatory' potential of technologies – in the broadest sense – is tremendous, and daunting, indeed.

What is striking about the current increasing use of techno-regulation as we are witnessing it in many Western countries today is that it takes place in a social climate of little debate – only a small band of regulators and scientists feel a need to address the legitimacy of these developments, to question whether it is *right* that both industry and governments may use technologies to hold us up to their (democratically endorsed or self-generated) standards. The trickiest part, of course, is that since the norms and values that are embedded into the technologies that are used for techno-regulation are *hidden from view* it becomes very difficult indeed for ordinary users to be critical of them, let alone to resist them (Leenes 2010, 2011). Of course, industry and state regulators have very good reasons to turn to technologies as a means of regulating behaviour: it is an efficient, cost-effective, convenient, foolproof and safe way to ensure that individuals stay within the norms set by these parties – whether they be adhering to the maximum speed or only buying DVDs from a single region. But as this chapter has revealed, they are currently overlooking the vast majority of means and possibilities to technologically influence human behaviour. On the one hand, one could argue this is good news: the less regulators know of these possibilities, the less they will use them to steer the behaviour of citizens. However, as especially the second half of this chapter reveals, technologies often contain a host of *unintentional*, *implicit* effects that neither regulators, nor designers, nor even users themselves are aware of. This is the case for any technology, so it may also apply to technologies that are used intentionally by regulators to steer the behaviour of their citizens. The artefacts used in the pursuit of realizing techno-regulation may contain mechanisms to enforce legal norms which were deliberately designed into them, but they may also embody norms of a different kind, viz. ones that no individual or group of people actively, deliberately designed into them (see also Hildebrandt 2011: 246). When there is insufficient insight into the techno-effects of measures taken by regulators to influence the behaviour of citizens through technological means, regulators may come to affect their behaviour in ways that are not intended, thus jeopardizing the legitimacy of their regulatory efforts. In the words of Lodewijk Asscher (2006: 71):

> Using code to replace law could mean that public goods or important values traditionally protected by the law can be compromised by those writing or controlling the code. [Techno-regulation] is not subject to an official system of democratic checks and balances and, therefore, it is all the more important to analyze the regulating qualities of software.
>
> The very features that make it a viable (and often attractive) alternative to legal regulation can have troubling public effects, at least as compared to legal regulation. Software regulation lacks forms of regulatory 'safety valves' (…).

If this is true for clear and explicit cases of techno-regulation, it is all the more so when the full range of techno-effects that we have discussed in this chapter comes in play.

What is more, the lesson to be learnt from 'Abort, retry, fail' is that users will feel infinitely frustrated when confronted with technologies that will offer them no choice – and by extension will offer the regulator full control and a perfect mechanism of force – while being fully aware that this is the case. And such frustration would surely over time lead to a rejection of these technologies. Of course, regulators could, therefore, choose the road they now often tend to take: hide the norm and the norm-setting itself from view by obfuscating both in the technological artefact. This way, regulators may gain complete control, and users will be none the wiser. However, since this approach seems to be odds with some of the fundamentals that we, as citizens of free and democratic societies, hold dear, we plead for the opposite approach instead: to leave individuals room for manoeuvring, freedom to choose, and, not unimportantly, have a sense of control over the technological and regulatory forces in their everyday lives. The guiding principle behind new regulatory measures that use technology to influence human behaviour ought therefore always to be that the compulsory pitfall of 'Abort, retry, fail' should be avoided.

As noted above, state and non-state regulators have valid reasons to use technologies' potential to influence human behaviour – and as this chapter has revealed this potential is far greater than the current debate on techno-regulation reveals. However, precisely because technologies can be used to call forth a host of implicit, automatic responses, and because the rules they set remain hidden from view, caution in the application of techno-regulation and its related techno-effects is of the utmost importance.

Acknowledgement The authors wish to thank Martin Pekárek and Mireille Hildebrandt for their willingness to challenge and debate the ideas put forth in this chapter.

References

Akrich, M. 1992. The de-scription of technical objects. In *Shaping technology/building society: Studies in sociotechnical change*, ed. W.E. Bijker and J. Law, 205–224. Cambridge, MA: MIT Press.

Akrich, M. 1995. User representations: Practices, methods and sociology. In *Managing technology in society: The approach of constructive technology assessment*, ed. A. Rip, T.J. Misa, and J. Schot, 167–184. London/New York: Pinter Publishers.

Asscher, L. 2006. 'Code' as law: Using Fuller to assess code rules. In *Coding regulation: Essays on the normative role of information technology*, ed. E. Dommering and L. Asscher, 61–91. The Hague/West Nyack: TMC Asser.

Baldwin, R., M. Cave, and M. Lodge. 2010. Introduction: Regulation – The field and the developing agenda. In *The Oxford handbook of regulation*, ed. R. Baldwin, M. Cave, and M. Lodge, 3–16. Oxford/New York: Oxford University Press.

Brownsword, R. 2008. So what does the world need now? Reflections on regulating technologies. In *Regulating technologies: Legal futures, regulatory frames and technological fixes*, ed. R. Brownsword and K. Yeung, 23–49. Oxford: Hart.

Brownsword, R., and K. Yeung. 2008. Regulating technologies: Tools, targets and thematics. In *Regulating Technologies: Legal futures, regulatory frames and technological fixes*, ed. R. Brownsword and K. Yeung, 3–23. Oxford: Hart.

Burgess, A. 2012. 'Nudging' healthy lifestyles: The UK experiments with the behavioural alternative to regulation and the market. *European Journal of Risk Regulation* 3(1): 3–30.

Cohen, J.E. 2012. *Configuring the networked self: Law, code, and the play of everyday practice*. New Haven/London: Yale University Press.

Dommering, E. 2006. Regulating technology: Code is not law. In *Coding regulation: Essays on the normative role of information technology*, ed. E. Dommering and L. Asscher, 1–17. The Hague/West Nyack: TMC Asser.

Duffy, B.R. 2003. Anthropomorphism and the social robot. *Robotics and Autonomous Systems* 42(3–4): 177–190.

Fogg, B.J. 2003. *Persuasive technology: Using computers to change what we think and do*. Amsterdam/Boston: Morgan Kaufmann Publishers.

Friedman, B. 1997. *Human values and the design of computer technology*. Stanford/Cambridge, NY: CSLI Publications; Cambridge University Press.

Friedman, B., and P.H. Kahn Jr. 2006. Value sensitive design and information systems. In *Human-computer interaction and management information systems: Foundations*, ed. M.E. Sharpe, 348–372. Armonk: M.E. Sharpe Inc.

Friedman, B., P.H. Kahn Jr., and A. Borning. 2002. *Value sensitive design: Theory and methods*. Washington, DC: University of Washington, Department of Computer Science & Engineering.

Frissen, V. 1994. The domestication of the telephone. In *Domestic technology and everyday life – Mutual shaping processes. Proceedings from COST A4 workshop in Trondheim*, Norway, ed. A.-J. Berg and M. Aune, October 28–30, 1993. Brussel: COST.

Frissen, V. 2004. *De domesticatie van de digitale wereld*. Rotterdam: Erasmus Universiteit Rotterdam.

Gaver, W.W. 1991. Technology affordances. In *CHI'91 proceedings of the SIGCHI conference on human factors in computing systems*, 79–84. New York: ACM.

Gaver, W.W. 1996. Affordances for interaction: The social is material for design. *Ecological Psychology* 8(2): 111–129.

Gibson, J.J. 1986. *The ecological approach to visual perception*. Hillsdale: L. Erlbaum Associates.
Gjøen, H., and M. Hård. 2002. Cultural politics in actions: Developing user scripts in relation to the electric vehicle. *Science, Technology & Human Values* 27(2): 262–281.
Haddon, L. 2003. Domestication and mobile telephony. In *Machines that become us: The social context of personal communication technology*, ed. J.E. Katz, 43–55. New Brunswick: Transaction Publishers.
Hildebrandt, M. 2008. Legal and technological normativity: More (and less) than twin sisters. *Techné* 12(3): 169–183.
Hildebrandt, M. 2009. Technology and the end of law. In *Facing the limits of the law*, ed. E. Claes, W. Devroe, and B. Keirsbilck, 443–464. Berlin/Heidelberg: Springer.
Hildebrandt, M. 2011. Legal protection by design: Objections and refutations. *Legisprudence* 5(2): 223–249.
Ihde, D. 1990. *Technology and the lifeworld: From garden to earth*. Bloomington: Indiana University Press.
Kerr, I.R. 2004. Bots, babes and the Californication of commerce. *University of Ottawa Law & Technology Journal* 1(1–2): 287–324.
Koops, B.-J. 2010. Ten dimensions of technology regulation: Finding your bearings in the research space of an emerging discipline. In *Dimensions of technology regulation*, ed. M. Goodwin, B.-J. Koops, and R.E. Leenes, 309–325. Nijmegen: Wolf Legal Publishers.
Kroes, P., A. Light, P.E. Vermaas, and S.A. Moore. 2009. *Philosophy and design: From engineering to architecture*. Dordrecht: Springer.
Latour, B. 1992. Where are the missing masses? The sociology of a few mundane artifacts. In *Shaping technology/building society: Studies in sociotechnical change*, ed. W.E. Bijker and J. Law, 225–259. Cambridge, MA: MIT Press.
Leenes, R.E. 2010. *Harde lessen: Apologie van technologie als reguleringsinstrument*. Tilburg: Universiteit van Tilburg.
Leenes, R.E. 2011. Framing techno-regulation: An exploration of state and non-state regulation by technology. *Legisprudence* 5(2): 143–169.
Lehtonen, T.-K. 2003. The domestication of new technologies as a set of trials. *Journal of Consumer Culture* 3(3): 363–385.
Lessig, L. 2006. *Code: Version 2.0*. New York: Basic Books.
MacKenzie, D.A., and J. Wajcman. 1999. *The social shaping of technology*. Buckingham/Philadelphia: Open University Press.
McGrenere, J., and W. Ho. 2000. Affordances: Clarifying and evolving a concept. In *Proceedings of graphics interface 2000 May 15–17, 2000*, 179–186. Montreal and Quebec.
Morgan, B., and K. Yeung. 2007. Regulatory instruments and techniques. In *An introduction to law and regulation: Text and materials*, ed. B. Morgan and K. Yeung, 79–151. Cambridge/New York: Cambridge University Press.
Nass, C.I., and Y. Moon. 2000. Machines and mindlessness: Social responses to computers. *Journal of Social Issues* 56(1): 81–103.
Nass, C.I., J. Steuer, E.R. Tauber, and H. Reeder. 1993. Anthropomorphism, agency, and ethopoeia: Computers as social actors. In *CHI '93 INTERACT '93 and CHI '93 conference companion on human factors in computing systems*, 111–112. New York: ACM.
Nass, C.I., J. Steuer, and E.R. Tauber. 1994. Computers are social actors. In *CHI'94 proceedings of the SIGCHI conference on human factors in computing systems*, 72–78. Boston/New York: ACM.
Norman, D.A. 1988. *The psychology of everyday things*. New York: Basic Books.
Oudshoorn, N., and T.J. Pinch. 2003. *How users matter: The co-construction of users and technologies*. Cambridge, MA: MIT Press.
Oudshoorn, N., E. Rommes, and M. Stienstra. 2004. Configuring the user as everybody: Gender and design cultures in information and communication technologies. *Science, Technology & Human Values* 29(1): 30–63.
Picard, R.W. 1997. *Affective computing*. Cambridge, MA: MIT Press.

Reeves, B., and C.I. Nass. 1996. *The media equation: How people treat computers, television, and new media like real people and places*. Stanford/New York: CSLI Publications/Cambridge University Press.

Silverstone, R., and L. Haddon. 1996. Design and domestication of information and communication technologies: Technical change and everyday life. In *Communication and design: The politics of information and communication technologies*, ed. R. Mansell and R. Silverstone, 44–75. Oxford/New York: Oxford University Press.

Thaler, R.H., and C.R. Sunstein. 2008. *Nudge: Improving decisions about health, wealth, and happiness*. New Haven: Yale University Press.

Turkle, S. 1984. *The second self: Computers and the human spirit*. New York: Simon & Schuster.

Turkle, S. 2007. *Evocative objects: Things we think with*. Cambridge, MA: MIT Press.

Van den Berg, B. 2008. Self, script, and situation: Identity in a world of ICTs. In *The future of identity in the information society: Proceedings of the third IFIP WG 9.2, 9.6/11.6, 11.7/FIDIS International Summer School on the Future of Identity in the Information Society*, ed. S. Fischer-Hübner, P. Duquenoy, A. Zuccato, and L. Martucci, 63–77. New York: Springer.

Van den Berg, B. 2010a. I-Object: Intimate technologies as 'reference groups' in the construction of identities. *Techne̕* 14(3): 176–193.

Van den Berg, B. 2010b. *The situated self: Identity in a world of ambient intelligence*. Nijmegen: Wolf Legal Publishers.

Van den Berg, B. 2011. Techno-elicitation: Regulating behaviour through the design of robots. In *Technologies on the stand: Legal and ethical questions in neuroscience and robotics*, ed. B. van den Berg and L. Klaming, 403–422. Nijmegen: Wolf Legal Publishers.

Van Oost, E. 2003. Materialized gender: How shavers configure the users' femininity and masculinity. In *How users matter: The co-construction of users and technologies*, ed. N. Oudshoorn and T.J. Pinch, 193–209. Cambridge, MA: MIT Press.

Verbeek, P.-P. 2005. *What things do: Philosophical reflections on technology, agency, and design*. University Park: Pennsylvania State University Press.

Weizenbaum, J. 1966. ELIZA: A computer program for the study of natural language communication between man and machine. *Communications of the ACM* 9(1): 36–45.

Yeung, K. 2008. Towards an understanding of design-based instruments. In *Regulating Technologies: Legal futures, regulatory frames and technological fixes*, ed. R. Brownsword and K. Yeung, 79–109. Oxford: Hart.

Chapter 5
A Bump in the Road. Ruling Out Law from Technology

Katja de Vries and Niels van Dijk

The authors would like to thank Sebastian Abrahamsson for his salient comments.

Abstract This article discusses the challenge posed by the upcoming field of techno-regulation to the study of law and its relation to new technologies. Technoregulation is often hailed as a new legislative tool for the intentional regulation of human behavior by means of technology. Instead of making law redundant, technoregulation could give a new impetus to classical debates in legal theory about the nature of law, by adding questions about the medium of law investigated in the light of the practice turn. If one understands law as a practice, what does this mean for the distinction between medium and content, which seems to underlie much of the debate on technoregulation? Both Hartian practice theory that frames law as a system of 'incorporeal' rules and more material approaches that explain law in terms of its mediality are analyzed. These will be discussed in the light of Latour's studies of the specificities of legal practices and technological practices, which seem to supersede the extremes assumed by both.

K. de Vries (✉) • N. van Dijk
Interdisciplinary Research Group on Law Science Technology and Society (LSTS), Faculty of Law, Vrije Universiteit Brussel, Pleinlaan 2, 1050 Brussels, Belgium
e-mail: edevries@vub.ac.be; nvdijk@vub.ac.be

M. Hildebrandt and J. Gaakeer (eds.), *Human Law and Computer Law: Comparative Perspectives*, Ius Gentium: Comparative Perspectives on Law and Justice 25,
DOI 10.1007/978-94-007-6314-2_5,

5.1 Introduction

Sometimes technological and scientific progress make existing practices obsolete: digital content which cannot be copied or distributed due to the restrictions of 'digital rights management' technology (see e.g. Lessig 2006); car ignition systems which only work when the driver puts the seat belt on (see e.g. Lessig 2006); information retrieval and decision support systems which are supposed to make the job of judges and public prosecutors more efficient and transparent (Lodder et al. 2001). Is techno-regulation, that is the intentional regulation of human behavior by means of technology (Leenes 2010), going to make law one of the practices ending up in the litter bin?

We argue that the rise of techno-regulation at the expense of law does not make the classical question 'what is law?' redundant – on the contrary, it gives it a new importance: is there something that makes law *worthwhile* defending against the onslaught of techno-regulation and, if there is such a laudable aspect to law, is it possible to integrate it within techno-regulation itself? While the discussions on the nature of law are thus resuscitated, they differ from their classical predecessors – such as the famous debate between Hart and Fuller on the separation of law and morality – in at least one important respect: they have to turn to the question of the *medium* of law, a question which has largely been neglected in legal theory until now. As Vismann rightfully observes 'legal studies lack any reflection on their tools' constituting a 'blind spot of jurisprudence' (2008: 11). Hart, for instance, does not concern himself with the question at all. The discussions on law and techno-regulation could thus, in turn, also open up new perspectives and investigations for legal philosophy.

This question of the technological medium of law also brings us to a second point. In the debates on techno-regulation we can distinguish different ways in which the relations between law and technology (and regulation) are articulated. On most accounts technology is represented as a material medium that incorporates and transmits policy choices, legal norms or rules. The latter two are either considered to have an essential connection to the technologies of writing or print,[1] or as medium independent entities that can be embodied in different technologies. In the last case this technological embodiment is perceived according to two extremes: as a neutral carrier of a legal rule that is transmitted without change, or as an element which itself radically changes the nature of legal rules or even law itself. However, in this chapter we will defend what might at first appear as a rather controversial statement, namely that neither law nor techno-regulation should be understood through the notion of rules.

The questions about the nature of law and its relations with and demarcation from other phenomena, form some of the basic questions of legal philosophy. However, a response to these issues cannot be separated from the specific way in which one approaches law as a legal philosopher. In this chapter these two issues of the specificity of law and its relation to technology will be investigated in the light

[1]Tien for instance speaks about law as 'textual rules' in this context (Tien 2004). Brownsword makes a distinction between 'paper rules' and 'real rules' (2008: 44). See further on this subject, below Sect. 5.8.1.

of what has been called the 'practice turn in contemporary theory'. This will lead us to explore the possibility of a practice-oriented approach to law. If one understands law as a practice, what does this mean for the distinction between medium and content, or dare we say matter and form, which seems to underlie much of the debate on techno-regulation? In these contexts we will analyze both Hart's 'practice theory' that enables him to formulate his concept of law, which has later been described as a system of incorporeal rules (MacCormick 1986), and more material approaches that explain law in terms of its mediality. We then investigate these conceptions of law in the light of Latour's studies of the specificities of legal practices and technological practices. Not unlike Hart's positivism this latter approach unburdens 'Law with a capital "L",' from a weight which it cannot carry: the relics[2] of 'sovereignty, law, morals, the social link, justice, politics and even religion' (Latour 2010: 267) and we could add humanity and autonomy.[3] In addition, Latour also unfolds a view on law, now with a lower and lighter case "l", which seems to supersede the 'extremes' assumed by the medial and incorporeal approaches.

5.2 Law Is Dead, Long Live Techno-Regulation?

At the *25th World Congress of Philosophy of Law and Social Philosophy*, in his keynote lecture entitled *Erosion of subjective rights by reason of technical development*, Sampaio Ferraz (2011) predicted the end of law in the next century. If he turns out to be right, the question is whether we should mourn the extinction of law. In *Bleak House* Dickens describes how legal proceedings can consume so much money and time that only the lawyers involved benefit from these endless proceedings – continuing even when the original dispute has long faded and the original litigating parties have all died in the meantime (Dickens 2005, orig. 1853: 544):

> 'My father expected a Judgment,' said Miss Flite.
> 'My brother. My sister. They all expected a Judgment. The same that I expect.'
> 'They are all – '
> 'Ye-es. Dead, of course, my dear,' said she.

Regulation by technology, on the other hand, bears the promise of cost efficiency, immediacy and integrity: car ignition systems do not ask for the fee of a judge, barrister or solicitor, they give their 'judgment' instantaneously, and cannot be bribed or prejudiced. Yet there might be something uncanny about relinquishing law completely (Brownsword 2005: 21):

> [T]here is a sense that the West Coast [of regulation by code] is a place to avoid. Is there more to this than the lawyer's or the moralist's instinct for self-preservation?

---

[2]Latour (2010: 267) refers here to La Fontaine's (2000) famous fable *The Ass That Carried Relics*.

[3]One of the founding principles of Actor Network Theory, to which Latour heavily contributed, is the principle of symmetry of humans and non-humans. This principle is necessary in anthropological research to prevent a precipitated *a priori* attribution of agency to human autonomy or intentionality and a neglect of the role non-humans in actions (1993: 94–96).

In the 1990s Lessig (2006) and Reidenberg (1998) sparked the debate on techno-regulation by juxtaposing law and technology as equal modes of regulation of human behavior. In Lessig's model regulatory goals can be achieved by choosing an optimal mix from the 'toolbox' of four different modes of regulation: social norms, law, market and architecture. He famously called the last mode regulation by 'code', both encompassing software encoded in hardware and more classical forms of techno-regulation such as speed bumps. Reidenberg speaks about policy choices which are to be embedded in technological networks or law. Law in this model is equated with a 'legal regulatory regime' and architecture as a regulator is called 'Lex Informatica' or 'code as law'.[4] These writings provoked several critical reactions. Gutwirth et al. (2008) argue that by placing law, technological encodings, the market and norms under the single denominator of regulation and forcing them to converge towards one common policy goal, no justice is rendered to their specificities. Depending on the practice to which a practitioner belongs, the set of aims, functions, rationales, responsibilities and challenges will vary. These differences would become annihilated when law and technology are turned into mere modes or instruments within general regulatory practices for the realization of policy goals. Since code as law does not take account of such differences, Lessig's optimal mix will not work according to Gutwirth et al. (2008). Tien (2004) and Brownsword (2005), from a different perspective, argued that treating architecture as an equivalent mode of regulation will endanger the very nature of law. These authors even argue that it might affect our moral agency of choice, since, as has been surreptitiously pointed out, in contrast to techno-regulation, in law the norm and its enforcement do not coincide. Thus techno-regulation only seems appropriate when a rule is unequivocal and does not need any discretionary interpretation (see Leenes 2011).

Hildebrandt and Koops (2007, 2010) criticize the 'code as law approach on the basis of its lack of democratic legitimization and its unambiguous self-enforcing character that leaves no room for deliberation. They, however, take a further step, viz. by claiming that in order to safeguard legal protection in the digital age, we have to make a move from 'law in the books' to 'law in other technologies'. They call this vision of law Ambient Law. It starts from the idea that historically law has always been incorporated in certain technologies (rituals, orality, the alphabet, printed codes). Historical changes from one technology to another have fundamentally altered the very nature of law itself and digitization will imply just such a change. On this view, contrary to Tien and Brownsword for instance, a change in the nature of law is not necessarily perceived as a danger, but as a new phase in the history of law. However, in order for digitally encoded regulation to be more than mere discipline through the 'rule of technology' (Hildebrandt and Koops 2010: 445) and to become '*law* in code', it will have to satisfy certain crucial requirements of constitutional democracy. The digital laws will have to be created by a democratic legislator and their application should be contestable in court.

---

[4] 'In essence, policy choices are available either through technology itself, through laws that cause technology to exclude possible options, or through laws that cause users to restrict certain actions' (Reidenberg 1998: 565).

Now, what is the nature of law that is at stake here? If law is a practice that has a certain specificity, what do we understand by this? In the debates surrounding techno-regulation we can detect different understandings of law. Firstly, in Lessig's instrumentalist approach law is rather classically presented as 'a command backed up by the threat of a sanction' (Lessig 2006: 340), the wording of which recalls the legal positivism of Austin's command theory. When Tien speaks about the danger of architectural regulation for the nature of law, he conceptualizes this nature as 'a system of rules' (Tien 2004: 3; contrasting it with architecture as a set of conditions), explicitly referring to Hart's concept of law. Hildebrandt and Koops seem to relate the nature of law more broadly to the foundations of modern constitutional democracy.

5.3 Incorporeal Rules or Brute Matter? Two Inescapable Truisms

What happens when legal rules are implemented in or supported by a new technology? Does it change what law is? Does law have a way to run its path in a medium-independent way? Normally the way to answering these questions is presented to us as a choice between the binary opposition of material determinism and, what we can call, incorporeal rules. When we start with the latter, we could say that what seems to complicate law as an object of study is that it has something to do with what is seemingly 'immaterial' or 'incorporeal'[5] (MacCormick 1986: 49–50):

> To take but one pertinent illustration, for every busload of passengers, there exist, in addition to the solid, physical, bus and the stolid, palpable, passengers, as many contracts of carriage as there are passengers. The existence of a contract between each passenger and Edinburgh corporation is obviously not a matter of physical or physiological fact, nor even indeed of psychological fact.

MacCormick, taking his cues from Hart, analyzes law in terms of a legal system that forms 'coherent sets of interrelated rules' (1986: 51–52). He distinguishes the plane of existence of law, which is characterized by its non-physical, non-spatial institutional nature, from the existence of 'brute facts' (1986: 49, 55).[6]

---

[5]This observation already goes back to the study of Roman Law. In his discussion of the difference between *res corporales* and *res incorporales,* concrete social institutions and abstract relations, Thomas remarks that 'le monde du droit, en particulier, est tout entier situé du côté de l'incorporel' (Thomas 1978: 112).

[6]Moreover, one could argue that this incorporeal approach is also more in accordance with the virulent ideas of modern information society than the materialist outlook. In our contemporary information society materiality should be a compliant neutral medium, and material particularities affecting the message seem mere impediments to the free movement of information: code should move freely from medium to medium, smoothing out any hindrance to universal movement and translation. Media formats have become interchangeable. The matter of different media has become irrelevant since they have all become interchangeable carriers of informational codes (Kittler 1986). The medium might have become the message, but it is a message that informs us that the medium has become irrelevant. Derrida makes a similar point when he states that: 'To relinquish materiality is even the driving force of translation' (Derrida and Mehlman 1972: 90–91).

A material determinist, to the contrary, might follow McLuhan in proclaiming that '*The Medium is the Message*' and add that the technological medium would indeed be the whole of the legal message.[7] To what extent could such media and technologies be said to determine or ground the law? (McLuhan 1994; Vismann 2008) The materialist might also follow Eisenstein and observe that law has always already been entangled with certain technologies in its modes of proceeding.[8] The printing press, as an agent of change, modified the conception of law as we know it. This argument could also be extended to new media like digital script (Hildebrandt 2008). Could there ever have been a Rule of Law, legal consistency, or equal legal treatment, without the invention of the printing press?[9]

A promising question seems to culminate into two seemingly inescapable truisms[10]: there is something incorporeal and something material about law. The reason for this might well be found at an earlier stage, that is, in the question itself, which contains two words – materiality (medium) and 'what law is' (the 'essence' of law) – that plunge us into a realm of some stubborn and opaque metaphysical assumptions whose origin can be found in the Aristotelian idea that every existing substance is composed by the binary of *morphè* ('form') and *hylè* ('matter'),[11] and the longstanding philosophical squabble whether the essence of something lies in the former (*pace* Aristotle) or in the latter (*pace* Rousseau and Marx).

---

[7]McLuhan does not distinguish matter and form in the classical sense, but between medium and message, and in his later work (McLuhan and McLuhan 1988) between figure and ground. McLuhan thus focuses on how a certain artifact (figure) changes the culture or environment (ground) in which it emerges: 'The ground of any technology or artefact is both the situation that gives rise to it and the whole environment (medium) of services and disservices that it brings into play' (1988: 5).

[8]Although Eisenstein takes inspiration from McLuhan's media-technological studies, she also explicitly reacts against the latter's technological determinism (Eisenstein 2005: xiii). Instead of his 'metaphorical' and 'abstract' thinking leading him to his sweeping deterministic statements, she urges for a more 'historical' and 'concrete' approach that focuses on the interactions between people and technologies in a variety of circumstances (Eisenstein 2005: 102).

[9]Hildebrandt states that 'the printing press was the condition of possibility for written law to be instrumental to the modern national state (providing the means for a detailed rule by law), democracy (providing the means to develop literacy on a full scale) and the rule *of* law (providing the need for an autonomous class of lawyers to interpret and sustain the intra-systemic coherence of law)' (2008: 185).

[10]Of course, we should underline, that we presented the arguments of the 'materialists' and the 'rule-based' approach in a very superficial way (we did not specify *how* the materiality of law matters or how rules – technological or material determinism, co-constitution, etc. – affect the practice of law) leading up to the triviality of the conclusion. However, there is also already some triviality in the question itself.

[11]'Now we speak of one particular kind of existent things as substance, and under this heading we so speak of one thing *qua* matter, which in itself is not a particular, another *qua* shape and form, in virtue of which it is then spoken of as a particular, and a third *qua* the product of these two. And matter is potentiality, while form is actuality' (Aristotle 1993, orig. ca 350 BC: Book II: 412a6).

5.4 The Practice of Law and the Price of the Practice Turn

It is interesting to relate the legal theories of Hart and MacCormick and the medial approach to law to, what has been dubbed, 'the practice turn in contemporary thought'. On this view, law is approached from the point of view of practices, as something we *do*. 'Most thinkers who theorize practices conceive of them, minimally, as arrays of activity' (Schatzki et al. 2001: 11). Understanding law as a practice also implies that it does not have a transcendental and immutable essence, but that its meaning lies in its repetitive use: like table manners, the practice of law does not have a golden standard outside but only within this repetitive use (for instance, each time the act of establishing a contract is performed its meaning within the practice of law is re-constituted). Understanding law as a practice, unburdened from its heavy relics, is an encouraging point of departure for research. The crucial question here thus becomes: how to approach law as a practice? We will first treat Hart's 'practice theory' and the medial approach to law, and then show how Latour's semiotic ethnography of law seems to mediate the problems of the two. Firstly, since Latour provides a concrete empirical account of legal practices in action (as opposed to Hart's general theory of law as a practice). Secondly, Latour's focus on the act of enunciation[12] does not limit or reduce his approach to law to just the material media that figure in legal practices. Furthermore, Latour's approach to law might offer an interesting way to bypass approaches to legal practice that seek to extract from it the 'form' or 'matter' that would constitute its essence. Maybe, it will even entail the promise to transform the very specter of hylemorfism itself.

This turn to 'law as a practice', however, also brings along a particular set of issues to be addressed. It raises the question how the researcher is to approach legal practice: does this practice turn in legal theory bring along an imperative to leave the theorist's armchair and embrace a more empirical approach? It also raises a problem of demarcation, because every practice becomes like any other: existing in repetitive actions. In a playful variation on Gertrude Stein's famous line, one could say: *practice is a practice is a practice is a practice*, but the challenge resides in showing in what sense a certain practice is a practice, but never a practice like any other practice.

5.5 The Medium of Law

We will start with the medial approach to law. We could trace this line of arguing back to studies of the effects of historical transitions of media, in particular writing and printing. On these kinds of accounts, important historical shifts from a mythical worldview to science and logic, from primitive to civilized man, are reconceptualized and explained as a shift from orality to literacy. The invention of the intellectual

[12]See for the notion 'act of enunciation' our discussion below in Sect. 5.6.

technology of the alphabet played a crucial role in these developments. Amongst others the development of political democracy (in ancient Greece), was 'a consequence of literacy' that became more widespread, since people could now read the laws (Goody and Watt 1963). Or as McLuhan puts it (1994: 84):

> It can be argued, then, that the phonetic alphabet, alone, is the technology that has been the means of creating 'civilized man'- the separate individuals equal before a written code of law. Separateness of the individual, continuity of space and of time, and uniformity of codes are the prime marks of literate and civilized societies.

In turn, Gutenberg's invention of the printing press with movable type around 1440, and the subsequent spread of printing presses to urban centers throughout European countries, also had important consequences. They led to what McLuhan dubbed the 'Gutenberg Galaxy' as 'the making of typographic man' (McLuhan 1994), or what Eisenstein has called the 'printing revolution' (Eisenstein 2005). These typographic technologies rationalized entire procedures of many domains including law with their principles of the repeatability, generality and homogeneity. After their introduction legal codes could now be easily reproduced in a uniform manner and distributed on a large scale throughout the territory. The very being of law was altered in these new 'technical forms': the media that are the whole of the legal message.

Whereas in these accounts the impact on law is only mentioned in the passing, the first wholesale media-technological analysis of the mediality of law has been made by Vismann. In her book *Files* she sets out to 'ground the law in files and records' (2008: 39). By focusing on the compilation of lists, i.e. kinds of writing that coincide neither with literacy nor with orality, she rejects the binary distinction between an oral culture of law and a literate culture of law that lies behind much of the historical research into law. These kinds of writings have nothing to do with the preservation or storage of texts, or the validity and security that is normally attributed to the relation between law and writing. Instead such lists control and regulate operations of transfer of goods, things and people and, consequently, belong to the register of administrative practices. The same goes for files which occupy an intermediary position between the written laws and the oral utterances in court. Vismann claims that the role of files in law, as a medium of legal transmission, has never been properly investigated. She calls files the 'variables in the universe of law' and explicitly excludes their 'content' from her studies. Instead she focuses exclusively on their 'external characteristics' like their materiality, mediality and their function as recording devices.[13]

---

[13]It might seem that Latour, with his emphasis on files and inscriptions also fits in the camp that approaches law through its material mediality, but he explicitly rejects assigning too much explanatory power to such technological devices (Latour 1986). In his studies of law, we will see that there is something more to law than this dimension, something he calls the legal regime of enunciation (see 4.7). Interestingly, Latour here refers to Eisenstein's account of the printing press, not as the cause for of scientific or legal change, but rather as a device of mobilization and immutability (Latour 1986).

As an example of this medial approach, we could mention the way in which she analyses how the historical shift to law as legislation was induced by a change in media technologies from scrolls to codices in the second century AD. Vismann states that (2008: 43):

> On the basis of their material, the media technologies scroll and codex determine differing concepts of time and law. Papyrus scrolls are linked to the purely actual, coextensive law of an imperial administration. In contrast, the organization of files as loose-leaf collections in connection with their independence from the act of writing predestines codices for the retroactive compilation of legal texts.

Codices enabled projects of compilation and codification that eventually culminated in the *Codex Justinianus, Institutes* and *Digests*. The shift from scrolls to codices promoted a more abstract approach to law and coincides with the first use of the word 'rules' (*regulae*) with regard to law (Berman 1983: 136). These rules were derived from cases, but were capable of being considered separately from them and compiled in 'books or rules', i.e. in codices. A prominent example is the concluding title D.50.17 of Justinian's *Digests* titled 'Concerning various rules of the ancient law', which provides the statement of 211 abstract rules of ancient law.[14]

5.6 Hart – The Concept of Law

In what follows we will take a closer look at Hart's *The Concept of Law* and his approach to legal practice. In order to enable an encounter with Latour's approach to law, we will first analyze Hart's attempt to write an essay in descriptive sociology and analytical jurisprudence, and secondly elaborate on Hart's demarcation of law as a practice by conceiving of it as a system of rules. Hart states that the goal of writing *The Concept of Law,* is not to provide a definition about the nature of law, but to 'advance a legal theory by providing analysis of the distinctive character of the legal system and an understanding of the resemblances and differences between law, coercion and morality as *types of social phenomena*' (Hart 1997: 17, italics KV and ND). This remark can serve as a starting point for our analysis of the role of method, social practice, essence, and demarcation in Hart. It becomes clear that law is approached as a type of social phenomenon about which a legal theory is to be produced.

---

[14] Yet even with the advent of codification we are still very far away from an understanding of law as a system of rules. A rule according to the classical and post-classical Roman jurist (see particularly D.50.17.1 of Justinian's *Digests*) was 'a short account of matters' (Berman 1983: 139), and thus 'rules must not be considered outside the contexts of the cases which they summarize' (1983: 137). It was only in the twelfth century that scholastic jurists began to conceive of law as systematic 'body' of abstract rules (1983: 136). Thus, while it is undeniable that shifts in techniques such as the one from scrolls to codices, or from handwritten to printed laws, stimulated a more abstract approach to law, the understanding of law as a systematic body of rules does not coincide with any of these two inventions.

5.6.1 A Practice Theory of Rules

In opposition to hypothetical legal theories – like Kelsen's pure theory of law – in which the existence of law is framed as something abstract, Hart frames it as a question of concrete social fact that can be determined by empirical research.[15] On the other hand, Hart states that he aims at providing a legal theory that is both general and descriptive to the extent that it 'seeks to give an explanatory and clarifying account of law as a complex social and political institution with a rule-governed (and in that sense 'normative') aspect' (Hart 1997: 239–240). There seems to be a tension between these two goals[16] that already becomes apparent in the introduction to the book. Hart subsequently both qualifies his book as 'an essay in analytical jurisprudence' which is 'concerned with the clarification of the general framework of legal thought' and as 'an essay in descriptive sociology' (Hart 1997: vi).

Here it still remains to be determined how Hart's approach relates to law taken *as a practice*. Later, especially in his postscript, Hart explicitly takes a practice-oriented approach to law. He describes his own enterprise as a 'practice theory of rules', which 'treats the social rules of a group as constituted by a form of social practice' (1997: 255). The legal theory that Hart proposes about law as a social phenomenon, takes account of the internal perspective of participants of a practice, but finally situates itself at the external point of view of a 'morally neutral descriptive jurisprudence'. In the end this internal perspective can be recorded as a fact on which the theorist can base his general descriptive conclusions (1997: 243–244). The problem is that Hart employs a concept of practice without indicating what he means by it, which is curious since it is introduced to 'constitute' or 'underlie' his crucial notion of a rule.[17] In this sense, we could say that he has a practice theory without a clear concept of practice. In *The Concept of Law* practice functions rather as a kind of abstract notion comparable to that of the external observer, who is at several occasions staged not as someone who has actually done empirical observations in practice, but as an abstract figure of thought, who is nevertheless capable of registering all kinds of facts about practices and making important deductions from such 'observations'. Later, in response to criticisms, Hart nuanced his methodological qualification by saying that *The Concept of Law* should itself not be seen as descriptive sociology but as 'providing the tools for descriptive sociology' (Sugarman and Hart 2005: 291). He furthermore states that all the important distinctions about law as a social phenomenon come from analytical

---

[15]For his rejection of Kelsen on these grounds, see Hart (1997: 292–293).

[16]This tension becomes even more explicitly articulated and pronounced in the writings of Neil MacCormick, one of Hart's students and disciples.

[17]Hart only gives a few examples throughout his book (stopping for a red traffic light, playing chess, taking one's hat off in church), but it could be seriously questioned if these are adequate for a full-fledged notion of practice. These are all models with rather binary options for the correctness of behavior. Turner has criticized the use of such simplistic and binary examples as the way to approach and think about practices. What would happen when we approach practices from a more multi-optional perspective, i.e. from the perspective of the orange traffic light (Turner 2001).

philosophy and are supposedly vital for engaging in any unambiguous project of sociology of law. Hart also remarked that he 'said far too little' in his book 'about the topic of adjudication and legal reasoning' (Hart 1997: 259) and that he was not really engaged by studies of law in practice and sociology of law (Sugarman and Hart 2005: 292).

In this sense Hart posits what the conceptual observer sees if he *would* observe practice – i.e. the very concepts of analytical jurisprudence that according to him *should* be the starting point of empirical sociological observation – independently of what any actual observer of concrete legal practices *does* in fact see. In this way the plane of law and the manner in which it is to be approached have already been unfolded in such a way that one *could* only recognize what is already put in from the start as a presupposition. We could ask by what right we should prefer such an 'approach' to law based on the conceptual 'observations' of an external observer, above the actual observations made from up close by the anthropologist, who empirically investigates these very processes and acts of legal reasoning and adjudication.[18] Why prefer an abstract 'practice theory' of law through descriptive armchair sociology, over a transversal ethnography of law in practice? This is the project that Latour has embarked upon in his ethnography of the French Council of State to which we turn below.

5.6.2 Demarcating Law as a Practice: Law as a System of Rules

One of the pivotal issues addressed in *The Concept of Law* is how to demarcate the practice of law from other ways in which we do things. Hart begins by distinguishing habits from social rules: the obligation to follow a social rule (e.g. *every man must bare his head in church* (Hart 1997: 10, 55) is not merely a matter of habitual convergent behaviour (1997: 86) (e.g. *drinking tea at breakfast every morning* [1997: 9, 52]), but also implies certain specific aspects such as the fact that deviations will lead to criticism and that the commitment of the participants to this social practice has an 'internal aspect' (1997: 55–57, 255 [i.e. an *internal attitude* that everyone *ought* to follow this rule]). Nevertheless, the obligation to obey certain social rules is *constituted* in social practice (1997: 254–255): e.g. the rule that a man must bare his head in church is only a rule as long as it is a generally accepted practice.

Hart's second step is to distinguish social from legal rules. Because Hart understands legal rules as being part of the larger realm of social rules, legal rules emerge and exist only within a social practice, in their repetitive use and acceptance. Yet,

[18] Galligan made a similar criticism of Hart on this point. 'A law and society approach needs to go beyond the analytical concept of acceptance and consider how officials behave in practice' (2007: 15).

Hart argues that there is something different about legal rules. He finds his answer to the demarcation problem in the *systematic* nature of law (1997: 107):

> If the question is raised whether some suggested rule is legally valid, we must, in order to answer the question, use a criterion of validity provided by some other rule.

Hart specifies that in order to 'do justice to the complexity of the legal system' (1997: 81) we need to distinguish between two kind of rules: primary, or so called 'rules of obligation', which impose a duty (e.g. 'it is forbidden to commit murder') and secondary, or so called 'rules of recognition', which confer power for the creation, alteration and even extinction of rules (e.g. 'a will must be signed by two witnesses' or 'a municipal regulation can only be altered if two thirds of the city council votes in favour of such a change') (1997: 155). Thus a certain municipal law is legally valid *because* it was made in accordance with the secondary legal rule describing how a County Council can bring a municipal law into existence.

> [The union between primary and secondary rules] may be justly regarded as the 'essence' of law (…) (Hart 1997: 155).[19]

How do we know that a secondary legal rule is valid? Only if there is, in turn, some other secondary rule that provides its validity. It is clear that we thus face a problem of infinite regress. Hart acknowledged this and introduced a so-called ultimate 'rule of recognition' (1997: 9) into his theory of law in order to bring such a regress to a stop. This ultimate rule of recognition is a 'judicial customary rule, existing only if it is accepted and practiced in the law-identifying and law-applying operations of the courts' (1997: 256)

> the rule of recognition exists only as a complex, but normally concordant, practice of courts, officials, and private persons in identifying the law by reference to certain criteria. Its existence is a matter of fact (1997: 110).

Summarizing, Hart characterizes law by its belonging to a legal system of rules, which demarcates it from a variety of other social phenomena. He does not discuss its ontological status. MacCormick (1986) however, used this idea of law's existence as a system of rules, so-called institutional facts, and opposed it to the existence of brute physical facts.

5.7 Latour – The Passage of Law

Comparing the work of analytical legal positivist Hart and the continental 'empirical philosopher' Latour (2010: x) is an enterprise that might seem unusual, as they belong to very different traditions of scholarship and philosophy.[20] Nevertheless, they might have more in common than one would think at first sight. Both authors

[19] When Hart speaks about the 'essence' of law, the word is placed in quotation marks to point to its inadequacy in relation to the anti-essentialist tradition.

[20] It is telling that Latour hardly mentions Hart, at best as an aside in a footnote, even though the latter is one of the biggest names in current legal philosophy (Latour 2004, 2010).

are situated within very different traditions of thought. Hart is a legal theorist whose theory of law can be positioned within the Anglo-Saxon tradition of analytical legal positivism (mainly the nineteenth-century variety of J. Austin) and has taken further inspiration from speech act theory, which was developed by Hart's colleague, friend and philosophical mentor J.L. Austin. Latour is a French philosopher and anthropologist who has become known as one of the leading figures within the field of Science & Technology Studies (STS) and is one of the originators of Actor Network Theory (ANT). His approach has been inspired by a mix of Greimasian semiotics and Garfinkel's ethnomethodology.[21]

And yet in spite of these most apparent differences in tradition, concepts and approach, Hart and Latour both share the desire to unburden the practice of law of unnecessary metaphysical ballast and exaggerated moral expectations: 'By demanding too much from it, we prevent it from transporting the only good that it is capable of carrying' (Latour 2010: 267). Both would probably nod approvingly at the anecdote recounting how Oliver Wendell Holmes, in his days as a judge at the Supreme Court, reciprocated the exhortation: 'Do justice, Justice!' with the reply: 'That's not my job!' (Dworkin 2006: 1). Both argue that law should not be confused with coercion or morality (e.g. Hart 1997: vi and 268; Latour 2010: 257–258 and 267): '[The Council of State] has survived every regime, including that of Vichy, owing only to its indifference to the nature of the sovereign' (Latour 2010: 270).

The attempt to unburden the ass of its religious relics (La Fontaine 2000) might sound like the way legal positivism separates law from its merits. Yet Latour is no legal positivist, at least not in the classical sense: the idea of a neutral description and the analytical theoretical approach, as found in the writings of Hart and other legal positivists, is fundamentally at odds with Latour's position. Instead of looking at the commonalities between Latour and Hart through the prism of legal positivism, their similarities can be understood from the fact that they both approach law as a practice. However, the way both authors turn to practice also marks their point of divergence. As already mentioned, Hart provides a general practice theory of law, whereas Latour provides a concrete empirical account of legal practices in action.

5.7.1 How to Study Law as a Practice? An Ethnography of the Council of State

Latour does not seem to use the term 'practice' as an explicit thematic concept in his analysis. He is rather focused on concepts like 'network', and 'mode of veridiction' or 'mode of existence'. The term 'practice' does however appear in some important phrases in which he describes his approach.[22] He gives the best characterization of

[21] See Latour (2005) for the different inspirations of his methods and thought in general.

[22] He remarks that the strength of science studies resides in '*paying close attention to the details of scientific practice*. Once we have described this practice from up close as other *anthropologists* do when they go off to live among foreign tribes, we will be able to raise again the classic questions that the philosophy of science attempted to solve without the help of an empirical grounding' (Latour 1999a: 24, italics KV and ND).

his approach in the preface to the English edition of his book *The Making of Law*, in which he documented the findings of his ethnographic studies of the French Council of State (*Conseil d'État*) (2010: 10):

> Although there is no clear description for what I'm doing, the closest is that of an empirical (not an empiricist) philosopher. This book tries, through the device of ethnography, to capture a philosophical question (…) that would be inaccessible philosophically (…): *the essence of law*. Knowing an essence does not lie in a definition but in a practice, a situated, material practice that ties a whole range of heterogeneous phenomena in a specific *way*. And it is on the search for this specific way that this book is entirely focused.

This approach makes it possible for Latour to avoid talking about the 'transcendence of the Law' (with capital "L") and substitute such talk with close empirical attention to the various details of practice.[23]

Latour's ethnographical research focuses on three points: the career paths of the members of the Council, the circulation of case files through the institution and the passage of law through the successful transfer of value objects. Here we are especially interested in these last two points. According to Latour the file is the central matter of concern within the Council of State. It 'traces and organizes all the activity of the Council. It forms the object of all types of care, of all conversation, and it allows continuous movement – without missing a step – from the most inarticulate complaint to the most sublime points of doctrine' (2010: 70). Latour followed all the stages of the logistical trajectory of these case files within the Council, along which they 'ripen' and undergo multiple modifications.[24] He claims that the file as a carton folder constitutes the material dimension of law in which every case will be physically enveloped. Its visibility allows the ethnographic researcher to trace all the particular movements of law. Just like Vismann who called files the variables of law and called the neglect of the study of the 'materiality' of files 'the blind spot of jurisprudence', Latour also exposes the absence in legal theories of the analysis of the materiality of files. In contrast to the former however this is not all there is to the law according to Latour.[25]

After having traced how files were dealt with within the Council of State, Latour proceeds to 'the heart of the matter': the passage of law. He is interested how jurists

---

[23] 'How can this be? Is there really nothing more elevated going on in this supposedly *supreme* court, beyond these infinitely small discussions on words and drafts?' (…) Darning, knitting and a ceaseless, patient, stubborn and pedestrian piece-working: a grey-on-grey that is much more beautiful and above all much more just, than the bright colors of passion' (Latour 2010: 68–9).

[24] Elsewhere one of us has argued that where the circulation of the file might be the object of concern within legal institutions like the council of State from a logistic point of view, this cannot be generalized to every other legal institution. We argue that more often the object of concern is the 'matter of dispute' or the 'matter of the claim' (Van Dijk 2011).

[25] Before his emphasis on regimes of enunciation Latour already limited the assignment of explanatory power to such material devices *per se*. Instead, he claimed, such devices are useful to the extent that they help an actor to solve an agonistic situation by aligning new allies for his or her solution (1986). From the present perspective, this logistic circulation of files would fall under what Latour calls the regime of enunciation of organisation (2008b).

'speak the law' (2010: 127) which, we understand, was even conceived as the original title of the French book.[26] In order to identify the passage of law in how jurists 'speak the law', Latour studied the processes of legal reasoning of jurists throughout the review meetings in the Council of State. The attention here thus shifts from the study of the circulatory paths of files and their materiality, to the analysis of the utterances of the jurists in order to understand the movements by which they make the law pass through them. He states that 'the sentences uttered by the members of the Council bear *explicit* signs of the changes of position they make with respect to the files that they are dealing with, and each of those signs indicates the transition, movement or metamorphosis of the particular force whose dynamic we are attempting to reconstitute' (2010: 129). Thus, for Latour, the essence of law can never be located in the static – independent of whether it is framed as the material or discursive side of the practice – but is to be found in the *passage* of law: the processes and ways of moving, transforming, tying, attaching.

5.7.2 Demarcating Law as a Practice: Law as a Regime of Reattachment

Latour chose the French Council of State as the institution which provided the best occasion to study 'pure' law. He has been criticized for this methodological choice by De Sutter and Gutwirth who claimed that his general theoretical considerations about the nature of law could not be drawn on the basis of this specific site of ethnographic study. Viewed from this perspective Latour's book can be understood as presenting a study of a particular institution and not of the nature of law itself (De Sutter and Gutwirth 2004).[27] In a reply, Latour (2004) responded by making a distinction between the 'Institution of Law' and the 'Enunciation of Law'. He argues that his study is ultimately directed at the isolation of the latter (Latour 2004), because the institution of law (of which the Council of State is a particular example) can only be understood through the legal regime of enunciation, that is, if we correctly recognize the way of truth production and the conditions of felicity or infelicity (Latour 2010: 9 and 129; Latour 2004: 35). As Latour states himself (see e.g. 1999b: 4, 2011: 309), understanding law as a 'regime of enunciation' belongs to a register of analysis which takes its inspiration from the discipline of semiotics, especially the work of Greimas.[28] The influence of semiotics on Latour's approach is not explicitly articulated in *The Making of Law*. However, in an article from 1999 he elaborates on the ways in which he is indebted to semiotics. There, he states that he

[26]The ambivalence of Latour's approach can also be seen in the genealogy of the title of his study. While it was published under the title *The Making of Law. An Ethnography of the Conseil d'État*, earlier Latour referred to the unpublished manuscript as 'Dire le droit, une ethnographie du Conseil d'Etat' ('saying the law' or 'expressing the law') (2002: 144, footnote 3).

[27]See also van Dijk (2011).

[28]See for instance Greimas and Landowksi (1976).

only preserves two concepts from semiotics: enunciation and mediation. Latour describes the first concept as follows (1999b: 3):

> The enunciation is an act of sending, mediation, delegation. (…) we can now define 'enunciation' as: the whole of the acts of mediation whose presence is necessary for the meaning [KV and ND tr.].

This redefinition brings the notion of enunciation to a new level, broader and yet more concise than in traditional semiotics. However, in *The Making of Law* and the short reply to Gutwirth and De Sutter (Latour 2004) we can trace also the use of several other semiotic notions.[29] We will hereafter first analyze the following semiotic characterizations of law: transfer of value objects (Sect. 6.7.2.1), acts of attachment (Sect. 6.7.2.2) and connotative keys for evoking a regime of enunciation (Sect. 6.7.2.3), before elaborating on the distinction between law as regime of enunciation and law as institution (Sect. 6.8.1)

5.7.2.1 The Transfer of Value Objects

If, as Latour argues in *The Making of Law*, law's essence is to be found in its movement of passage, what is it that brings these dynamic processes of transformations, translations and passes to an end, or at least a temporary end?

> And when this process comes to an end, it is never because pure law has triumphed, but (…) because the actors themselves consider that certain value objects have indeed been transferred and that conditions of felicity have indeed been fulfilled (2010: 192).

To put it differently: if to extract legal enunciation does not mean that we 'discover someone or something, neither that we discover an essence, but a process, a movement, a passage, literally a pass, as meant when this word is used with regard to ball games' (Latour 1999b: 3), towards *what* is all this movement of passage going? To answer this question Latour refers in the first place to the transfer of *value objects*, which is a notion imported from Greimasian semiotics. We will discuss the notion of value object below in more detail. Secondly, Latour mentions that the *conditions of felicity*, a term which he derives from Austin's speech act theory, must be fulfilled (e.g. a passage of statements, files, acts and legal practitioners which results in a legally invalid contract, has clearly failed to fulfill all conditions of felicity, which is indicated by certain explicit signs, such as the lack of a signature). The juxtaposition of the concepts *value object* and *conditions of felicity* which, at least at first sight, derive from two rather distinct disciplines, raises the question how they relate to each other: are they equivalent or does each of them have its own particular function?

Latour spent a large part of his study (2010: see in particular chapter 4) identifying the value objects which are transferred in the Council of State. Therefore it is worthwhile to begin by taking a closer look at this concept. In Greimasian semiotic

[29] In this chapter we will limit ourselves to the extrapolation of a model of law as a regime of enunciation with the purpose of engaging with the debate on techno-regulation. A more sustained and critical discussion of law as a *semiotic* regime will be elaborated upon in a subsequent chapter by the same authors, which we hope to publish in 2013.

theory a value object is what makes the actants[30] of a narrative move; it is the carrot dangling before the mouth of a donkey. The value object arises 'from the relationship between actantial subjects and objects: any subject's need or desire for a particular object makes the latter valuable, turning it into an *objet de valeur* in the process' (Martin and Ringham 2000: 97). Once the subject of a quest is united with a value object, which can be very concrete (a diamond, a lost testament, a hidden treasure, etc.) or abstract (happiness, knowledge, the victory over evil, etc.), the story comes to an end: Bluebeard's wife discovers the horrible truth behind the secret door and is united with her value object (knowledge), the wicked fairy luring the princess to touch the spinning wheel is partly united with her value object (death, evil), the prince kisses the Sleeping Beauty and obtains his value object (breaking the spell, good), etc. As the example of the Sleeping Beauty shows, a narrative can contain a whole series of transfer of values (death – life – partial death – life). Even though a value object will often be an end which is pursued out of a need or desire, a semiotic analysis does not provide a psychological or mimetic, but a formalistic operational description: for instance, the kissing episode from the Sleeping Beauty can be described as: $[\mathbf{S1} \rightarrow (\mathbf{S2} \cap \mathbf{O1})]$.[31]

In law there are some very particular value objects, the transfer of which makes the actantial subjects tick. During his studies in the Council of State Latour studied the sentences uttered by the councilors, and looked for explicit signs[32] indicating transfers of value. Moreover, he looked – borrowing from speech act theory – for the signs which allow the members of the Council to judge whether transfers should be considered felicitous or not. As an example, we could mention Latour's description of the first value object, which is the authority of a councilor (2010: 129):

> [...] her capacity to speak uninterrupted, and to gain her colleagues' support for her opinion. This particular 'value object', the members' authority with respect to their colleagues, changes from session to session, and throughout their entire career at the Council dealing with cases and files.

Apart from the authority of the councilor at stake, Latour identifies nine other value objects[33] which are modified during the ordeal: the procedural progress of the

---

[30] In this chapter we use the words *actor* and *actant* as synonyms, but in Greimasian semiotics the latter notion is more prevalent.

[31] S1 = Subject 1, 'the Prince'; S2 = Subject 2, 'the Princess', O1 = Object of Value 1, 'breaking the spell'; ∩ = Union; ->= Action. See for an extensive semiotic analysis of the Sleeping Beauty: Martin and Ringham (2000: 148–167).

[32] The semiotic assumption that the transformations made in enunciation can be retraced through markers or signs within the statement, is pivotal for Latour's argument: 'Although mental reasoning is inaccessible to the observer equipped only with a notebook, the sentences uttered by the members of the Council nevertheless bear explicit signs of the changes of position they make with respect to the files that they are dealing with, and each of those signs indicates the transition, movement or metamorphosis of the particular force whose dynamic we are attempting to reconstitute' (2010: 129).

[33] Latour's list of ten value objects raises the question whether this list is exhaustive. It seems likely that further research could expand the list. Another question is whether the conditions of felicity of *every* value object need to be satisfied in every case, in order to speak of a successful passage of law.

claim, the logistic organization of cases, the interest of the cases (which is a measure of their difficulty), the authoritative weight of texts, the control of the quality of the legal work (which verifies the conditions of felicity reflexively), the hesitations that provide a room for maneuver before producing linkages, the legal means (*moyens*) that allow for certain actions, the internal coherence of law, and the limits of law with justice and public indignation. The modification of each of these value objects halts or speeds up the passage of law (2010: 140–141):

> The passage of law first manifests itself in the modification that all of our value objects undergo in the course of the ordeal, through which their circulation is either accelerated or slowed down.

The concept *value object* gives specificity and direction to the passages described as legal. The value objects function as attractors towards and through which the dynamic of law proceeds.

5.7.2.2 Acts of Attachment

Latour argues that whereas the mode of enunciation of Fiction is that of disengagement (*débrayage*), the mode of enunciation of Law is that of retracing and retying all disengagements. He even calls law the enunciation of Attachment (2004: 37):

> It does what no other regime of enunciation does: it keeps track of all disengagements, to tirelessly reconnect statements to their enunciators, via the perilous routes of signatures, archives, texts and files (Latour 2010: 276).

This legal regime of enunciation gives rise to questions such as: Who was the speaker of this enunciation? To whom was it addressed? Where and when was it uttered? Although the act of enunciation, which gives sense to a statement, is absent and only implicitly present in the markers of enunciation of the statement, in law the whole dynamic is directed towards the explicitation of these absents: '*this* enunciator, *that* enunciatee, *here* at this spot, in *that* situation' (Latour 2010: 15). Moreover law has specific procedures like qualification, imputation, authentication, placing signatures, etc., to make these re-attachments strong and reliable (2010: 274):

> Everything happens as if law were interested exclusively in the possibility of re-engaging the figures of enunciation by attributing to a speaker what he or she said. Linking an individual to a text through the process of *qualification*; attaching a statement to its enunciator by following the sequences of signatures; *authenticating* an act of writing; *imputing* a crime to the name of a human being; *linking* up texts and documents; *tracing* the course of statements: all law can be grasped as an obsessive effort to *make enunciation assignable* [italics KV and ND].

The endless process of re-tracings and re-attachment reminds vaguely of Hart's test of whether a rule is legal or not. As we showed before, Hart argues that only when a rule can be traced down to the ultimate rule of recognition it can be said to be legal. By tying a particular legal rule to the ultimate rule of recognition it is tied to law in its totality, which gives *The Concept of Law* a particular tautological flavor. A similar move is made by Latour when he establishes in the last chapter of *The*

Making of Law that we enter the regime of enunciation of law when a local, specific case is tied to 'Law *as a totality*' (2010: 254, 256–257):

> it seems that there is law when it is possible to mobilize a certain form of totality with regard to an individual case, irrespective of how tiny it may be – and this is precisely why we call some reasoning 'legal'.

Reformulated in semiotic terms the 'unquestionable sender' (*destinateur*) of all the speech acts of the actors in the passage of law is 'the Law with a capital "L"' (2010: 254): for the passage of law it is essential to be re-attached to this ultimate enunciator bearing the name Law. So far *The Concept of Law* and *The Making of Law* do not differ as much as one would assume at first sight. However, what clearly differentiates Hart from Latour is that for the latter it is unacceptable to state that the essence of legal practice can be found in a *system* of legal rules – accepting the existence of such a discursive sphere, region or domain (Latour 2004: 39) would be in complete contradiction with the non-modernist character of his work (Latour 1993). Instead Latour shifts the focus from *what* must be attached towards *how* it is attached. Law as a mode of enunciation is thus not tied to a field, region or system, but it 'can go everywhere and make everything coherent' (Latour 2010: 264). The strength of Latour's re-conceptualization of law as the regime of enunciation of attachment is that it seems to equip us with a very formal and minimalist way to address the problem of demarcation. Whereas Hart needs to introduce a whole complex system of legal rules to address the question whether we can demarcate coercion (a gunman forcing us to hand over our wallet) from law (a government taxing its citizens), Latour's answer to this question[34] seems more parsimonious: if the letter of the tax office can be re-attached to Law as its enunciator it can be called legal, otherwise it is a scam.

5.7.2.3 Clef de Lecture

A last point Latour makes to characterize this legal regime of enunciation and to distinguish it from a legal institution, is by evoking the concept of a 'key':

> I quite often use, as a synonym for the mode of existence, the idea borrowed from semiotics of regimes of enunciation. Just like prepositions, regimes of enunciation set up what comes next without impinging in the least on what is actually said. Like a musical score, the regime merely indicates the tonality, the key in which one must prepare to play the next part. So this is not about looking for what is underneath the statements, their condition of possibility, or their foundations, but a thing that is light but also decisive: their mode of existence (2011: 309).[35]

[34] Interestingly, both Hart and Latour address the question how to distinguish between a policeman and a gunman (Hart 1997: 19*ff.*) or a 'thug with a baseball bat' (Latour 2010: 257–258).

[35] Latour continues: 'It tells us 'what to do next', as Austin would say; his idea of illocutionary force could quite easily be another useful synonym here. Illocutionary force, one will recall, is not about the statement, but tells how one should entertain the felicity conditions so as to avoid category errors, such as mistaking a fictive narrative for a description, or a request for a prohibition. Whether we are concerned with a preposition, a regime of enunciation, a mode of existence, or an illocutionary force, the vector is the same' (2011: 309).

We see here that Latour explicitly links the concept of regime of enunciation to that of a 'key'. We can understand this latter concept in a double meaning: musical and unlocking. When following the musical comparison, a regime of enunciation would thus constitute the musical key on a score sheet, in terms of which the notes that follow can be said to be harmonious or off-key. In making a distinction between legal regime of enunciation and legal institution, Latour makes a comparison with reading a novel in which we can distinguish between what is said – the storyline – and saying that the novel is a book of fiction. He calls the latter a key of understanding (*clef de lecture*). Where in the case of fiction this key of enunciation has to be extracted from the analysis of many different storylines, in the case of law this key has to be extracted from 'the totality of acts, texts and institutions which one calls legal' and to which it 'gives all its sense' (2004: 37). A key of understanding is a particular mode of send-off (*envoi*) into a certain register of intelligibility – like Law or Fiction – without which one does not understand a thing about the narrative that follows. In the case of fiction we could provide the following example: when a speaker utters the sentence 'Once upon a time' the listener is able to understand that the subsequent storyline will unfold in the register of fiction.[36] Latour states that (2004: 38):

> In the same way each time a child says 'You don't have the right to take my marbles!', he engages in a discussion that is about to commence on the rules on the game of shooting marbles, a type of veridiction which presupposes a particular lecture of what will follow – and which will derail when the discussion ends with a black eye.

Now, and this point is especially important for our present discussion, framing a regime of enunciation as such a key of understanding, allows us to say that law does not only exist by being connected to legal institutions. In the case of the child 'there is (still) no verbal process, no judge, no lawyer in robe, no civil code, etc' (2004: 38). Instead we are permitted to state that there is law 'everywhere a bit' and each time such connotative phrases are enunciated. When discussing the same point with regard to distinguishing political institutions from the political regime of enunciation, Latour states that (2003: 145):

> One can be a Member of Parliament and not talk in a political way. Conversely, one can be at home with one's family, in an office, at work, and start talking *politically* about some issue or other even if none of one's words have any apparent link with the political sphere.

The examples mentioned actually point our attention to the everyday settings in which a certain mode of truth production can be evoked by different acts of enunciation. A child in the schoolyard can evoke the whole legal regime of enunciation with regard to a game of marbles and, in the evening at home at the dinner table may trigger a debate in the political key of enunciation about the topic.

---

[36]It might be important to stress here that there are many different regimes of enunciation according to Latour, e.g. Fiction, Technology, Science, Law, Politics, Religion, etc. Though Law, as we will clarify below (Sect. 5.8.2), clearly has a specific 'trajectory', it should not be confused with the narrativity of the regime of Fiction. The latter always relies on a send off or shifting out from the act of enunciation, whereas the latter is characterised by a reattachment (see before, Sect. 5.6.2.2) to the act of enunciation.

5.8 Beyond Incorporeal Rules and Material Media?

In the discussions about legal positivism and the mediality of law we have subsequently seen an ontological distinction between the existence of physical objects (like buses) and the existence of law as a system of incorporeal rules, and a distinction between the medium of legal transmission and the content or message that is transmitted. Latour's focus on the act of enunciation does neither reduce law merely to the material media as they figure in legal practices, nor does it limit it to a fixation on a system of incorporeal rules in a practice theory. This allows Latour to bypass approaches to legal practice that seek to extract its 'form' or 'matter'. Latour stated that enunciation is 'an act of send-off, of mediation, of delegation' (1999b: 3), an act that makes something pass. In the case of law, the specific manner – the regime – in which this act of enunciation is performed is that of 'attachment'. By stating that what characterizes law is the way it *attaches* the local to the totality of law as its enunciator, gives a novel approach to address questions like: 'Did the printing press affect what law is?', 'Does a prohibition to copy implemented in 'digital rights management' technology differ from the prohibition in the legal codex', etc.? Following Latour one does not focus on material mediality but on the mediality of the act of enunciation. Thus, when faced with a technological innovation, the question becomes whether the specific legal way of enunciation is preserved. However, this 'regime of enunciation' is not all there is in Latour's approach: there is also the contrasting notion of 'institution'. In the following section, we will take a closer look at this equivocal duo.

5.8.1 Institution – Regime of Enunciation

Distinguishing a regime of enunciation from an institution is an interesting conceptual move which merits detailed attention, since it seems to underlie most of Latour's more recent work which he describes as a 'programme of systematic comparison of enunciation regimes' (Latour 2003: 144). While the opposition with 'institution' is still absent in Latour's early (1999b) philosophical exploration of the notions 'enunciation' and 'regime of enunciation', it has become a returning characteristic in his later, more detailed and empirical studies of particular regimes of enunciation. Yet, Latour's use of the notion institution as opposed to enunciation is far from obvious and prone to confusions. The Latourian understanding of institutions radically diverts from the more common understanding of this notion: 'Institutions are systems of established and embedded social rules that structure social interactions' (Hodgson 2006: 18). As such institutions are quite ubiquitous: language, money, law, systems of weights and measures, table manners, and organizations can all be called institutions. Thus, Hart's conceptualization of law as a system of rules can be understood as a definition of law as an institution (at least, as reformulated by MacCormick 1986), whereas in Latour the institution of law almost seems to be the complete opposite: it is the heterogeneous positivity from which a regime of enunciation can be extracted. The Latourian notion of institution is difficult to grasp in his writings, but it seems close to his notion of network, itself a complex notion.[37] Latour describes an institution as an 'ensemble of ingredients' (2003: 144), a '*bric à brac*'[38] (2004: 39) or, as was mentioned in the case of law, as 'the totality of acts, texts and institutions'[39] (2004: 37). These heterogeneities can nevertheless be labeled in a general sense: 'institutions like Science, Religion and Law' (2004: 35). Latour addresses this issue by arguing that despite the fact that 'institutions like Science, Religion and Law are indefinitely mixed, like the veined marbles of San Marco in which no figure is clearly recognizable' (2004: 35), there is always 'a particular regime which plays the role of the dominant' while the other regimes function 'as harmonics only' (2004: 35). To stress this point Latour evokes the image of an assemblage made out of Lego bricks (2004: 39–40):

> The bricks themselves are of multiple shapes… Now let kids play the game. They will produce shapes – *institutions* – of which the segments which are more or less long will be, let's say, LAW, because the attachment is of the type LAW, even though a given brick can be recaptured, according to another segment, by the attachment POL[ITICS]. In the *colorful* ensemble that is produced, one can say, according to the *intensity* of bonds, that 'overall that is really more law than something else', 'that is in fact more politics than something else'. Of course, this will always be wrong, because the bricks are diverse, heterogeneous, etc., of various colors, and nevertheless it will never be fully wrong because the 'dominant', to use the discourse of music, will be given by a particular type of attachment or vibration or contamination [KV and ND tr.].

When not using the discourse of music to describe this type of 'attachment or vibration or contamination' that can be extracted from an institution, Latour speaks of 'a regime of enunciation'.

The picture that emerges from these writings is that a regime of enunciation is to be viewed as a certain *mode of connecting* or assembling that maintains something in presence, whereas an institution is the assemblage of the elements *connected this way*, i.e., that which is maintained in presence and where the specific enunciation becomes institutionalized. There is a curious relation between the two: a legal institution is the heterogeneous positivity from which the regime of enunciation of law can be extracted, but this regime of enunciation is that which has already permitted us to understand the institution as legal. Or rather, let us propose the following interpretation of the distinctions between network, institutions and regime of enunciation.

---

[37] In another article Latour opposed the regime of enunciation with his notion of a 'network'. (Latour 2008a, b).

[38] 'If we would study the legal institution, strictly speaking, it becomes crucial to distinguish the types of transmission in this *bric-à-brac* that they compose and maintain in existence. Immense portions of its networks depend in fact, for their solidity and durability, on morals, politics, technology, economy, etc., as much as on the type of attachment and legal vehicle proper' (Latour 2004: 39, KV and ND tr.).

[39] Here Latour seems to shift between two different uses of the word institution: there is the institution of Law (one is almost inclined to write *Institution*, with a capital 'I') but also the variety of institutions (for instance, the Council of State) through which the former is constituted.

One can distinguish between tracing how a certain network is laid out (making possible certain actions and transformations) and the understanding that the kind of transformation that takes place is legal. On the first task one will find that the *network* consists out of a variety of different actors: instruments, people, procedures, settings, texts etc., and a variety of ways in which these are connected together. Potentially, one could endlessly follow how this web unfolds without making a cut (in the same way that Latour [1988] described the process of the discovery of lactic acids by Pasteur and traced their subsequent proliferation throughout the whole of France up until the most isolated wine farmer). We could call this the extensive approach referring to the horizontal direction of extension in which the network is traced. One could, however, also focus within this unfolded web upon the tone or color of the *connection* by which the elements are assembled together. We could call this the intensive approach referring to the kinds of intensity of connection that are established within these networks. Now, in the pursuit of the latter task, one will find a heterogeneity of differently colored threads. In some places of the web however, we can distinguish zones with a certain dominant color. This enables us to 'cut the network' and call the assemblage of elements in this zone a certain *institution*.[40] Of course this cut is an artificial demarcation, since one can always take hold of a differently colored thread within the zone that enables one to flee and be led away to different zones,[41] but the cut is useful to the extent that it enables us to recognize the territory on which we have arrived.

5.8.2 *The Legal Trajectory of Enunciation*

Now, although the interpretation given above may help in understanding the relations between networks, regimes of enunciation and institutions, it might also deceive in its colorful simplicity. It might thus be useful to zoom in on the connecting threads, in this case the legal ones, when we thus speak about the intensity of the type of connection established. Whereas in the discussion of the semiotic analysis of the legal regime of enunciation the elements (transfer of value objects, *act*s of attachment, key of interpretation) might have seemed somewhat dispersed, we will now try to bring them together to understand the particularities, described as the color-tone of the legal threads, of legal enunciation. We could understand these connecting threads as the timeline of a trajectory. This trajectory is initiated by the evocation of a key of understanding, like 'You don't have the right..!', most often in the breakdown of everyday societal activities into a conflictual situation, which sends the discussion that is about to follow off in a legal direction. Through this act a behavior, thing or person is linked to the kind of a concept that might later be linked to constructed sequences of (statutory) articles, (case-)documents or (doctrinal)

[40] For this notion of cutting the network see Strathern (1996).

[41] We are here alluding to Deleuze's concept of a 'line of flight' that can lead to a deterritorialization. For the use of this concept see Deleuze and Guattari (1987).

texts and that will enable the mobilization of a legal totality. This happens when our small conflictual scene is followed up by the involvement of lawyers who further occupy themselves with the conflict and, through their specific acts, reinforce its proceeding in the legal tone. The matter in dispute is now also subjected to the transfer of value objects (which only seem applicable to law as a professional practice[42]) engaging the legal practitioners, and will terminate when the legal conditions of felicity have been fulfilled.

At the same time it is good to notice that the evocative key of understanding does not set in stone what is going to happen afterwards – the trajectory could, for instance, derail if the involved parties decide to settle things with their fists. Moreover, the sentence 'You don't have the right..!' has a certain ambiguity. We could ask whether the phrase 'you don't have the right to take my marbles' does actually evoke the legal regime of enunciation, or whether we are rather transposed into the registers of morality, ethics or organization. What kind of right is evoked here? A legal right, maybe a right of property, a moral right of indignation, or does it resort to an interpretation of the right way of playing the game of marbles?[43] However, let us assume that none of these is the case and a conflict develops in the legal mode: in what sense does it differ then from the mode of techno-regulation?

5.9 Law and Technology

5.9.1 A Bump in the Road

After having described this Latourian view on law, we can now return to the discussion of techno-regulation and focus on two aspects: the understanding of law as a system of rules and the understanding of technology from a legal perspective. Hart's concept of law is one dominated by the notion of *rules*. So is the current debate surrounding techno-regulation. Unsurprisingly, when law and techno-regulation are juxtaposed, the pivotal question becomes what happens when a rule embedded in text is implemented in a different technology. A traditional paper rendition of rule,

[42]It is interesting to note that the main point of focus of Hart is also *professional* practice. He distinguishes between an active aspect of the existence of law, consisting in the operations of law-making by legislating officials, law-identification and application by the court officials and experts (lawyers) (1997: 61), and its passive aspect that becomes manifest in the 'general social practice' of ordinary citizens who acquiesce in the results of these official operations (1997: 55).

[43]The problem is that the answer to these questions is underdetermined here, since we do not know anything else about the uttered phrase. In this case it implies that, in its present abbreviated form, the uttered phrase has not yet sufficiently distinguished the regime that is to be evoked. This leads to the question whether phrases like 'once upon a time' and 'you don't have the right' can be assigned such a weighty function of connotative key in characterizing the uniqueness of a certain regime of enunciation. Much more might be needed for such evocation. These 'additionals' will have a lot to do with the details of practices, issues, circumstances and consequences.

whether it is legal or not, would leave room for debate, interpretation and for 'a practice around the rule' (Brownsword 2008: 44) adjusting its paper meaning. Brownsword reminds us that 'paper rules are one thing; the real rules are something else' (2008: 44). Compared to a paper rule a 'techno-rule' is considered to be more rigid: 'it does not allow for exceptions that the written legal rule allows' (Hildebrandt and Koops 2010: 453). Framed in these terms the challenge of techno-regulation becomes the translation of textual rules into techno-*rules* whilst keeping in mind the limitations and allowances of the *medium* in which it is implemented. How to translate the following rules: 'do not drive faster than 50 km/h' into a speed bump?; 'Do not bring the key outside the hotel' into a key (Latour 1991)?; 'Lighters should not be operable by children younger than 51 months' *into* a lighter (Hildebrandt and Koops 2010)? Latour's approach of practices as different regimes of enunciation, however, allows for a refreshingly different understanding of both law and the regulatory capacity of technology, as it neither relies on the notion of a rule nor on a medium as its carrier.

This can be clarified with an example drawn from the context of traffic. Let's imagine the following sequence of events: a car ignores a speeding sign and drives too fast through a residential area. A hiker who has to get out of the way of the car quickly, shouts '@#$#%^! You are not allowed to drive so fast here!' and phones the police. In the meanwhile the car continues to speed, until it drives over a speed bump which makes it bounce, damages its chassis and forces it to slow down. When the car finally stops, an alerted cop has managed to register the speed of the car with the help of a camera and qualifies the act of driving as an infraction of the official speed limit. A few months later the driver is found guilty of speeding by the district judge and has to pay a high fine. In this example we can distinguish many elements which affect the course of events: the car, the driver, the hiker, the speed bump, the phone, the camera, the judge, etc. We can trace the relationships between these 'actants' (Latour 2005) according to different modes of enunciation: law and technology.[44] Depending on which of these modes is followed, the study of the example will be sent off in very different trajectories.

5.9.2 *Law as Tracing Through Reattachments*

We will first focus on the legal trajectory. As described earlier legal acts reattach enunciations to their enunciator and to the totality of law. The exclamation of the hiker and the qualification by the policeman can be considered the first step in this modality of enunciating, introducing a key for the legal mode of reattachment that follows. This subsequent process can consist of many steps. For instance, photos of

[44]We could even distinguish more regimes of which the speed bump would be part. As Gutwirth remarks, 'the same object can thus well have several dimensions. A "sleeping policeman" is a moral, technical, legal and political being all at once' (2010: 27).

the license plate and the damaged chassis are sent to the police station where a file is created. Based on the pictures that link the registered license plate number of the car to the act of speeding, the infraction can be imputed to the name of the driver, by tracing the license plate in a register. Then the file is eventually handed over to the prosecutor who, based on his or her own considerations and hesitations, has certified the legal qualification of the speeding infraction, summons the driver to appear in court. The driver might hire a lawyer who could link the act to the legal concept of 'extenuating circumstances' (the driver might have been speeding home in relation to an accident which had befallen his or her child), or to the faulty execution of police procedures (the police might have already been surveilling the driver for a while without a valid mandate), the competence of the court (the act occurred outside of the court's jurisdiction) etc. In short a host of value objects is brought in circulation with regard to the case and its proceeding will only come to a halt when the judge condemns the driver in his verdict, of which an official copy is sent to the driver, and the legal consequences ensue: the driver has to pay a fine. We thus have a long chain of events in which an enunciator (the driver) is eventually linked back to his enunciation (driving too fast) through a whole chain of mediating files, procedures, legal means, pieces of evidence, witnesses, statements, legal operations. Thus, the legal mode is one of retracing, reattachment: the traffic sign, the driver and the car all become connected and *traced back* to the totality of law – it is always about bringing a retro-attributive trajectory to the fore, which, in our example, can be evoked *onwards from* the moment a concrete car passes the traffic sign with a certain speed.

5.9.3 Technology as Delegational Folding

A second mode of enunciation is technology. Latour has explored this modality in several studies.[45] The speed bump is often used as paradigmatic example of *regulation through technology*. Interestingly, Latour has also studied this so-called 'sleeping policeman' to exemplify the *technological regime of enunciation* as such (Latour 1992, 244; 1999a, 188–9). A whole network is folded within the speed bump: the municipality that proposed to place it, the speed regulations that organized the proposal, the policeman for whom the speed bump will come to act as a stand in, the engineers who worked out the programs of action, the budget which constrained the project, the manufacturer who made the asphalt, the construction company that placed it at the right spot on the road, etc.[46] Each of these steps transforms the identity

[45] For an extensive Actor-Network ethnography of a technological project see Latour (1996). For a very relevant short analysis of the example of the speed bump according to this approach, see Latour (1999a: chapter 6).

[46] It might be that the example of the speed bump is too simple for requiring such an elaborate technological network. We could however also think of the other examples of techno-regulation like the automatic gates in subway stations that only open when one is able to show a valid transportation card.

of the technological project that is at stake in this network through a detour. Latour considers this detour, this actorial, temporal and spatial shift, to be essential to the technological regime of enunciation. When all of these actants are aligned successfully, the technological object (the speed bump) will eventually come to act independently of the network that produced it and therefore it can function as its spatio-temporal stand-in, the place-keeper or *lieu-tenant*. Latour calls this function a relation of delegation. All these actants are both present and absent within the technological object once it is produced: they are all folded within the speed bump, but seem very absent at the moment when it acts in its own particular way on the action of the driver-car assemblage by slowing it down or even damaging it. The network which produces and maintains a technology is black-boxed or folded. Normally, a driver simply uses a car to drive, without having any need to reflect on the mechanisms, factory workers, road maintenance organization, the actants involved in oil supply etc. Only in a situation of breakdown – the chassis is broken, there is an oil crisis, the road maintenance is on a strike, etc. – the network keeping the car in existence becomes urgent. This whole network of actants might also be brought to the fore when an ethnographer wants to describe the actor-network in which the speed bump is embedded, or when it becomes involved in a legal case (e.g. a concerned citizen contests its placement because the concrete was not made according to the regulations in this field). Yet, normally all of this remains black-boxed, invisibly folded within the speed bump, overshadowed by the relative independent way in which it seems to act on another actant: the car acts on the actions of the driver, allowing him or her to move at high speed.

5.9.4 Law Versus Technology

Contrary to the mode of law, the technological mode of existence of the speed bump does not rely on any reattachments but instantaneously acts on the action of the car-driver assemblage, immediately distributing its consequences (to the car's suspension and chassis) all in the very action itself.[47] No legal value objects, keys of understanding, or hesitative operations of attachment are involved in this case. Everything seems to happen on the spot, immediately; without legal means or media.[48] In this sense law and technology are very different (Latour 2010: 272–273):

[47] In contrast Latour remarks that it is specific for law if 'punishment is not decided on the spot but later, elsewhere, on the basis of a file, by other people who stall for a long time, by means of a regular procedure, before stating their decisions, which you receive in the form of a letter delivered by a postman' (Latour 2010: 257).

[48] We could say that in the trials through the technological projects leading *up to* the placement of the speed bump on the road, all that will come to pass it will have been *traced in advance* as a certain general type of actor [car] and action [speeding]. This becomes even clearer in the case of software technologies that 'qualify' persons, things or actions according to certain general 'social ontologies'. Semantic Web technologies are a prominent example.

> The humblest technique – this lamp, this ashtray, this paper-clip – mixes periods, places and totally heterogeneous materials; it folds them into the same black box, [making] those who use them (..) act, by diverting the course of their action. Law is incapable of that. It is the least technical of all forms of enunciation (…) No acceleration, no delegation, no stunning innovation. Once again, nothing replaces law, if not the renewed expression of law itself. For an essential reason that we shall soon discover, law, unlike techniques, is neither folded nor delegated.

5.10 Techno-Regulation: A Future Without Law?

5.10.1 Techno-Regulation: A Legal Understanding of Technology

So what about the role of rules in the understanding of the speed bump? Does this artefact not embody and enact a traffic rule? If we look at the speed bump from the perspective of techno-regulation, one could indeed say that it does something which is not unlike the act of legal enunciation: this so-called 'sleeping policeman' (Latour 1992: 244; 1999a: 188–189) *qualifies* the driver as committing an infringement on the speeding limit by causing the car's suspension and damaging its chassis and as such seems to instantaneously relate an action (driving with a certain speed) back to its enunciator (the driver). However, we must realize that understanding the event in this way is already a legal projection on technology. In this sense we could say that much of the debate on techno-regulation, from a Latourian perspective, should be seen as a legal articulation of technologies (which is no wonder, since nearly all participants to this debate are legal scholars!). This perspective has its merits, but, just like all legal fictions[49] it should not lead us to confuse this projection with the technological *modus operandi* that answers to very different requirements. It is known that each discipline has this tendency of over projecting its own mode of operation upon others. Latour offers us a way of thinking to resist such reductions and to start understanding technology from its own set of requirements. In this sense it offers us a prolegomena for thinking about techno-regulation. In order to articulate the relations between legal, technological and regulatory practices, we first need to understand what is specific to each of these.

We started this chapter by discussing the rather specific understandings of both law and technology that figured within the debate of techno-regulation. Law was understood as a system of rules, orders backed by threats of the sovereign or the guardian of constitutional democracy. Through a rather large detour we have gained a different conception of law that neither depends on rules, nor asks its fragile threads of attachment to carry the heavy burden of relics. In this chapter we have

[49] According to Latour, fiction, like technology, is a regime of enunciation which always involves an actorial, spatial and temporal shift-out (1999a, 1999b).

mainly focused on law, but the same arguments would apply to technology. Like law, technological practices have their own set of constraints and complexities. If we resist the temptation to provide a simplistic picture of both, it also becomes very difficult to maintain the regulative model according to which rules, norms and policies are simply embodied in both law and technology as means to regulative ends. Instead of thinking in terms of embodied rules, we force ourselves to focus on the transformations that entities undergo when they pass through a particular practice and how they are articulated through the constraints proper to it. Now it becomes clear that through all the detours of technology, through all the co-foldings with all kinds of other requirements that have to be taken into account in a technological project (economical, political, organizational, habitual, legal) something quite different comes out than what we started with. As we can see, political policies might be just one of these requirements that have to be folded into a trajectory that has a rather different direction: the production of a technology that is capable of existing by itself, independent of its makers. Each of these intervening requirements that are taken into account will transform the technology that is under construction, to such an extent that the so called 'originally envisioned technology' is no more. Similarly, in law, even when we choose to focus on a relatively straightforward speed prohibition, there is no way of telling what will happen when this humble legal provision is squashed between the immense complex dispersions of a concrete dispute and the totality of the law that will have to be mobilized. Both the *modus operandi* of technology and the mode of proceeding of law, we could say, have their ways of resisting the regulative instrumentalizations proposed.

After having described the regime of enunciation of law and technology, we should not jump too easily to conclusions about what belongs to the former and to the latter. When in discussions about law, we speak about 'law in the books', we should realize that such a legal codex[50] is as much a technology as the ones that figure so prominently in the debate on techno-regulation: a speed bump,[51] a CD with digital rights management (DRM) code sold to software developers,[52] or a compact disc protected by DRM code[53] – they are all black-boxes that through a detour of

[50]The legal codex creates an actorial (the textual rules act as a stand-in for the legislator producing it, which becomes inscribed in them as their 'law maker'), temporal (the 'law maker' has become more permanently consultable) and spatial shift (on the bookshelf a new actant resides).

[51]The speed bump (Latour 1999a: 189) also creates an actorial (the bump replaces the engineers and the policeman and acts on the behavior of car drivers), temporal (the bump is on guard day and night) and spatial shift (a new actant resides on the road where it slows down or damages cars).

[52]The DRM technology creates an actorial (the technology will function as a stand-in for the copyright infringement organizations and the software developers and installs a different world of maneuver for pirates and hackers), temporal (the technology always fulfills its protective function when the music is accessed) and spatial (the 'blood hound' now exist as a new actant in the CD-ROM drive) shift-out.

[53]The protected music CD creates an actorial (the creation of the CD replaces the musicians, differentiates appropriate from inappropriate musical players, a connaisseur of good CD recordings etc.), temporal (listening to the music is not limited to its live performance, but can always be listened to) and spatial (a new actant is lying on top of my stereo) shift-out.

delegation guide actions. It has become common place to talk about information technologies in terms of a hardware/software distinction, which bears a certain alluring analogy to the classical understanding of law in terms of incorporeal rules embedded in material media. As we argued before, this 'legal' way of looking at things has contaminated the techno-regulation debate in general, but this is even more so where software and hardware are involved. However, instead of bifurcating a codex or a piece of IT technology in such way, it might be more fruitful to look at them as assemblages which belong to the technological regime of enunciation. Thus, for instance if we want to understand DRM technology without an ontological divide, we have to understand that the technological network producing this technology is also tightly interwoven with other technological networks that produce either compact discs, computers, electricity circuits etc.[54] These distinctions however, are horizontal as it were: from network to network, instead of vertical: a rule in a carrier.

Similarly, in order not to understand a legal codex according to a bifurcation of materiality and incorporeal rules, it would be worthwhile to engage in an ethnographic study of the very networks in which legislation is constructed, to prevent a perspective in which laws (as codices) are somehow taken as *prêt-a-porter*. We will then expect to see the deployment of a network that joins together a multiplicity of different activities: societal issues that will lead to the gathering of political assemblages, administrative and organizational activities in which scripts[55] will be produced that are supposed to address such issues, the involvement of legal practitioners who will have to translate and transform these scripts into legalese according to their own conditions of felicity, the technological activities at publishing houses that eventually will have to fold these scripts, with a heterogeneity of materials, printing techniques, political agendas, counter-agendas, into a book that will be called the legal codex. This perspective is necessary to avoid being lured to talk about these processes in terms of a certain vocabulary of 'big terms' - like rules, incorporation, implementation, objects, or medium - that shortcuts our understanding of these complex processes. Instead we have to first understand and unravel the complex fabric of threads that are here run together.

[54]This is an additional complication in relation to the examples of the codex and the speed bump.

[55]'A script is a set of goal-oriented instructions that delegate to some other actors more or less specific tasks depending on those actors competences' (Latour 2008b). 'Organisation' is the name given by Latour to the mode of enunciation which subsists by scripting actors and by actors that script. This mode of enunciation is entangled with many other modes. We have already seen in Sect. 5.7.1 (footnote 25) how organisation was intertwined with law. Organisation also has very strong ties with technology. Akrich (1992) describes for instance how designers endeavor to inscribe a script into technologies that contain prescriptions for the hypothetical actors that will come to use the technology and that will have to be *de-scribed* by the ethnographer of technology.

5.10.2 A Technological Future Without Law?

Let us imagine a future where society is ruled through scripts incorporated in technology. The way in which this is done is not through mere 'rule by technology' or 'technological discipline', but the scripts are embedded in the technology in a transparent way, they are democratically legitimized, and democratically contestable. Moreover the technology is scripted in such an advanced way that it is able to deal with all kind of nuances and could quickly adapt to change. Nobody ever receives a high legal bill, the technology acts instantaneously and in a fair and unbiased way. However, within this (clearly imaginative) techno-regulation utopia one thing is missing: the legal regime of enunciation as described by Latour. No reattachment to the totality of law is ever made again. Let's also imagine that in our utopia every bookshelf is still filled with codices, but they only act as monumental pieces of historical evidence or blue prints for further regulation through information-technological means. We will then be in a situation in which every bit of script is created in accordance with a 'rule of law'. But when no legal acts of reattachments are enunciated these technological intermediaries will not partake in legal enunciation. The question we want to propose is whether within such a future, we would not be deprived of an important way of partaking in existence, namely the *legal* way? Will we not have lost a crucial ability to maintain a continuity in our acts, through all the dispersed ways in which we will be doing whatever it is we might do?

References

Akrich, M. 1992. The de-scription of technical objects. In *Shaping technology/building society: Studies in sociotechnical change*, ed. W.E. Bijker and J. Law, 205–224. Cambridge, MA: MIT Press.

Aristotle. 1993, orig. ca 350 BC. *De anima: Books II and III with passages from book 1*, Trans. D.W. Hamlyn. Oxford: Clarendon Press.

Berman, H.J. 1983. *Law and revolution*. Cambridge, MA: Harvard University Press.

Brownsword, R. 2005. Code, control, and choice: Why east is east and west is west. *Legal Studies* 25(1): 1–21.

Brownsword, R. 2008. So what does the world need now? reflections on regulating technologies. In *Regulating technologies: Legal futures, regulatory frames and technological fixes*, ed. R. Brownsword and K. Yeung, 23–48. Oxford: Hart.

De La Fontaine, J. 2000, orig. ca 1668. The ass that carried relics. In *Selected fables*, 35. Mineola: Dover Publications.

Deleuze, G., and F. Guattari. 1987. *A thousand plateaus*. Minneapolis: University of Minnesota Press.

Derrida, J., and J. Mehlman. 1972. Freud and the scene of writing. *Yale French Studies* 48: 74–117.

De Sutter, L., and S. Gutwirth. 2004. Droit et cosmopolitique. Notes sur la contribution de Bruno Latour à la pensée du droit. *Droit et Société* 56/57(1): 259–289.

Dickens, C. 2005, 1853. *Bleak house*. New York: Barnes & Noble.

Dworkin, R. 2006. *Justice in robes*. Cambridge, MA: Belknap Press of Harvard University Press.

Eisenstein, E. 2005. *The printing revolution in early modern Europe*. New York: Cambridge University Press.

Galligan, D. 2007. *Law in modern society*. Oxford: Oxford University Press.

Goody, J., and I. Watt. 1963. The consequences of literacy. *Comparative Studies in Society and History* 5(3): 304–345.
Greimas, A.J., and É. Landowski. 1976. Analyse sémiotique d'un discours juridique: la loi sur les sociétés commerciales et les groupes de sociétés. In *Sémiotique et sciences sociales*, ed. A.J. Greimas, 79–128. Paris: Éditions du Seuil.
Gutwirth, S. 2010. Composer avec du droit, des sciences et le mode technique: une exploration. In *Les technologies de l'information au service des droits: opportunités, défis, limites*, ed. D. Le Métayer, 24–42. Brussels: Bruylant.
Gutwirth, S., P. De Hert, and L. De Sutter. 2008. The trouble with technology regulation from a legal perspective. Why Lessig's 'optimal mix' will not work. In *Regulating technologies. Legal futures, regulatory frames and technological fixes*, ed. R. Brownsword and K. Yeung, 193–218. Oxford: Hart Publishers.
Hart, H.L.A. 1997. *The concept of law*. Oxford: Clarendon.
Hildebrandt, M. 2008. A vision of ambient law. In *Regulating technologies: Legal futures, regulatory frames and technological fixes*, ed. R. Brownsword and K. Yeung, 175–191. Oxford: Hart.
Hildebrandt, M., and B.-J. Koops. 2007. *A vision of ambient law*. FIDIS Deliverable 7.9: The Future of Identity in the Information Society (FIDIS), Brussels.
Hildebrandt, M., and B.-J. Koops. 2010. The challenges of ambient law and legal protection in the profiling era. *The Modern Law Review* 73(3): 428–460.
Hodgson, G.M. 2006. What are institutions? *Journal of Economical Issues* 40(1): 1–25.
Kittler, F. 1986. *Gramophone, film, typewriter*. Stanford: Stanford University Press.
Latour, B. 1986. Visualization and cognition: Thinking with eyes and hands. *Knowledge and Society* 6: 1–40.
Latour, B. 1988. *The pasteurization of France*. Cambridge, MA: Harvard University Press.
Latour, B. 1991. Technology is society made durable. In *A sociology of monsters: Essays on power, technology and domination*, ed. J. Law, 103–131. London: Routledge.
Latour, B. 1992. Where are the missing masses? The sociology of a few mundane artifacts. In *Shaping technology/building society: Studies in sociotechnical change*, ed. W.E. Bijker and J. Law, 225–258. Cambridge, MA: MIT Press.
Latour, B. 1993. *We have never been modern*. New York/London: Harvester Wheatsheaf.
Latour, B. 1996. *Aramis, or, the love of technology*. Cambridge, MA: Harvard University Press.
Latour, B. 1999a. *Pandora's hope: Essays on the reality of science studies*. Cambridge, MA: Harvard University Press.
Latour, B. 1999b. Petite philosophie de l'énonciation. Pour Paolo – à la mémoire de notre amie commune Françoise Bastide. In *Eloqui de senso. Dialoghi semiotici per Paolo Fabbri*, ed. P. Basso and L. Corrain, 71–94. Milano: Costa & Nolan.
Latour, B. 2002. Si l'on parlait un peu politique? *Politix* 15(58): 143–165.
Latour, B. 2003. What if we *talked* politics a little? *Contemporary Political Theory* 2: 143–164.
Latour, B. 2004. Note brève sur l'écologie du droit saisie comme énonciation. In *Pratiques cosmopolitiques du droit. Cosmopolitiques. Cahiers théoriques pour l'écologie politique*, ed. F. Audren and L. De Sutter, 34–40. Paris: L'Aube.
Latour, B. 2005. *Reassembling the social: An introduction to actor-network-theory*. Oxford: Oxford University Press.
Latour, B. 2008a. Coming out as a philosopher. Paper presented at the Discourse for the acceptation of the Siegfried Unseld Preis, Frankfurt, Sept 2008.
Latour, B. 2008b. What's organizing? A meditation on the bust of Émile Boutmy in praise of Jim Taylor. Paper presented at the what is an organization? materiality, agency and discourse, Montréal, 21 May 2008.
Latour, B. 2010. *The making of law. An ethnography of the Conseil d'État*. Cambridge: Polity Press.
Latour, B. 2011. Reflections on Etienne Souriau's 'Les différents modes d'existence. In *The speculative turn: Continental materialism and realism*, ed. L. Bryant, N. Srnicek, and G. Harman, 304–333. Melbourne: re.press.

Leenes, R.E. 2010. *Harde lessen. Apologie van technologie als reguleringsinstrument (Hard lessons. Apology for technology as a regulatory tool)*. Tilburg: Universiteit van Tilburg.

Leenes, R.E. 2011. "Technoregulering: regulering of 'slechts' disciplinering" ("Technoregulation: regulation or 'mere' disciplination"). *Recht der Werkelijkheid* 32(1): 47–52.

Lessig, L. 2006. *Code: Version 2.0*. New York: Basic Books.

Lodder, A.R., A. Oskamp, and A.H.J. Schmidt. 2001. IT support of the Judiciary in Europe, ITeR. eJure: Available at: www.ejure.nl. Last accessed 20 Oct 2012.

MacCormick, N. 1986. Law as institutional fact. In *An institutional theory of law: New approaches to legal positivism*, ed. N. MacCormick and O. Weinberger, 49–76. Dordrecht: Reidel.

Martin, B., and F. Ringham. 2000. *Dictionary of semiotics*. London: Cassell.

McLuhan, M. 1994. *Understanding media. The extensions of man*. Cambridge, MA: MIT Press.

McLuhan, M., and E. McLuhan. 1988. *Laws of media: The new science*. Toronto: University of Toronto Press.

Reidenberg, J.R. 1998. Lex informatica: The formulation of information policy rules through technology. *Texas Law Review* 76(3): 553–584.

Sampaio Ferraz, T. 2011. Die Erosion subjektiver Rechte als Folge der technischen Entwicklung (Patentrecht, Urheberrecht)/Erosion of subjective rights by reason of technical development (Patent, Copyright). Paper presented at the Internationalen Vereinigung für Rechts- und Sozialphilosophie (IVR) World Congress, Frankfurt am Main, 14–20 Aug 2011.

Schatzki, T.R., K. Knorr-Cetina, and E. von Savigny. 2001. *The practice turn in contemporary theory*. London: Routledge.

Strathern, M. 1996. Cutting the network. *The Journal of the Royal Anthropological Institute* 2(3): 517–535.

Sugarman, D., and H.L.A. Hart. 2005. Hart interviewed: H.L.A. Hart in conversation with David Sugarman. *Journal of Law and Society* 32(2): 267–293.

Thomas, Y. 1978. Le droit entre les mots et les choses. *Archives de philosophie du droit* 23: 93–114.

Tien, L. 2004. Architectural regulation and the evolution of social norms. *International Journal of Communication Law & Policy* 9: 1–14.

Turner, S.P. 2001. Throwing out the tacit rule book. Learning and practices. In *The practice turn in contemporary theory*, ed. T.R. Schatzki, K. Knorr-Cetina, and E. von Savigny, 120–130. London: Routledge.

Van Dijk, N. 2011. Approaching law through conflicts. *Law and Method* 1(1): 44–63.

Vismann, C. 2008. *Files*, Trans. G. Winthrop-Young. Stanford: Stanford University Press.

Part II
Law and Literature

Chapter 6
Prefatory Remarks on Part II: Law and Literature

Jeanne Gaakeer

We are what we imagine we are: reality itself is the supreme fiction

O'Hagan (2010: 22)

Abstract This chapter forms the introduction to part II of this volume. The depiction of science and technology has fascinated literary writers for centuries, from ancient Greek tragedy to contemporary literature. If technology and literature share a long history, so do law and literature as the two strands of Law and Literature, 'law as literature' and 'law in literature' show. The combined interest in law, literature and technology in part II, then, has its focus on questions pertaining to the topic of code, both as constraint and option.

6.1 Man and/or Machine?

The depiction of science and technology has fascinated literary writers for centuries. From ancient Greek tragedy where the topic of the limitations of an unrestrained application of *technè* comes to the fore, showing that there is a tragic sense to all technical and technological knowledge, with Sophocles' *Antigone*, a play not incidentally centered on the uses of "code" as a case in point (Tabachnick 2004), to contemporary literature with, for example, Christa Wolf's novel *Störfall* on the topic of the human subject and technology after the Chernobyl nuclear disaster.

J. Gaakeer (✉)
Department of Jurisprudence, Erasmus University Rotterdam,
Burgemeester Oudlaan 50, 3062 PA, Rotterdam, The Netherlands
e-mail: gaakeer@law.eur.nl

M. Hildebrandt and J. Gaakeer (eds.), *Human Law and Computer Law: Comparative Perspectives*, Ius Gentium: Comparative Perspectives on Law and Justice 25,
DOI 10.1007/978-94-007-6314-2_6, © Springer Science+Business Media Dordrecht 2013

The standard association of modern technology and literature is Mary Shelley's 1818 novel *Frankenstein*. This fictive depiction of technological progress is already anticipated, however, in a small passage in Jonathan Swift's *Gulliver's Travels* (1726). In the part of the Academy of Lagado where 'the projectors in speculative learning resided', the narrator encounters a huge machine, an engine so to speak of knowledge, that can write books because in it are pieces of paper with 'all the words of their language in their several moods, tenses, and declensions, but without any order', so that when an iron handle is turned 'the whole disposition of the words was entirely changed' and all the available knowledge in the world could, in principle at least, be connected in 'a complete body of all arts and sciences' (Swift 1977: 227, 229). This wonderful literary precursor of computational and corpus linguistics also,[1] is emblematic of the human fascination for the idea of code in its various forms and its interconnection to control and power. Furthermore, it already suggests that code is made by us, as Lawrence Lessig emphasizes (Lessig 2006: 6). Satiric as Swift's portrayal is, it also offers a sobering thought to all technocrats in the sense that literature has foreseen what technology could accomplish in the twentieth century.[2] In another sense it also ties in with the rise of the mechanistic worldview that became the hallmark of modernity, i.e. the mechanistic concept of 'man as a machine' traced back philosophically to Descartes' *Traité de l'homme* (1648) and De la Mettrie's *L'homme machine* (1748). In literature, a later source would be Aldous Huxley's *Brave New World* with the first example of man as a truly technologically determined creature.

Viewed with a different lens, it also shows the root of the disciplinary struggles between 'The Two Cultures' as C.P. Snow (1993) called them in his eponymous 1959 Rede Lecture when he made the distinction between scientists and non-scientists and grouped under the latter heading those working in the humanities, thereby diminishing the culture they stood for. This dismissal of the humanities was fiercely contested by F.R. Leavis (1962) who demanded a place for literature as the 'third realm' on the view that the existence of literary works is rooted in human minds that constitute and reaffirm their own humanity. Leavis read Snow through the prism that he himself put forward, viz. that of a technocrat who pretended to speak authoritatively on behalf of the natural sciences, and thus the controversy can also be understood to take place on the plane of ideology rather than (merely) in 'disciplinary terms' (Ortolano 2009; Gaakeer 2011).

If technology and literature already share a long history, so do law and literature. With literature as a linchpin, because '… it creates autonomous figures that may be

---

[1]The professor assures the author that 'he had emptied the whole vocabulary in his frame, and made the strictest computation of the general proposition there is in books between the number of particles, nouns, and verbs, and other parts of speech' Swift (1977: 229).

[2]For an overview of 'Landmarks in Fictive Images of Technology', see Chandler (1995); Chandler's main focus being on science fiction, with utopian views on societal dependence on artificial intelligence in the form of robots etc., it is only fair to note here Henry James's early contribution to narratives of decoding and surveillance, the short story 'In the Cage' (2005, orig. 1919), and Ri Tokko's (pseudonym of Ludwig Dexheimer) *Das Automatenzeitalter* (2004, orig. 1930).

used as terms of comparison with experience or with other constructions of the mind' (Calvino 1987: 36), the second part of this volume therefore aims to address interdisciplinary possibilities of the three fields. It does so on the view that while law, technology and literature are different fields, they can nevertheless be complementary as forms of cultural reflection.

6.2 Law, Literature and Technology

In *Law and Literature*, a traditional axis of research is 'law *as* literature', following Benjamin Cardozo (Cardozo 1925) who advocated a focus on language as a form of human behavior so that the central task of both law and literature is seen as a coming to terms with a claim for meaning and to redirect the lawyer's attention to the fact that interpretation, be it of the codified text of law or of the invisible, but implicit code in force in any specific context, demands our active participation.

Cardozo's own approach was mainly directed at the legal professional's development of a feeling for legal writing styles, and this seemingly neutral agenda made this line of thought go relatively long unnoticed. These past few decades, however, we witness a tremendous proliferation of this subject, ranging from the rhetorical analysis of judicial opinions and Peircean semiotics to epistemological considerations of narrative as a general ordering principle (or code) of meaningful action. Unsurprisingly the subject of statutory and constitutional interpretation became prominent in this axis when the French poststructuralist ideas on philosophical deconstruction found their way into the law school and adherents of Critical Legal Studies began to use deconstruction as a tool for unmasking the rule of law, i.e. for 'trashing' law so that it will reveal its true ideological core hidden in the depths of both common law and codified civil law. In a more constructive vein Ronald Dworkin (1982) and Stanley Fish (1982) debated the Dworkinian idea of law as a 'chain novel' with the claim that any interpretation in law is, on the one hand, strongly embedded in a specific tradition, the coherence of which limits the range of new interpretations, while on the other hand legal interpretation is also always explicitly future-oriented in the new proposal of meaning it brings forward.

The 'law *in* literature' axis is devoted to research primarily concerned with the analysis of the literary depiction of law or, more generally, of literary works with law-related topics. The idea is that literary works with legal themes, however remote perhaps at first sight from the traditional jurisprudential themes, can give us insights into the struggles and tensions created by law as code in the sense of the regulation by an important institution in society of the lives of individuals.

It traces back to John Wigmore's list (1908) of 'legal novels' drawn up for the benefit of the legal professional and aims at a discussion of the normative aspects of law. In contemporary 'law *in* literature' an especially flourishing field is that guided by the idea that literature appeals to the emotion as well as to the intellect, and that this quality represents a valuable trait for lawyers in that it can help them develop not only the necessary legal imagination and interest in the circumstances of the case, but also their capacity for empathy towards to other. An empathic ability on this view is the ability to identify oneself with the other and his situation, and this implies both an affective understanding of the other and the capacity to act accordingly, and that is an ethical gain.

Interestingly, the idea of literature as a humanizing force that provides an antidote to what Max Weber so eloquently coined as the *Entzauberung*, the disenchantment of the world when science became a dominant societal force, is at work both in contemporary *Law and Literature* and *Literature and Science*. It challenges the sometimes profound positivist belief in the possibility and transparency of objective knowledge and human progress, with each and every aspect of life calculable and governable, and in doing so provides a vehicle for critical reflection when it comes to dealing with the influence of new technologies on law.[3] It is interesting, and a sobering thought to boot for purposes of this volume's topic, to recall that Francis Bacon put 'literature' under the heading of the results of new technologies, 'Again, it is well to observe the force and virtue and consequences of discoveries; and these are to be seen nowhere more conspicuously than in those three which were unknown to the ancients, and of which the origin, though recent, is obscure and inglorious; namely printing, gunpowder, and the magnet. For these three have changed the whole face and state of things throughout the world; the first in literature, the second in warfare, the third in navigation; whence have followed innumerable changes; insomuch that no empire, no sect, no star seems to have exerted greater power and influence in human affairs than these mechanical discoveries' (Bacon 2000: 114; Hildebrandt 2008). The late Cornelia Vismann is therefore quite right to point to an earlier bond of literature and law when she discusses how the increased demand for scribes after the 30 Years War led to a new class of civil servants in Prussia under king Frederick Wilhelm I, i.e. secretaries who were not jurists by formal training but who on account of their earlier training in language and literature (esp. poetry) considered themselves superior to what they deemed one-sided black-letter jurists (Vismann 2008: 103). Obviously the structure that the scribes brought to the often unruly body of law relates to the topic of law as code, 'Cultural technologies arrange and order … the things that are to be examined *as* culture. The law is what is generated by technologies of culture. Files are what make up the law' (Vismann 2011: 309, italics in the original).

Viewed from the point of view of the history of ideas, such interdisciplinary ventures that attempt as it were to 're-enchant' law and legal culture(s) and/or science and scientific culture(s) by welding them with the humanities can also be thought of in terms of a counterreaction to the differentiation of academic disci-

[3] An early example of such influence can be seen in the way in which the body-oriented sciences such as craniology, physiognomy and phrenology, all based on the idea that the human body is itself a code that, when read well, provides valuable information, together culminated in criminal anthropology. As introduced and developed by Cesare Lombroso (1835–1909) it has as its central tenet the claim that a person's character and disposition as well as features such as inborn criminality can be judged from the face and the outward appearance of his bodily characteristics, and that, subsequently, a person's acts are determined (Gaakeer 2005).

plines and social power structures that characterized late nineteenth-century western societies. In retrospect the tendency of scholarly fields to become autonomous disciplines contains something of a paradox when we consider that literature and literary theory, whose formation into autonomous disciplines also occurred in the nineteenth century, are now brought on to counterbalance law and science.

James Boyd White's seminal publication *The Legal Imagination* (1973) unites both the 'law *as*' and the 'law *in* literature' perspective in that he looks upon law as a culture and a language that proposes a certain form for the world. More importantly, also for purposes of this volume, is his contribution on the very idea of interdisciplinarity, in law and elsewhere. He consistently voices the argument that any form of speech is a form of translation that has its deficiencies and exuberances. White defines translation as the literary art '… of confronting unbridgeable discontinuities between texts, between languages, and between people' (White 1990: 235). These discontinuities are, firstly, the given that a reduction of meaning necessarily takes place whenever a person chooses the meaning he or she will use from the range of possibilities offered, and thus (often implicitly) dismisses other options. Secondly, there is the idea of meaning as culture-specific modes of speaking that qualify or undercut it (White 1990: 257). Lawrence Lessig calls the result 'the transformed significance' of a term once it is translated (Lessig 1993: 1202).

To White, interdisciplinary research is comparable to translating texts in that interdisciplinarity is a construction of new meaning and the composition of a new form of language. As such it engenders a new culture. The idea of translation as integration implies that truly interdisciplinary work should not come to a stop at a mere exchange of findings between disciplines, for that would be at the most transdisciplinary work, but should rather aim at articulating the specificity of our acting with languages, both legal and otherwise, so that the foundations of both disciplines can be understood in their mutual connection, and a new discursive community is founded on that basis. White rejects the idea of disciplines as separate entities that may or may not be conjoined, as well as the notion that disciplines are containers full with chunks of knowledge called data that can be used elsewhere without further ado. To him, integrative knowledge is not '… the transfer of "findings" from field to field, nor the transportation of "method" … but a bringing to consciousness of the nature of our own intellectual and linguistic practices' (White 1990: 19). To lay bare the analogies between law and other disciplines is therefore the essence of translation. As a normative ideal it precludes any tendency to think in terms of the conveyance of entities of meaning (Gaakeer 2012). Another similarity between *Law and Literature* and *Law and Science* can be perceived in the research focus on the narrative structure of legal and scientific discourse and its effects as far as style, rhetoric and the use of metaphor is concerned (Bono 1990). On the view that such research lays bare hidden or unspoken conceptual, epistemological premises, as is also noted from a perspective of cultural studies by Mieke Bal whose view that metaphors have cognitive relevance is illustrated with references to philosophers of science such as Isabelle Stengers (Bal 1994: 40–41; Bal 2002: 29), the importance of interdisciplinary cooperation for the humanities themselves becomes pertinent, also in view of the issue of representation which remains acute in literature as much as in science and law

(Clarke and Dalrymple Henderson 2002). Dimock and Wald (2002: 706) therefore also ask, 'How should the humanities come to terms with changes in our experience of the world and in the new forms of knowledge and conceptual exchanges now emerging?' To them, this is not only a question after the possible influence of the humanities on scientific developments and evaluations but it is also a question after the effects of scientific developments on the humanities and/or their methodologies, i.e. '… how are the humanities affected by new technologies such as the Internet and electronic archives?' (Dimock and Wald 2002: 707).

As far as this volume concerns, this topic will not be specifically addressed, but it is nevertheless worth noting here in these prefatory remarks, given important questions pertaining to the topic of code, such as whether contemporary uses of hypertext still allow us to speak of authorial intention. What is more, from the point of view of traditional literary theory and criticism, Stanley Fish (Fish 2012: 2–3) recently lamented that the original start of literary research has always been an interpretive proposition serving as a heuristics for textual analysis, whereas the reverse is now the case in the digital humanities: 'first you run the numbers, and then you see if they prompt an interpretive hypothesis. The method, if it can be called that, is dictated by the capability of the tool.' But how are we to proceed when we don't know what we are looking for or why? If technology allows us to cover substantively more texts than traditional research, the research data may directly be taken from the digital files. As a result 'The answer is not to go to the text "armed with a hypothesis" but "with a machine that is ready to reorganize the text in a thousand different ways instantly"' (Fish 2012: 6). In short, the question would be, 'what if 'code' takes over?' And that question also brings us back to the topic of the construction of the human – or should we by now say the posthuman? – by new technologies and that of technology's influence on human thought (Hayles 1999, 2012).

6.3 Constraints and Options: Technology – Language – Law

On the basis of the above, to us as editors of this volume, Caudill's argument is therefore most congenial: 'Because of the significance of scientific knowledge for law, I am convinced that a merger of law-and-literature and literature-and-science, perhaps a law, literature, and science project, would be useful to a lawyer's understanding of science, science, and scientific narratives in legal contexts' (Caudill 2003: 8). The second part of this volume is a modest proposal to contribute to such an attempt, on the view that '[T]he notion of multidisciplinary collaboration, particularly when it involves the inclusion of insights associated with the humanities within the practices of a seemingly technical discipline, is familiar to those in law and literature studies' (Caudill 2009: 431).

Such collaboration not only allows, but also invites us to think through the evaluative and interpretative implications and epistemological commitments involved in law, technology and literature. Not to pit the one against the other since they obviously share an intellectual history and a cultural matrix (Thiher 2005), or replace the primacy of the one field with that of another, but to seriously engage in a discussion of what may well prove to be a fruitful new *ars combinatoria* in legal theory rather than a new Library of Babel as in the eponymous short story by Jorge Luis Borges.

From a perspective of *Law and Literature*, Gaakeer's interest is in what it means for us as recipients and users of new technologies not of our own design that our perceptions are influenced, in what this means for our idea of the human, and, last but not least, for the idea of (the rule of) law, the re-invention of which would seem called for if we conjure up dark technological scenarios. Inspired by current legal-philosophical scholarship on subjects such as data-mining and profiling, she raises a number of questions pertaining to a humanistic view of technology by means of an analysis of the German author-lawyer-philosopher Juli Zeh's *Corpus Delicti*, a novel in which the juridical-political ideal of around-the-clock observation, lack of privacy, control and prevention works to the detriment of the protagonist Mia Holl. On the postmodern view, expressed by theorists like Foucault and Deleuze, that disciplinary society's sites of confinement have broken down, she asks what the possible consequences of new technologies are for law and the human if, as seems to be the case already in many fields, technology outpaces law, and law seems to vacillate between thus far deeply-ingrained legal principles and unconditional acceptance of technological developments.

Durante takes as his starting point the conception of semantic information as proposed by Floridi. On this view data are to be looked upon as both constraints and affordances that constitute the resources that the epistemic agent can use to construct information and hence knowledge. Since knowledge is indispensable to construct normativity, legal as well as technological, Durante then investigates the consequences of his premise. To him, despite similarities and dissimilarities, what unites legal and technological normativity is their basis in épistèmè. Via this lens, both legal and technological normativity may be understood as a set of constraining affordances, i.e. constraints that both delimit and afford a range of possibilities. Durante proceeds by investigating the conditions of a creative response to the problem of (in)determinacy of meaning. To him it consists of an imaginative construction of ourselves, the narration of which we are unable to accomplish on our own because in this creative response resides a wider concept of autonomy and normativity, one that may well be consistent with the Rule of Law. Inspired by Paul Auster's *Oracle Night* (2004), Durante looks into the nature of writing, in order to understand whether and to what extent the (automatic) production of knowledge allows our own indeterminacy to live through the constraints of legal and technological normativity.

Almog deals with the issues of personhood, privacy and surveillance by means of an investigation into the relation between the role of law and the rule of law in Ridley Scot's 1982 film *Blade Runner*. To her, *Blade Runner*, on the one hand, is a cautionary tale that ultimately and in spite of exciting cinematographic elements reveals a dark, dystopian realm. On the other hand, it brings to the fore the importance of a thorough discussion of the very idea of legal personhood in an age of new technologies when the question after the construction of the human has been replaced by that after the construction of the non-human. Following Derrida, Almog compares *Blade Runner* to Philip K. Dick's *Human is?* in order to highlight the issue of exclusion and inclusion. Throughout her chapter she asks us to consider whether the use of new technologies can and should be controlled, and if so, how. To her, *Blade Runner* can serve as a warning against the abuse of legal instruments as much as of technological possibilities.

References

Bacon, F. 2000. Aphorism 129. In *Novum Organum Scientiarum*, ed. F. Bacon (New Instrument of Science), in the edition of the *Past masters British philosophy series 1600–1900*, ed. M.C. Rooks, Charlottesville (Virginia) U.S.A., Intelex Corporation 2000, from *The New Organon book 1*, available at: http://www.nlx.com/collection/26. Last accessed 23 June 2011.

Bal, M. 1994. Scared to death. In *The point of theory: Practices of cultural analysis*, ed. M. Bal and I.E. Boer, 32–47. Amsterdam: Amsterdam University Press.

Bal, M. 2002. *Travelling concepts in the humanities: A rough guide*. Toronto: University of Toronto Press.

Bono, J.J. 1990. Science, discourse, and literature: The role/rule of metaphor in science. In *Literature and science, theory and practice*, ed. S. Peterfreund, 59–89. Boston: Northeastern University.

Calvino, I. 1987. Two interviews on science and literature. In *The uses of literature*, ed. I. Calvino, 28–38. New York: Harvest.

Cardozo, B.N. 1925. Law and literature, *Yale Review*, 489–507. Ed. M.E. Hall. Repr. (1947), *Selected writings of Benjamin Nathan Cardozo, the choice of Tycho Brahe*, 339–356. Albany: Fallon Publications.

Caudill, D.S. 2003. Law-and-literature, literature-and-science, and enhancing the discourse of law/ science relations. *Journal of the Legal Profession* 27(1): 1–22.

Caudill, D.S. 2009. Synthetic science: A response to rabinow. *Law & Literature* 21(3): 431–444.

Chandler, D. 1995. Landmarks in fictive images of technology, available at: http://users.aber.ac.uk/ dgc/chrono.html. Last accessed 1 May 2012.

Clarke, B., and L. Dalrymple Henderson (eds.). 2002. *From energy to information, representation in science and technology, art, and literature*. Stanford: Stanford University Press.

Dexheimer, L. 2004, orig. 1930. *Das Automatenzeitalter*. Berlin: Shayol Verlag.

Dimock, W.Ch, and P. Wald. 2002. Literature and science: Cultural forms, conceptual exchanges. *American Literature* 74(4): 705–714.

Dworkin, R. 1982. "Law as interpretation" and "My reply to Stanley Fish". In *The politics of interpretation*, ed. W.J.T. Mitchell, 249–270 and 287–314. Chicago: University of Chicago Press.

Fish, S. 1982. Working on the chain gang: Interpretation in the law and literature criticism. In *The politics of interpretation*, ed. W.J.T. Mitchell, 271–286. Chicago: University of Chicago Press.

Fish, S. 2012. Mind your P's and B's: The digital humanities and interpretation, 1–6, available at: http://opinionator.blogs.nytimes.com/2012/01/23/mind-your-ps-and-bs-the-digital-humanities-and-interpretation. Last accessed 4 May 2012.

Gaakeer, J. 2005. 'The art to find the mind's construction in the face': Lombroso's criminal anthropology and literature: The example of Zola, Dostoevsky, and Tolstoy. *Cardozo Law Review* 26: 2345–2377.

Gaakeer, J. 2011. The future of literary-legal jurisprudence: Mere theory or just practice? *Law and Humanities* 5(1): 185–196.

Gaakeer, J. 2012. Iudex translator: The Reign of finitude. In *Methods of comparative law*, ed. P.-G. Monateri, 252–269. Cheltenham/Northhampton: Edward Elgar.

Hayles, N.K. 1999. *How we became posthuman: Virtual bodies in cybernetics*. Chicago: University of Chicago Press.

Hayles, N.K. 2012. *How we think: Digital media and contemporary technogenesis*. Chicago: University of Chicago Press.

Hildebrandt, M. 2008. A vision of ambient law. In *Regulating technologies*, ed. R. Brownsword and K. Yeung, 175–191. Oxford: Hart.

James, H. 2005, orig.1919. *In the cage*. London: Martin Secker, available at: http://www.gutenberg.org/files/1144/1144.txt. Last accessed 15 May 2012.

Leavis, F.R. 1962. *Two cultures? The significance of C.P. Snow*. London: Chatto and Windus.

Lessig, L. 1993. Fidelity in translation. *Texas Law Review* 71(6): 1165–1268.

Lessig, L. 2006. *Code version 2.0*. New York: Basic Books.

O'Hagan, A. 2010. *The life and opinions of Maf the dog and of his friend Marilyn Monroe*. London: Faber and Faber.

Ortolano, G. 2009. *The two cultures controversy: Science, literature, and cultural politics in post-war Britain*. Cambridge: Cambridge University Press.

Snow, C.P. 1993, orig. 1959. *The two cultures*, S. Collini (introduction). Cambridge: Cambridge University Press.

Swift, J. 1977, orig. 1726. *Gulliver's travels*, ed. P. Dixon and J. Chalker and M. Foot (introduction), Harmondsworth: Penguin.

Tabachnick, D.E. 2004. Techne, technology and tragedy. *Techné* 7(3): 91–112.

Thiher, A. 2005. *Fictions refracts science: Modernist writers from Proust to Borges*. Columbia: University of Missouri Press.

Vismann, C. 2008. *Files, law and media technology*. Stanford: Stanford University Press.

Vismann, C. 2011. In judicio stare: The cultural technology of the law. *Law & Literature* 23(3): 309–323.

White, J.B. 1973. *The legal imagination, studies in the nature of legal thought and expression*. Boston: Little, Brown and Co.

White, J.B. 1990. *Justice as translation: An essay in cultural and legal criticism*. Chicago: University of Chicago Press.

Wigmore, J.H. 1908. A list of legal novels. *Illinois Law Review* 2: 574–593.

Chapter 7
Control, Alt, and/or Delete? Some Observations on New Technologies and the Human

Jeanne Gaakeer

'The technology to abolish truth is now available'

Joseph (2005a: 18)

Abstract With "Control, Alt, Delete, username, password" we daily gain access to the digital world. Failure to comply? Access denied! From a perspective nourished by the fields of *Law and Literature*, and *Law and the Humanities*, this chapter focuses on the influence of new technologies on our idea of the human and the idea of (the rule of) law. It aims to formulate some questions pertaining to a humanistic view of technology by means of an analysis of the German author-lawyer-philosopher Juli Zeh's novel *Corpus Delicti*. This novel's main theme is a state's obsessive and omnipresent health concerns that prove to be an inescapable ideology with devastating consequences for its citizens. The juridical-political ideal of around-the-clock observation, lack of privacy, control and prevention that transpires in this novel works to the detriment of the main character Mia Holl who observes that law is a game that we all have to play. While disciplinary society's sites of confinement may have broken down, new technologies introduce new forms of disciplining the human and this development speaks for our attention to the risks of an uninformed application of technology in and for law.

J. Gaakeer (✉)
Department of Jurisprudence, Erasmus University Rotterdam,
Burgemeester Oudlaan 50, 3062 PA, Rotterdam, The Netherlands
e-mail: gaakeer@law.eur.nl

M. Hildebrandt and J. Gaakeer (eds.), *Human Law and Computer Law: Comparative Perspectives*, Ius Gentium: Comparative Perspectives on Law and Justice 25,
DOI 10.1007/978-94-007-6314-2_7, © Springer Science+Business Media Dordrecht 2013

7.1 Introduction

"Control, Alt, Delete, username, password" is what we automatically do, everyday and without giving it any further thought, in order to gain access to the digital world. Failure to comply? Access denied! It is stating the obvious to claim that new information and communication technologies have permeated our lives for quite some time now and at an accelerated speed to such an extent that we take most of them for granted. On the view that 'a culture is defined by what it can name' (Manguel 2010: 204), what interests me, from a perspective nourished by the field of *Law and Literature*, or, more broadly, *Law and the Humanities*, is not only how as recipients and users of new technologies not of our own design, our perceptions of the world around us, and hence our epistemological assumptions are influenced by them, but also what all this means for our idea of the human, the invention of whom Shakespeare is credited for (Bloom 1999), and subsequently, what it means for law.

Would Shakespeare recognize a digital representation of the human of the kind described as 'Digital-Me', a device, as yet a fantasy but a very serious one, that hints at what mobile communication and ambient intelligence can accomplish together: one's digital replica that can be programmed to perform one's own tasks as a kind of personal assistant that impersonates its owner, for instance when he or she does not want to be disturbed, and in doing so takes its owner's decisions independently, or rather as if it were its owner, and also knows when to switch on the real 'me'.[1] Does this conjure up the idea of a split personality or a many-worlds philosophy? Would this be human progress or would it seriously affect a human being's autonomy should this fantasy come true?

In order to discuss these and other questions pertaining to a humanistic view of technology generated by contemporary scholarship on technological views and predictions for the near future, I will first point to what struck me as most significant in my readings on the subject, and why. Then I will turn to the aims of literary-legal scholarship and its possible contribution, and to literature in the form of a novel by the German author Juli Zeh for further illustration.

7.2 New Kids on the Law Block?

My focus for purposes of this article is on current legal-philosophical scholarship on subjects such as profiling, data-mining and ambient intelligence as interrelated technological visions, the new kids on the block so to speak when it comes to their legal implementations. My view is informed here by what Hildebrandt and Gutwirth call the cross-disciplinary perspectives of a number of European scholars (Hildebrandt and Gutwirth 2008) and by a number of Dutch studies on the way in which the government, or rather, information-Government a.k.a. *i-Government* (Böhre 2010;

[1]I derive this example from Van den Berg (2010: 171).

Prins et al. 2011; Buruma 2011) regulates and makes use of digital technologies. What strikes me in the descriptions and analyses of profiling (Hildebrandt 2008a: 19) and/or data-mining of groups or one individuated subject (Van der Hof and Prins 2008: 111), given that these technologies use algorithms to arrive at results in the form of predictions about human behaviour, is the way in which aspects of volition are dealt with. If the data subject is targeted without his being aware of it, and acts on that, i.e. shows a certain kind of behaviour, is this to be called an exercise of his free will? Does the subject in this way show his or her preferences?[2] Even if we allow for the fact that humans act out of habit most of the time so that the question of volition does not turn up, consciously at least (Hildebrandt 2008a: 27), the point remains that (in)voluntary participation is immediately connected to a model of thought that has individual autonomy at its heart.

In classical economics and in traditional interdisciplinary *Law and Economics*, to make a comparison by way of example, the goal of the individual participating in the marketplace is said to be wealth-maximization, i.e. maximization of individual preferences. On the meta-level, the starting point is a methodological individualism that works from the presupposition that participants always choose rationally. This assumption, however, mistakenly leaves out the fact that participants often have to make their choices while in a situation of dependence, rather than independence. Once autonomy and freedom of choice are not only taken to justify both the freedom of the market and its goal of wealth-maximization, but also form the basis for decision-making in law, the poverty of a world so created reveals itself in its impotence to satisfactorily deal with human values. Here is also the political perspective. From a humanistic point of view, Robin West argued that Kafka's fiction provides us with a clear picture of the horrors of a world in which consent legitimates everything. The supposed freedom to engage in transactions is false because there is a strong contrast between the 'outward descriptions imposed upon the transactions in which Kafka's characters engage and the radically different inward experience of those transactions by the parties involved' (West 1985: 384, 1986), as the fates of Joseph K. in *The Trial*, of Georg in 'The Judgement' and of the eponymous hunger-artist clearly show. Richard Posner took a stand against this criticism, claiming in terms of the liberal, night-watchman state, that the state should refrain from interfering in the Pareto-optimal transactions of its citizens. He did so because to him law is 'a system of rules' (Posner 1986: 1433).

Such view on law suggests a positivistic hermeneutics favouring the idea that meaning is obvious. This touches one of *Law and Literature*'s major topics: the function of language and the representation of reality. In economic and technological environments, language easily becomes the supposedly neutral vehicle for the communication of information in which 'facts' are entities in the world easily transmissible by words. On this view, words are encoded thoughts, i.e. our perceptions

[2]The same goes when we think of uses of ambient intelligence applied to, for example, the concept of contract. If the intelligent application/ambient-intelligence system 'independently' of its user enters into an obligation that is legally binding, whose risk is it when things go wrong? What does this mean for the legal concept of consideration?

of these very same facts. In philosophical terms it is the idea of the correspondence theory of the *adequatio rei et intellectus*, i.e. when the 'thing' and our understanding of it are thought to coincide. *Law and Literature* is vehemently opposed to this idea because such a language view disregards the influence of our conceptual framework on our valuation of the world. Roland Barthes succinctly put the contrast thus, 'Language is literature's Being, its very world', whereas '[A]s far as science is concerned language is simply an instrument, which it profits it to make as transparent and neutral as possible: it is subordinate to the matter of science (workings, hypotheses, results) which, so it is said, exists outside language and precedes it' (Barthes 1970: 411). This view is related, in short, to the Cartesian idea(l) behind the view that scientific knowledge is theoretical knowledge, the chunks of which can easily be conveyed by means of a neutral instrument called language, from one brain to the other. Turned the other way around, as Heidegger elaborated upon in his *Introduction to Metaphysics* (Heidegger 2000), our articulation of reality as we perceive it by means of language is the result of a process of selective interpretation on the basis of the perspective we take. This opens up possibilities at the very same moment that it delimits when that which is not spoken of remains obscure in the background.[3]

And there is a related point too. Is law a mere system of rules or is it a culture of argument that addresses questions of value and community? It is here that I think a common ground can be created for a discussion of how new technologies are to be regulated by law because 'information dependence' of technologies' users is an important issue. As Van der Hof and Prins argue for new technologies, 'In other words, the use and "value" of personal data cannot be separated from the specifics of the context (social, economic and institutional settings) within which these data are collected and used' (Van der Hof and Prins 2008: 112). Thus, our being *unconscious* of the fact that we leave a digital trail with practically our every move, including the unconscious generation of clickstream data when we visit the world wide web, shows that '[T]he real problem is *how* personal data are processed, in what context and towards what end' (Van der Hof and Prins 2008: 117). Furthermore, together with, if not prior to the determination of this problem, the question would have to be addressed of how to create a public awareness of the fact that all too often our attitude is casual (if not downright careless if we consider what appears on Facebook, which information we give away readily, and so on and so forth) and subsequently have a public debate on these issues. It would seem that paradoxically while new technologies have opened (cyber)space for us, the *agora* has diminished in size (Mitchell 2000: 176). In order to reach this aim of a public debate, the public needs to be informed about the hazards of new technologies, for here too when it comes to misinformation the consequences at the juridical-political level of human equality are not to be underestimated. That is to say, how can one at all decide about what (not) to do under the circumstance that the self a.k.a. the data subject has become objectified as a designed product.

---

[3]See White (1990: 257) for the related argument that any form of speech is a form of translation with deficiencies and exuberances.

And while I fully agree with those scholars who focus on the effects of all this on concepts of individual privacy, autonomy and control, or discrimination (Hildebrandt 2008b), I would also encourage us to think in terms of the bad chance that someone else is going to decide for us, state ideology writ large, and that we are easily lulled into complacency when the services rendered by ambient intelligence technology aim at presenting the least inconvenience while providing the maximum benefits. It is all a matter of good reading: of human behavior, including human interaction, of hidden premises and codes, overt and covert, by means of which these are governed, if only because of the dialectical connection between human behaviour and technology, with each new development necessitating an infinite regress of new forms of protection and disclosure. I would resist the idea of the unspoken presupposition behind technology's anticipation on its user, at least as far as design is concerned, and that is that of the average human who is taken as the measure. In short, I would advocate reading technologies with an ethics of responsibility. And so I would have a bit of a quibble beyond the semantic with Mireille Hildebrandt when she writes, 'As long as the technologies enable us to make our own choices, inducing but not enforcing a change of habit, the technology is regulative of our behavior' (Hildebrandt 2008b: 174), especially where she also refers to the Thomas-theorem, 'if men define situations as real, they will be real in their consequences', and translates it to the idea that, 'if machines define a situation as real, it is real in its consequences' (Hildebrandt 2011: 513, 2010: 172). When it comes to privacy Hildebrandt convincingly shows the methodological importance of Paul Ricoeur's distinction between one's *ipse* identity (the way one perceives oneself in the course of lifetime's development) and one's *idem* identity (the way in which the other perceives me, for example as a legal subject when the situation is legal), but what matters in the context of new technologies, as far as I am concerned, is to 'see oneself as another' and that literally in order to be aware of how smart environments 'think' of us (Hildebrandt 2008c: 312, 2010), for Hildebrandt is right when she claims that in order to understand my own actions I must understand how others understand my actions. It is the classical hermeneutic challenge, also, of figuring out what the underlying question was, when one has to confront the text or action that is the answer. So whose 'free will' is it anyway? To me, the basic question behind new technologies is not 'so what?', but 'what if?' It is astounding to read, for example, that Apple and Google and the likes of them are already forum shopping when they look for places where to establish their companies: they go to Ireland because as a result of the financial crisis the Data Protection Authority there consists of only four people who are obviously unable to check everything (Thomas 2010: 15).

All this is just to say that it would seem that contemporary technological developments are out of line with our more traditional ways of thinking about the human, his values, and his behaviour so that the risk of Orwellian 'doublethink' about technological applications looms large when decisions are made with an eye on future use only rather than also on present infractions of principles and values. And while *i-Government* may not be designed out of an evil genius, we cannot deny the fact that information spreads like an inkblot and function creep is a real risk (Böhre

2010: 78, 93; Van der Hof and Prins 2008: 119). Brave New World has an ironic ring to it, for what if function creep is the default, and 'delete' in the definition given by Viktor Mayer-Schönberg (2009), the virtue of forgetting (i.e. data being 'forgotten' at some point in time) in the digital age is not? Then the disruption of the individual's freedom as far as life choices are concerned is a reality we have to reckon with. Anticipating my literary analysis below in Sect. 7.4, I would like to point to what Trojanow and Zeh have recently argued, viz. that the transparent human is no longer a free person and that the fundamental dilemma that does not go away after calm deliberation is the question of how we can defend the value of any new system while at the same time we are in the process of abolishing the value of freedom (Trojanow and Zeh 2009: 14, 58).

7.3 Narrative Knowledge

So the question after the human matters immensely and obviously also from a point of view of law. As Garreau put it, 'The law is based on the Enlightenment principle that we hold a human nature in common. Increasingly, the question is whether this stills exists', and so he asks, 'What will this mean? (…) Will we soon pass some point where we are so altered by our imaginations and inventions as to be unrecognizable to Shakespeare or the writers of the ancient Greek plays?' (Garreau 2005: 8, 21). That would be on the view that 'without Shakespeare we would not have seen ourselves as what we are' (Bloom 2011: 8), with our passions, virtues and vices.

An interesting and, as I hope to show, legitimate lens through which to view this subject would be a humanistic one. Given considerations of space I cannot do justice to the diversity of approaches that have developed since the revival of lawyers' interest in a humanistic approach to law in the 1970s that led to the interdisciplinary field of *Law and Literature*.[4] Suffice it to say that from the very start emphasis on the development of the (legal) imagination by means of literary works has been most prominent since James Boyd White's seminal *The Legal Imagination* (White 1973). On the view that law and literature are both producers and products of culture so that they reflect as much as critique, ideally at least, the prevailing societal convictions and conventions, the investigation of the literary creation of human experience may help us understand the ways in which narratives construct and reconstruct reality and how we as the authors and readers of legal narratives have to acknowledge that law's instrument is an institutional language that also imposes its conceptual framework on its users so that it behoves us to develop our linguistic sensibilities. Hence, too, the importance of attention to 'another view' and that includes attention to a broad range of aspects of alterity, not in the least because law

[4]The division of Law and Literature is by now exhaustively documented, both as far as the Anglo-American strands and European topics are concerned. Various overviews can be found in Gaakeer (1998, 2011), Dolin (2007) and Lachenmaier (2008).

is socially also organized as power. So fostering the imagination as the capability to enter imaginatively into the lives of others also helps foster a capacity for empathy. Obviously, this also goes for those involved in scholarly ventures other than law.

I am inspired by Lyotard to ask how we confer legitimacy on new technologies in a postmodern world, on the view that technological as well as legal narratives are narratives legitimating a specific kind of knowledge with their concurrent strategies of inclusion and exclusion leading to residue and loss. In a related context Lyotard speaks in terms of lost narratives, i.e. when for whatever reason (e.g. because it is 'not done' in any given professional or scholarly setting, or because the question simply doesn't crop up) it is impossible to address certain issues that are nevertheless felt to be important, if only by a relatively small group of people. This impossibility is not necessarily a cause for alarm or regret, because while, 'Most people have lost the nostalgia for the lost narrative', 'It in no way follows that they are reduced to barbarity. What saves them from it is their knowledge that legitimation can only spring from their own linguistic practice and communicational interaction' (Lyotard 1991: 31, 41). There's the rub, then. What we need most is an awareness of our linguistic practices. We need the kinds of expertise that help define both the dominant narratives and the lost narratives, to reflect on them in order to preclude repeating old mistakes. Put differently, now that the design-choices of new technologies are made without us, their users, and we have to be content to deal with what is offered, including its regulation by law, we should turn to fiction because of its metaphorical potential – seeing the one as the other – in order to engage in a dialogue between disciplines.[5]

Another reason why attention to the unity of two often disparately perceived subjects as law and literature can help shed light on the interrelation between law and technology is that we can read literary works as unorthodox jurisprudential texts. There is a good epistemological reason too, to do so, as Juli Zeh puts it succinctly, '"But literature (...)finds the truth? Or is it creating its own?"' (Zeh 2003: 144), i.e. a question that draws our attention to an epistemological clash so often perceived (or should we say cultivated?) between the humanities and the natural, 'hard' sciences. This is also important now that etymologically *narrare* in the sense of telling stories and *gnarus*, knowing, have the same root. So uncertainties resulting out of our postmodern contesting of old truths, and epistemological dualism generally, can find an antidote in narrative knowledge. In other words, both the practice that is law and the practice that is technology merit our discursive attention. If it seems that technologies develop relatively autonomously, an interdisciplinary approach is all the more called for. Again, the humanities provide a starting point, with Erasmus' working definition of knowledge, for example, as a reminder of the importance of attention to language and narrative, 'In principle, knowledge as a

[5] My literary source of inspiration here is, 'The masters of information have forgotten about poetry, where words may have a meaning quite different from what the lexicon says, where the metaphoric spark is always one jump ahead of the decoding function, where another, unforeseen reading is always possible' (Coetzee 2008: 23).

whole seems to be of two kinds, of things and of words' (Erasmus 1978: 666). Attention to the linguistic pitfalls and peculiarities of the discourse on the technological would thus be called for.

The issue is acute in that for a subject as consequential as law, including the very concept of the rule of law, the reaffirmation or reinvention of the human in the sense of the legal persona seems called for if we conjure up dark scenarios. I think here in terms of Walter Benjamin's lesson as found in his seminal essay 'The Work of Art in the Age of Mechanical Reproduction' (1936). Benjamin contrasts the idea of the presence of the original work of art as a condition for authenticity with the consequence of technical reproduction that 'can put the copy of the original into situations which would be out of reach for the original itself' (Benjamin 1999, orig. 1936: 214), i.e. it detaches what is reproduced from its traditional domain. The process of mass production has social significance, so Benjamin claims, but at the same time it is destructive when it results in a loss of cultural value of the original. Loss of uniqueness means loss of tradition and loss of autonomy of the original work, as well as the genesis of a new way of looking at "the thing". Applied to technology, this means that technology affects our perceptions of who we are. As a result, changes in technology, when looked upon as a cultural product, will lead to changes in the ways we perceive the world around us. This process may, on the one hand, be a liberation of what is perceived as an outdated ways of doing things. On the other hand, when applied to law as it deals with the effects of technology, the idea of 'reproduction', such as of sensitive information pertaining to individual privacy in the form of biometrical data, when embraced as beneficial to people's lives without reflection on the consequences, runs the risk of introducing a form of what, if we think of a legal theorist such as Carl Schmitt, may best be called a societally disconnected aesthetics[6] of the legal and the political, the history of which has shown that it entails the danger of totalitarian dominance, or at best an instrumental attitude. So what Benjamin argued with respect to art in the age of mechanical reproduction also goes for the human in relation to new (digital) technologies, and we should be wary of technologies when viewed in terms of epistemological determinism, and of literal engineers of human souls.

Put simply, technology develops its own narratives and with them its own discursive idiosyncracies, cognitive metaphors included,[7] and that is all the more reason to further the discussion by questioning the assumptions behind the discursive *topoi* of technology, be they legal, moral or cultural. Now one might, of course, rebut and argue that earlier body-oriented sciences based on the idea that the human body proffers valuable information (such as craniology, physiognomy and phrenology together culminating in Lombrosian criminal anthropology), also influenced law and yet the human in its traditional (Renaissance and Enlightenment) form lives to tell. My point, however, following Benjamin, is that contemporary technologies are influential at a far larger scale an at a far greater speed, and that this necessitates new legal norms to be enacted to help form new interrelations between the human and

[6]Ironically, the ancient Greek sense of aesthetic is 'perceptive'. See Bloom (2011: 16).

[7]Consider, for example, the metaphorical titles of various paragraphs in Böhre (2010).

his artifacts, and between human beings as such, in order to prevent the risks noted above such as discrimination.

In the context of technological influences on law, while we still admit that who or what is to count in law as an independent unit with rights and responsibilities is a fiction, a legal construct, based on law's rulings that define subjecthood, the quest after our identity and, with it, the quest after self-knowledge does not evaporate. What, then, are the fictions of the self? The classical questions remain: Is a human being a person, or is it a mind with a body as extension? Is it a material objector just part of a collective representation? Translated to the concepts of commodification and self-ownership, is the human a tenant or a freeholder of his own body? Will 'Digital-Me', for example, be granted consciousness and, if so, will that be the key to its personhood and thus to its capability to assert its existence and its possible dominance over the original, but mechanically reproduced 'me'? The paradigm shift in scientific thought that technological advancements have brought about has not yet been fully understood in and by law. New technologies are as yet as 'undecided' as they are 'undecidable' from a legal point of view. Therefore law's attempts at codification of new norms suffer the consequences. If, for example, technology has already outpaced the laws regulating the legal persona, many concepts held dearly since the Enlightenment become unsettled. Again, the idea that literary fiction can help form law's truth dimension gains relevance.[8]

Since Christopher Marlowe transformed the German legend of Georg Faust into *Doctor Faustus* and Galileo Galilei found himself in trouble with ecclesiastical authorities, the epistemological question after the limits of human knowledge and the related ethical, as well as juridical-political question whether or not it is justified to introduce new technological endeavours when we cannot fully size up the possible risks, has held the stage. So when law has new concepts under construction by way of answers to matters technological, the question whether the legal subject still absorbs the human person remains acute. That is another reason to probe technology's narratives, if we foreground the constitutive power of law.

With this in mind I turn to literature in order to exemplify how particular concepts of law and legality operating in author-lawyer-philosopher Juli Zeh's novel *Corpus Delicti* as a part of the human condition in a postmodern control society can offer a narrative of 'what may happen' as Aristotle conceived the task of the poet (Aristotle 1994, orig. 350BCE: I, ix) and thus help clarify some aspects of the interrelation between law and technology.

7.4 Control, Alt and/or Delete?

My choice is also inspired by the fact that Juli Zeh (Bonn, 1974) is an author who is fully committed to the public cause. As a public intellectual with two law degrees to her name, she is 'a notable exception' (Herminghouse 2008: 268) in Germany to the

[8] 'What is seen, heard, and imagined at the same time – that truth. A sort of relationship is established between our attention to what is furthest from us and what is deepest in us' (Joseph 2005b: 12).

pattern that older male intellectuals are dominant when it comes to publicly voicing their opinions on political topics. She not only contributes to the debate on important societal issues, for example election campaigns, Wikipedia and Linux open-source development (Herminghouse 2008: 268), but she does so on a regular basis with her literary output, in interviews and by taking legal action given her concerns about the current rise of the control society. An example of the latter is that on 28 January 2008 Juli Zeh lodged a complaint with the German Constitutional Court against the German government because of new legislation introducing the biometrical passport (Zeh 2008). In an interview with the Berlin correspondent of the Dutch newspaper *Trouw*, Verbij, on 4 September 2008, Zeh voiced concern that her complaint would be filed in the Court's office of European affairs rather than in the office for home affairs. If in the former, then the complaint would not stand a chance on the view that the European Union stretches the limits when it comes to security. The complaint would be better off with the office for home affairs given the German government's reluctance to collect its citizens' personal data in view of the horrors of the Nazi past. Why this kind of involvement? Because Zeh firmly believes 'that society needs intellectuals to take public positions on matters of general concern', and that '[li]terature per se has a social and, in the broadest sense of the word, political function. (…) [it] bears the responsibility to close the gaps that are exposed through journalism's attempt to present a supposedly "objective" – and therefore distorted – picture of the world (…) I want to give readers ideas, not opinions, and to give them access to a non-journalistic, but nonetheless political view of the world' (Herminghouse 2008: 270, 277).

Zeh wants the reader to think about the text she is reading, i.e. she wants the literary text to be a call to conscious reflection and subsequent action, and an antidote to the numbing influence of modern media with their predominant format (the genre and the stylistics) of the soap-opera, the one-liner, the soundbite, the cliffhanger and other superficial ways of infotainment. Or, as Herminghouse (2008: 276) points out, 'Zeh stresses the Aristotelian notion of mimesis, which differentiates between reality and its interpretation in artistic representation.' What matters from a hermeneutic point, then, is not, or not merely, the search for the intention behind the text, but to 'a world unfolded in front of it', as Paul Ricoeur claims (Ricoeur 1989: 93).

Originally written as a play set in the year 2057, *Corpus Delicti* was first performed at the Ruhr Trienale festival in September 2007. Its narrative is, as Zeh herself explained, a philosophical debate on individual freedom and responsibility in a literary form (Verbij 2008). In the novel *Corpus Delicti, ein Prozess*[9] we read about a state's obsessive and omnipresent health concerns and 'healthcare' that together prove to be an inescapable ideology with devastating consequences for its citizens. Having appropriated the responsibility for the physical well-being of the people to which everything is subordinated, the state takes all the measures necessary to reach its goal but what is camouflaged as prevention of illness quickly turns out to be harmful to privacy and the free will.

[9]Zeh (2009), hereinafter CD. All translations are mine.

The novel starts with the fictional: the preface to Heinrich Kramer's book dedicated to promote the state's ideology and policy, *The Health Principle as a Legitimacy of the Body Politic* (CD: 8), already in its twenty-fifth edition. The Health Principle is not only pervasive in all strata of society, it is a doctrine with a Hobbesian twist in the sense that the individual – methodological individualism is the key – is thought of as having subjected himself to the principle for the purpose of forming a society – the society that guarantees the individual's health –, and totalitarian in that once the *pactum subjectionis* is made the state's health is what matters most now that all the healthy bodies together form the body politic, comparable to the image of the individual persons' bodies on the frontispiece of Hobbes' *Leviathan*, so that each breach of the contract is seen in terms of treason. If the individual is guaranteed a life free from illness and fear on the basis of The Method, with all the laws functioning as the nervous system of a healthy body does, then of course any infraction, any violation of the law is an attack on the organism itself, one that is pictured by means of the virus metaphor (CD: 201). Punishment must therefore be meted out immediately as the protagonist Mia Holl, and her brother Moritz before her, find out when they seek to destroy their own bodies, by suicide in Moritz' case, by allowing private grief over Moritz' death to take precedence over physical fitness in Mia's case, for in this state. 'The body is everything' (CD: 158).

Heinrich Kramer, then, a man who moves with the naturalness of a man who has access to every place as we will soon find out, is not just a well-known author and television personality, he is the *auctor intellectualis* and the personification of The Method, as the practical application of the doctrine is aptly termed. And it is "In the Name of the Method" that Mia Holl is tried for incitement against The Method and is sentenced to being kept frozen for an indeterminate period. How this came about is what we learn in the rest of the narrative.

The scene is set with the judge, a young woman named Sophie, and the public prosecutor Bell together with the attorney Rosentreter in a kind of administrative settlement of easy cases. In each case, the picture of the suspect is projected on the wall. Later we learn that this is possible because all citizens have a microchip under their skin so that their each and every move is registered. Moritz, for example, is unhappy when the sensor in his upper arm comes into contact with the sensors found on the side of all roads (CD: 90). Fiction? Future? One only has to think of the Locationgate affair in 2011, when Apple through what was called a software error was able to register the exact location of any iPhone. While Steve Jobs explained that Apple did not track its users, one can imagine the anxiety. The same goes for the programme Prey that protects computers against theft: once you report your computer as missing, the Prey-website shows all the relevant, privacy-sensitive data, i.e. the computer's IP-address, its location based on the mobile networks and the use made of wifi (did anyone say (wireless) fidelity?).

Enter Mia Holl, a biologist whose crime consists of her having neglected her duty to report. She has failed to hand in the data on her sleep and nutrition, and neither has she sent in the results of her blood pressure and urine tests. What is worse, the curve of her sports performance, strictly monitored as well, shows a sudden drop. So she is invited to come to court for what is euphemistically called an explanatory conversation. Heinrich Kramer who has been present all the time during the judicial deliberation goes to invite Mia. It is interesting to note that both criminal law and criminal procedure in this state have familiar features and yet, at the same time, are at odds with law as we know it today in Western Europe. This adds an effect of alienation, not in the least when the reader realizes that quite a number of legal measures are applied indiscriminately to all citizens, i.e. including those not under suspicion of having committed a crime. Thinking about committing a crime is not prohibited, or should we say, not yet, when the legislation aimed at preventing acts of terrorism is brought to mind (Trojanow and Zeh 2009: 67). Mia is furious that Kramer enters her life in this way because she holds him responsible for her brother Moritz's suicide in jail after he had been charged with and convicted of the rape and murder of Sibylle Meiler, his blind date whom he found dead at the meeting point. Moritz's sperm was found in the dead woman's body and since, according to The Method, 'The DNA-test is infallible. Unfallibility is a cornerstone of The Method' (CD: 37), a conviction is a mere legal routine, even though Moritz has vehemently pleaded not guilty and has consistently argued, 'You sacrifice me on the altar of your infatuation', a cry that a bystander will later on repeat when Mia is sentenced (CD: 34, 257).

Since Mia does not show signs of physical or social disturbance – the human psyche is of no concern to The Method – , her grief over Moritz's death is incomprehensible to the system. Mia therefore avoids showing any outward signs, hoping to fool the system of constant surveillance by not using the toilet equipped with sensors so that it will not record any change in her gastric juices when she has to vomit. Epistemological doubt is not an option, says Kramer, but Mia points to the fact that any man-made rule is by definition fallible as history shows when paradigm changes occur. Combining syllogistic reasoning and the confirmation bias, Kramer contends that doubt leads to casuistic decisions and that is 'the reign of the heart's arbitrariness' (CD: 38), i.e. the equity of the king's conscience in legal terms. That Moritz has consistently pleaded his innocence in the face of overwhelming technical evidence shows that he repudiates The Method. In order to investigate this methodologically unthinkable discrepancy between private and public interest in the case Moritz, Kramer even wants to interview Mia for the paper Healthy Common Sense (CD: 42), a name that has an uncanny resemblance to 'das gesundes Empfinden des Volkes' as a criterion for judicial decisions in Nazi Germany. In a scene reminiscent of Kafka's Joseph K.'s arrest, two guards come to take Mia to a physical exam, after which she is taken to court to account for her offence against The Method. Judge Sophie, like Kramer before her, is unable to grasp the concept of private grief that Mia herself explains is the cause of her wrongdoings. Linguistic subversion of reality generally is the first sign of totalitarian tendencies as Victor Klemperer shows in his description of the language of the Third Reich in *Lingua Tertii Imperii* (Klemperer 2000). What is more, James Boyd White has argued that when words lose their meaning and the linguistic empire of force reigns (White 1984, 2006), it becomes impossible to find a common language with which to speak about law and justice. That is what the case Mia Holl painfully shows. Furthermore, the equality of speakers that is both a precondition and a product of a culture of argument that aims for justice, is sorely lacking when the state's Method is the sole directive. If recognition of our common humanity rather than exclusion on the basis of a lack of commitment to The Method, then, and equality before the law – and that includes the availability of a common language with which to tell one's story and be heard – are no options, there is irony in the observation that law is a game that we all have to take part in and play along with, if we look at the double meaning in the German word 'mitspielen' (CD: 74), especially when the juridical-political ideal of around-the-clock observation, lack of privacy, control and prevention work to the detriment of the individual. What then is left of autonomy, of finding one's own destiny in life, of deliberately entering into civil bonds to form a state and a society? Mia finds that out very soon when her preliminary hearing ends abruptly because, as her defence attorney Rosentreter points out, her case has 'elements relevant to the legal protection of The Method' (CD: 73). If this is the good news, the state of exception cannot be far behind for a crime against The Method is an act of terrorism. A network of reactionary activists called Right to Illness, a right that of course cannot be recognized by a healthy common sense, has drawn public attention. Würmer, host of the talkshow What Everybody Thinks, interviews Kramer on the subject. To Kramer, these anti-Methodists are still committed to that gross error of Enlightenment thought, individual freedom, because they claim that (the right to) illness is the recognition that one is free. This, of course, is an act of terror against the state. So when Moritz thought of life as an offer that you can refuse, that is to say only worth living if you have the liberty to choose death, he deliberately chose to be an enemy of The Method. For the law, truth is a subjective matter: believing and knowing are interchangeable so one should use one's common sense in borderline cases and decide what is true on an instrumental basis rather than on the basis of validity.

So a combined reading of the lawyer-poet Lawrence Joseph's warning I use as an epigraph that, 'The technology to abolish truth is now available', and *Corpus Delicti* may help alert us to the possible outgrowths of information technologies. That is even more so because Kramer thinks in terms of establishing offender profiles of terrorists and the difficulties involved with that, also as far as linguistic change is concerned as the case of Moritz's being named a terrorist shows. Ultimately Mia is charged with abuse of toxic substances: she smoked a cigarette in the open air near the brook where she and Moritz used to go. At her arrest she is asked whom she was going to meet there and when she answers 'Nobody' this leads to a hilarious argument by the district attorney that surely this Nobody is a pseudonym of one of the members of Right to Illness, i.e. proof of Mia's defiance of The Method. Rosentreter in the meantime has his own, parallel agenda for trying to trip The Method up: he has fallen in love with a woman who is literally out of his league because of Methodologically determined immunological incompatibilities that preclude their marrying and having children.

What Rosentreter finds out is that Moritz who suffered from leukaemia in the old days underwent a stem cell transplant with as a result that he took over his donor's blood group, immune system and DNA: Walter Hannemann is Moritz's donor and he is the man who raped and killed Sibylle Meiler. This unexpected dénouement leads to Mia's release but not for long. After having denounced Kramer's epistemology that the will to live encompasses a right to health and hence the justification of The Method, Mia is again arrested. She abandons her trust in the human body if that is no longer described in terms of flesh and blood but merely as the collective view on what a normal, healthy body is supposed to be. As a consequence, she denies the legitimacy of a form of law that depends for its success on the total control of its citizens, and abandons her trust in science if it rejects the free will. Public opinion then turns against The Method with mass demonstrations as a result, and since all now think Mia innocent, even Würmer voices a critique of The Method. He pays for it dearly, for in an Orwellian exercise of 'doublethink'[10] he ends up being identified as the terrorist behind Nobody and ends up as a witness for the prosecution. Mia does not relent. 'I stand for what you really think,' she cries, 'I stand for *what everybody thinks*. I am the *Corpus Delicti*' (CD: 218). What to Mia was a statement made in private, is public business in Kramer's worldview.[11] Kramer demands the destruction of the infectious thoughts that are the source of the current pollution of The Method, goes to see Mia in jail and charges her with being responsible, should Right to Illness kill innocent people (by then he has tapped Mia's confidential telephone conversations with her attorney). When Mia refuses to plead guilty, Kramer brings her food and beverage in her prison cell, thus obtaining her fingerprints that are subsequently found on a tube of botulinum in her house: technical evidence of her terrorist goal of destroying society, destroying mankind. That settles the case, of course, but still Mia does not relent. Not even when Kramer suggest that, 'In especially significant and highly explosive situations, when there is a present danger for the greater good, it would seem that one will have to fall back on outdated measures' (CD: 234). To which threat Mia replies, 'The Middle Ages are not an epoch. Middle Ages are the name for human nature' (CD: 235).[12] In a final act of defiance, Mia takes the needle that Rosentreter has smuggled into her cell, thrusts it into her arm, takes out the chip that identifies her, and gives it to Kramer as a token of remembrance, 'Take it. This is me' (CD: 248). In this celebration of the eucharist of transparency – remember the Christian liturgical phrase *Hic est corpus meum* – the chip coincides with the human being, and Mia's code is cracked. For her crimes, this offender by conviction who is prepared to die for her cause should not, however, get the supreme punishment, says Kramer, because then she would obviously be satisfied for it would mean that she is respected as a free human being: 'The penalty honors the offender!' (CD: 255). And so Mia is sentenced to a state of suspended animation by freezing, a 'Kaltstellen' as

[10]The theme is recurrent in Zeh's works. In her 2010 novel *Schilf* the whole plot turns on this intentional form of linguistic distortion (Zeh 2010).

[11]The first important literary work on the topic of privacy in terms of public and private interests is Edith Wharton's short story '"Copy": A dialogue', about former lovers, one now a successful writer, and their dispute about the letters they exchanged earlier on in their affair.

[12]It would seem that we have returned to the state of nature in which Hobbes situated the war of all against all. See also Dietz Müller-Dietz (2011: 91) on the link between torture and Orwell.

it says in German and that literally and figuratively.[13] When at the very last moment the prosecutor enters the room and tells her that the president of the Council for The Method has pardoned her and she will be sent to a resocialisation camp instead, Mia refuses to believe that she is saved. She demands that she be kept there. Only when Kramer has the last laugh and cries, 'Go home ... You are ... free!' (CD: 263–264), she realizes that she, the game, all is over. Control, alter(nate), and delete? Does Mia end in oblivion or is she destroyed? Does she choose her own doom or is she conditioned to? If this novel shows us one thing, it is that 'The right perception of any matter and a misunderstanding of the same matter do not wholly exclude each other' (Kafka 1978: 238–239).

7.5 O Brave New World That Has Such People In't?

Zeh's nightmarish portrayal of the road to Wellville (Boyle 1993) is timely when we think of contemporary healthcare insurance companies' tendency to put the blame on the patient's bad nutritional habits, his smoking addiction or his lack of physical exercise when it comes to paying treatments. The link between prevention of illness and electronic surveillance made in Zeh's novel is all the more reason, then, to think about what it means when one becomes or wants to become an outsider.[14] Mia Holl out of her own indomitable free will, or should we say spirit, opts out, and as a legal subject suffers the consequences given the circumstance that the state's utopia has devastating effects on civil and human rights. But what if one is excluded by the ones in control over your data? What then is left of the autonomous subject in the Kantian sense? (Müller-Dietz 2011: 90) As Trojanow and Zeh recently argued, freedom is not a gift made by the state to its citizens, it is a precondition of any thought about the state (Trojanow and Zeh 2009: 15–16). So those who think of their constitional

[13]In contradistinction to any fair trial (article 6 European Convention for Human Rights), the decision is ready before the trial, because the judge – Sophie has by then been replaced by judge Hutschneider – draws a piece of paper from the file, supposedly written before the court was in session (CD: 260). That is of course also why the judge refuses to write down in the minutes of the session that Mia's last wish is to smoke a cigarette, presumably because the minutes too have been written beforehand. What is more, there is no separation of powers: the judge is also the executioner! See also Linton (1996: 7) for a comparable example in Shakespeare's Richard III in which the indictment with which to accuse Hastings of treason is prepared after his arrest and beheading, saying that the play, 'offers the playwright an opportunity to point out the power that documents have to determine the way reality will be perceived.' I am inspired to mention these examples here by the seminal work of the late Cornelia Vismann on the role of files in and on law (Vismann 2007, 2008), for, as Grafton astutely points out 'control of files meant control of the organization' (Grafton 2009: 165).

[14]In an interview on German television (Zeh 2011), Zeh pointed out that one of the themes of Corpus Delicti is that today people are all too often held responsible for their own illnesses by insurance companies. That is to say, if you fall ill, you must have done something wrong, an argument as old as the Book of Job.

rights only when they are harmed, entirely miss the point. In our era of communication the keyword is information, to know means to be able to control, and control means power as Mitchell already pointed out as early as 1995 when he wrote 'Out there on the electronic frontier, code is the law' so that '[A]t a technical level, it's all a matter of the software's conditionals – those coded rules that specify *if* some condition holds, *then* some action follows' and as a result 'control of code is power' (Mitchell 2000: 111–112).

If vital information in the form of personal data are used and function creep sneaks in, for example when commodities in supermarkets come with a RFID-Chip in order to cater to the customer's needs by means of her profile, and this very same identification by means of the chip also enables the location of humans and things, then what happened to Mia Holl is not just a fictional, or at most a future nightmare, but a clear and present danger. So from a humanistic point of view, the fact that we are built from living cells as much as from data and not only equipped with a body but also with a mind, favours a reading of *Corpus Delicti* as a call to arms to resist an instrumental use of humans before it is too late.

To Zeh, then, the greatest human problem is that we do not know when to stop when we have produced something good. She points to the work of the Austrian artist-writer Bernhard Kathan whose *Schöne neue Kuhstallwelt*'s main argument I read as a metaphor for ambient intelligence. The basic idea in Kathan's work is that through new technologies dairy farming has completely changed. The cows move about freely, yet – as the human being in Rousseau's famous opening of *The Social Contract*, born free but everywhere in chains, be they visible or invisible -they are fully 'managed': the doors of the cowshed open by means of the cow's electronic identification, the feeder 'knows' what to feed each individual cow, and by its very movements the cow's milking time is 'recognized'. The result is a very efficient form of herd management that is applicable also to hospitals, homes for the elderly, prisons, and universities. It is a model of power and control. Just like cows we are 'forced' rather than 'free', i.e. we exchange freedom for the coercion to have to choose what other have decided is on offer, as noted above in Sect. 7.2 is the case with so many new technological developments. Just like the cows, we are the consumers of our own Hobbesian subjection, and in the same way that the architecture of the cowshed constitutes the cow's freedom to act, modern technologies organize the lives of humans in contemporary societies by destinations made by third parties (Kathan 2009: 26, 269). Both animal and human are thus commodified, they become objects as lifeless as machines while the technical apparatus takes over and transforms into the really living being. In short, what and who lives becomes transparent, whereas technology dresses in a cloak of opacity. The cows constantly produce 'text' in the sense of data by means of the machines they are hooked up to, and are at the same time objects of descriptions by others, as are we, courtesy of Apple. Kathan points to Aldous Huxley's *Brave New World* and the view unfolded in the novel that humans are forced to slavery but they do not recognize this as such, they do not feel forced because they love the situation that they are in (Kathan 2009: 251). So much for the ideal of Renaissance man, of human individuality. Dependence rather than autonomy prevails. When, with a variation on the old Kantian dilemma, the question of how to insist on the authority of science while preserving the autonomy of law returns with a vengeance, Kafka's doorkeeper may have been replaced by electronic devices, but that other question remains the same: what if the door does not open?

From Foucault we learned how the disciplinary societies that developed in the late eighteenth and nineteenth centuries organized various sites of confinement governed by intricate codes of their own design: the prison, the factory, and the school, with the prison as the ultimate site. And as Deleuze forcefully argued, while in our era these sites of confinement may be breaking down, disciplinary societies are immediately replaced by control societies. To him, '[T]he various forms of control, on the other hand, are inseparable variations, forming a system of varying geometry whose language is *digital* (though not necessarily binary)' (Deleuze 2002: 318). Deleuze reads Kafka as the author at the point of transition between the two kinds of society. In *The Trial* Kafka described the judicial expression of the disciplinary society as apparent acquittal i.e. between two confinements and at the same time the mode of endless postponement of the trial of Joseph K. as the characteristic of in constantly changing control societies. Recall Mia Holl's experience and you know what Deleuze means. In control societies, Deleuze claims, 'the key thing is no longer a signature or number but a code: codes are *passwords* whereas disciplinary societies are ruled (when it comes to integration or resistance) by *precepts* (lit. '*mots d'ordre*', ordering words, directives in contrast with '*mots de passe*' that regulate systems of individual moves). The digital language of control is made up of codes indicating whether access to some information should be allowed or denied' (Deleuze 2002: 319). Human beings are no longer whole, i.e. no longer individuals, but rather the sum of their 'dividual' parts that are used depending on the needs felt by the user. Marketing, then, is the new instrument of social control, and Deleuze is proved right by the sales of new generations of i-phones, i-pads and so on, and electronic tagging is used as a control mechanism to fix human beings' positions, but this new system of domination leaves us in the dark as to why sometimes the door doesn't open.

So if we agree with Foucault and Deleuze that disciplinary society's sites of confinement have broken down, what then are the possible consequences of new technologies for law and the human? For it would seem that the main effect already to be perceived now that technology seems to have outpaced law in many fields, is that law and legal systems seem to vacillate between traditional, deeply-ingrained principles and (unconditional) acceptance of the new by means of *ad hoc* decisions, or rather an uninformed application of technology in and for law. To me, one reason may be that we have not paid enough attention to the question that Heidegger asked to show the importance of our questioning of what we perceive in this world: what is this phenomenon that we call technology? With Heidegger we can connect the arguments so far.

First there is the linguistic aspect. At the very moment that we use language to name 'things' in the world, we select and hence we restrict options. Inevitably we do so, given the lack of a *tabula rasa*, from the perspective that we ourselves already take. On this view, language usage is a continuous process of deciding what will be said, so that we need to be aware of this selective interpretation that we make, and of the risks of conceptualization and reification. In my view, Heidegger's contribution to the issue of law and technology is that, as already noted above in Sect. 7.2, he emphasizes that the process of reciprocity – man forms and is formed by language and reality – does not preclude us from falling into the trap of thinking that language is 'just' the objective tool 'we' use to describe 'the world'. In other words, it is man's *hubris* to think that this mediation is neutral. Here, I think, is the root of the problem we also face in applications of new information technologies.

Homo faber that man obviously is, ever since he first created tools, fails to understand fully and hence tends to underestimate the consequences of an uninformed application of technology that leads to an uniformed implementation in law by means of codification. That is to say, we all too often do not realize what is deliberately left out, or just forgotten to incorporate, i.e. the residue, the loss, the lost narrative. In the sense that technological possibilities are augmented beyond the traditional scope of human progress, we run the risk of being trapped in our conceptual frameworks and being ill-prepared for changes in perspective, either for good or for bad. That is a problem of legal epistemology that we will do well to provide with other disciplinary perspectives such as the ones afforded by the humanities. That is why I would argue that we can learn important lessons from Heidegger's phenomenological distinction between *techné* and technology, between technology as a human activity and technology as a means to an end. Focused as we are today on implementing technological innovations by means of legal rules, with rights and guarantees prominently present, without, however, reflecting on the *what* of technology itself, mistakenly pushes Heidegger's distinction to the background. That is all the more reason to foreground it here.

Heidegger asks us to return to the Greek roots of the term technology with *technikon* meaning that which belongs to *techné*. He points out that, '*techné* is the name not only for the activities and skills of the craftsman, but also for the arts of the mind and the fine arts. *Techné* belongs to bringing-forth, to *poièsis* (…)' His second point is that, 'From earliest times until Plato the word *techné* is linked with the word *épistèmè*. Both words are names for knowing in the widest sense. (…) Such knowing provides an opening up. And as an opening up it is a revealing' (Heidegger 1977: 13). On this view, as Heidegger claims, 'Technology is not equivalent to the essence of technology (…) the essence of technology is by no means anything technological. Thus we shall never experience our relationship to the essence of technology as long as we merely conceive and push forward the technological, put up with it, or evade it. (…) But we are delivered over to it in the worst possible way when we regard it as something neutral; for this conception of it, to which today we particularly like to do homage, makes us utterly blind to the essence of technology' (Heidegger 1977: 4). The combined definition of technology as 'a means to an end' and 'a human activity' suggests that when it comes to implementing new technologies the question will not only be "to what end?", but also "in what way does an instrumental conception affect the human?", and that is even more so now that Heidegger also offers the caution, 'The will to mastery becomes all the more urgent the more technology threatens to slip from human control' (Heidegger 1977: 5).

When it comes to causality Heidegger argues that we mistakingly think of technology purely as production and application, that is to say that we think in terms of the *causa efficiens* only, disregarding other aspects such as the *causa materialis* (the material out of which something is made), the *causa formalis* which refers to the shape into which that material enters, and the *causa finalis* or the purpose for which that something is made. While one may argue, of course, that this is all very well for classical Greece but does not apply to modern technology, based as it is on the exact sciences, this disregards another fundamental question that Heidegger asks, i.e. 'Of what essence is modern technology that it happens to think of putting exact science to use?' (Heidegger 1977: 14). For if 'Code is never found; it is only ever made, and only ever made by us' (Lessig 2006: 6) then we are also responsible for what the legal imagination can bring forth, for we live in webs of significance we ourselves have spun and every culture has its own way of imagining the real (Geertz 1973: 5). So we must not be epistemologically and methodologically naïve and accept, like the cows in Kathan's example, that as a result of modern technology as we have come to use it, we ourselves have been reduced to 'being at hand' or 'on hold' only, objects that stand reserve for purposes of further ordering by others. This is what Mia Holl experiences when she realizes that she has internalized the system when she tells her guards that surely they do not think she did not hand in her data on purpose. Lest we once again divorce *physis* from *technè* and *poièsis*, and use them as direct opposites rather than work from their interrelations, we should (re)turn to the humanities to learn about poetic revealing in its original sense in order to reveal by reflection the core of contemporary technologies in their applications so that we may be able to ask the right questions. If we don't, *thesis*, ordinance, a.k.a. *nomos*, law in the sense of what is generally accepted as an ordered whole, becomes predominant. So we should not accept at face value what is held before us as technology, and in doing so reduce our ethical thought on the subject to a discussion of the current trends rather than foreground the question after the human. Science, too, 'must always be on its guard lest it mistake its own linguistic conventions for objective laws' (Calvino 1987: 45). The argument made by Matthew Arnold to emphasize the importance of the humanities, therefore still holds. Aldous Huxley's grandfather, Thomas Huxley, took Arnold to task because Arnold supposedly asserted '*literature* to contain the materials which suffice for thus making us know ourselves and the world.' However, Arnold did not deny that knowing about modern science and its results is also required from an educational and cultural perspective, but what he meant was that scientific knowledge is 'a knowledge of things', whereas 'the humanist's knowledge is (...) a knowledge of words' (Arnold 1882: 2, 4). Historically, what runs through the debate like a continuous thread is what Erasmus argued, as noted above, that knowledge can be of things and of words, and that argument still holds. On the view described above, we should continue to ask what the new scripts are, i.e. the organizing linguistic frameworks that facilitate human understanding and that at the same time contribute to their own continuation as knowledge structures (Sherwin 1994), and what they mean for the idea of the human. This, of course, would include keeping at the forefront a reflection on the human and the

Enlightenment values underlying law with their penchant for autonomy, privacy, civil and human rights, on the view that these too are epistemological frameworks. We should, in short, ask whether we dominate technology or whether technology dominates us. One the one hand, the developments in the digital world have made the human the nodal point of relations and connections in a global network, with as a result new forms of being together, of 'societies', and that at a far larger scale than ever experienced before in human history. On the other hand, one might question both the belief of individual autonomy behind the choices we make when entering this global network, and the effect of our going global in this way on the human self. I was particularly struck when one of my students, a Frenchman in the international students' exchange programme, told me that he lamented the fact that when he wanted to talk to a fellow student who lived in the same building, he sent him an e-mail or text message instead of going to visit him in his room. That is to say, he recognized the effects of his behavior on human relations and the risk of loneliness and alienation they entailed, and yet found it difficult to discontinue this behavior. This example goes to show new technologies affect the human and suggests alternative framings to help save the day for the human, lest we are impoverished rather than empowered. This is not to argue for a renewal of the Luddite manifesto, but it is an unsimple truth that new technologies change the constitution of the human self, of human identity. If we are to continue the conversation on our uniqueness, however historically contingent it may be, then intersubjectivity in the form of interdisciplinary research is inescapable. I find support for my view that the humanities can greatly contribute here, in what Nicholas Carr points to in *The Shallows, what the Internet is doing to our brains*, i.e. that 'What's stored in the individual mind – events, facts, concepts, skills – is more than "the representation of distinctive personhood", that constitutes the self (…) It's also "the crux of cultural transmission", so that it behoves us to be careful about digitalisation and its effect on the human mind because there is a direct link with our concept of knowledge too (Carr 2010: 196). Connected to the topic of law, language and technology, the question will be whether technology will further the disenchantment of the world with an ongoing belief in the possibility and transparency of objective knowledge and human progress, and in doing so divorce the analytical and the narrative components of law, or whether we can agree that scientific rationality and the imagination both have a function in order to bring things back to a human proportion. In this world of technology, we would therefore do well to emphasize the reciprocal relationship between those disciplines that address the human condition from all possible angles. Rather than emphasize the Control function, then, we should focus on the Alternate function button to see if there is anything interesting underneath the surface of contemporary debates on new technologies. If that does not help, the three-finger salute Ctrl-alt-del may help interrupt any malfunctioning field so that we can make a fresh start and with Shakespeare's Miranda in *The Tempest* (V, I, 186–187) continue to ask, 'O brave new world that has such people in't'?[15]

[15] Shakespeare, W., *The Tempest*, Act V, scene 1, lines 186–187.

References

Aristotle. 1994, orig. 350BCE. *Poetics*, section I, part IX. Trans. S.H. Butcher, available at: http://classics.mit.edu/Aristotle/poetics. Last accessed 1 July 2011.

Arnold, M. 1882. Literature and science, electronic edition by Ian Lancashire, available at: http://www.chass.utoronto.cw/~ian/arnold.htm. Last accessed 1 July 2011.

Barthes, R. 1970. Science versus literature. In *Structuralism: A reader*, ed. M. Lane, 410–416. London: Jonathan Cape.

Benjamin, W. 1999. orig. 1936. The work of art in the age of mechanical reproduction. In W. Benjamin, *Illuminations*, H. Zorn (trans.) and ed. H. Arendt, 211–243. London: Pimlico.

Bloom, H. 1999. *Shakespeare, the invention of the human*. London: Fourth Estate.

Bloom, H. 2011. *The anatomy of influence, literature as a way of life*. New Haven/London: Yale University Press.

Böhre, V. 2010. *Happy landings*, a Dutch study on the biometrical passport ordered by the *Scientific Council for Government Policy* (the WRR), available at: www.wrr.nl. Last accessed 1 July 2011.

Boyle, T.C. 1993. *The road to Wellville*. London: Granta Books.

Buruma, Y. 2011. Het recht op vergetelheid. Politiële en justitiële gegevens in een digitale wereld. In *De staat van informatie (The state of information)*, ed. D. Broeders, C.M.K.C. Cuijpers, and J.E.J. Prins, 165–221. Amsterdam: Amsterdam University Press.

Calvino, I. 1987. Two interviews on science and literature. In *The uses of literature*, ed. I. Calvino. New York: Harvest.

Carr, N. 2010. *The shallows: What the internet is doing to our brains*. New York/London: W.W. Norton & Co.

Coetzee, J.M. 2008. *Diary of a bad year*. New York: Viking.

Deleuze, G. 2002. *Postscript on control societies, Karlsruhe ZKM/Center for Art and Media and MIT*. Papers on the occasion of the exhibition 'CTRL [SPACE] rhetorics of surveillance from Bentham to Big Brother', Karlsruhe, 317–321.

Dolin, K. 2007. *A critical introduction to law and literature*. Cambridge: Cambridge University Press.

Erasmus, D. 1978, orig. 1518. On the method of study, de ratione studii ac legendi interpretandique auctores. In D. Erasmus, *Collected works of Erasmus, literary and educational writings 2: de copia/de ratione studii*, B. McGregor (trans.) and ed. C.R. Thompson. Toronto/Buffalo/London: University of Toronto Press.

Gaakeer, J. 1998. *Hope springs eternal: An introduction to the work of James Boyd White*. Amsterdam: Amsterdam University Press.

Gaakeer, J. 2011. Law, language and literature: Their interrelations in law and literature. In *Law and method*, ed. B. van Klink and S. Taekema, 215–235. Tübingen: Mohr Siebeck.

Garreau, J. 2005. *Radical evolution: The promise and peril of enhancing our minds, our bodies – and what it means to be human*. New York/London: Doubleday.

Geertz, C. 1973. *The interpretation of cultures*. New York: Basic Books.

Grafton, A. 2009. *Worlds made by words*. Cambridge, MA: Harvard University Press.

Heidegger, M. 1977, orig. 1954. The question concerning technology. In *The question concerning technology and other essays*, ed. M. Heidegger, W. Lovitt (trans. and introd.), 3–35. New York: Harper & Row.

Heidegger, M. 2000, orig.1935. *Introduction to metaphysics*. Trans. G. Fried and R. Polt. New Haven/London: Yale University Press.

Herminghouse, P. 2008. The young author as public intellectual: The case of Juli Zeh. In *German literature in a new century: Trends, traditions, transitions, transformations*, ed. K. Gerstenberger and P. Herminghouse, 268–284. Oxford: Berghahn Books.

Hildebrandt, M. 2008a. Defining profiling: A new type of knowledge. In *Profiling the European citizen, cross-disciplinary perspectives*, ed. M. Hildebrandt and S. Gutwirth, 17–45. Dordrecht: Springer.

Hildebrandt, M. 2008b. Legal and technological normativity: More (or less) than twin sisters. *Techné* 12(3): 169–183.
Hildebrandt, M. 2008c. Profiling and the identity of the European citizen. In *Profiling the European citizen, cross-disciplinary perspectives*, ed. M. Hildebrandt and S. Gutwirth, 303–326. Dordrecht: Springer.
Hildebrandt, M. 2010. Privacy en identiteit in slimme omgevingen. *Computerrecht* 6: 273–282.
Hildebrandt, M. 2011. Criminal liability and "Smart" environments. In *Philosophical foundations of criminal law*, ed. R. Duff and S.P. Green, 507–532. Oxford: Oxford University Press.
Hildebrandt, M., and S. Gutwirth (eds.). 2008. *Profiling the European citizen, cross-disciplinary perspectives*. Dordrecht: Springer.
Joseph, L. 2005a. Poem "I Note in a Notebook". In *Into it*, ed. L. Joseph. New York: Farrar, Strauss and Giroux, 18.
Joseph, L. 2005b. Poem "Inclined to Speak". In *Into it*, ed. L. Joseph. New York: Farrar, Strauss and Giroux, 12.
Kafka, F. 1978, orig. 1925. *The trial*. Trans. W.E. Muir. London: Penguin.
Kathan, B. 2009. *Schöne neue Kuhstallwelt*. Berlin: Martin Schmitz Verlag.
Klemperer, V. 2000. *The language of the third Reich: LTI, Lingua Tertii Imperii, a philologist's notebook*. London: Athlone Press.
Lachenmaier, B.M. 2008. *Die law as literature-Bewegung*. Berlin: Wissenschaftlicher Verlag.
Lessig, L. 2006. *Code version 2.0*. New York: Basic Books.
Lyotard, J.-F. 1991, orig. 1979. *The postmodern condition: A report on knowledge*. Trans. G. Bennington and B. Massini. Minneapolis: University of Minnesota Press.
Manguel, A. 2010. *A reader on reading*. New Haven/London: Yale University Press.
Mayer-Schönberg, V. 2009. *Delete: The virtue of forgetting in the digital age*. Princeton: Princeton University Press.
Mitchell, W.J. 2000, orig. 1995. *City of bits: Space, place, and the Infobahn*. Cambridge, MA: MIT Press.
Müller-Dietz, H. 2011. Zur negatieven Utopie von Recht und Staat – Am Beispiel des Romans "Corpus Delicti" von Juli Zeh. *Juristen Zeitung* 2: 85–95.
Posner, R.A. 1986. The ethical significance of free choice. *Harvard Law Review* 99(7): 1431–1448.
Prins, C., et al. 2011. *i-Government*. Amsterdam: Amsterdam University Press.
Ricoeur, P. 1989. *Hermeneutics and the human sciences*. Trans. and ed. J.B. Thompson. Cambridge: Cambridge University Press.
Sherwin, R.K. 1994. Law frames: Historical truth and narrative necessity in a criminal case. *Stanford Law Review* 47(1): 39–83.
Thomas, C. 2010. Select before you collect. *De Groene Amsterdammer*, November 4, 14–19.
Trojanow, I., and J. Zeh. 2009. *Angriff auf die Freiheit*. München: Carl Hanser Verlag.
Van den Berg, B. 2010. Ambient intelligence: Wat, wie en … waarom? *Computerrecht* 6: 267–272.
Van der Hof, S., and C. Prins. 2008. Personalisation and its influence on identities, behaviour and social values. In *Profiling the European citizen, cross-disciplinary perspectives*, ed. M. Hildebrandt and S. Gutwirth, 111–124. Dordrecht: Springer.
Verbij, A. 2008. Interview Juli Zeh. *Trouw*, September 4, available at: www.trouw.nl/achtergrond/deverdieping/article184555.ece. Last accessed 1 July 2011.
Vismann, C. 2007. Files, not literature. In *Figures of law, studies in the interference of law and literature*, ed. G. Hofmann, 163–173. Tübingen/Basel: A. Francke Verlag.
Vismann, C. 2008. *Files, law and media technology*. Trans. G. Winthrop-Young. Stanford: Stanford University Press.
West, R. 1985. Authority, autonomy, and choice: The role of consent in the moral and political visions of Franz Kafka and Richard Posner. *Harvard Law Review* 99(2): 384–428.
West, R. 1986. Submission, choice, and ethics: A rejoinder to judge Posner. *Harvard Law Review* 99: 1449–1456.

White, J.B. 1973. *The Legal Imagination: Studies in the nature of legal thought and expression*. Boston: Little, Brown & Co.

White, J.B. 1984. *When words lose their meaning*. Chicago: University of Chicago Press.

White, J.B. 1990. *Justice as Translation, an essay in cultural and legal criticism*. Chicago: University of Chicago Press.

White, J.B. 2006. *Living Speech: Resisting the empire of force*. Princeton: Princeton University Press.

Zeh, J. 2003. *Die Stille ist ein Gerausch, eine Fahrt durch Bosnien*. München: Btb.

Zeh, J. 2008. Verfassungsbeschwerde Zeh, available at: http://zelos.zeit.de/2008/06/Verfassungsbeschwerde28012008.pdf. Last accessed 1 July 2011.

Zeh, J. 2009. *Corpus Delicti, ein Prozess*. Frankfurt am Main: Schöffling &Co.

Zeh, J. 2010. *Schilf*. London: Harvill Secker.

Zeh, J. 2011. Interview with Die Bananenrepublik, 24 May 2011, available at: http://www.youtube.com/watch?v=_2LJ2ymYwKk&feature=player_embedded. Last accessed 1 July 2011.

Chapter 8
Law, Normativity, and the Writing. *Oracle Night* and Human Indeterminacy

Massimo Durante

> *Thoreau said he had three chairs in his house, Ed remarks. One for solitude, two for friendship, and three for society. I've only got the one for solitude. Throw in the bed, and maybe there's two for friendship. But there's no society in here.*
>
> Paul Auster (2004: 65)

Abstract Both legal and technological normativity may be understood as a set of constraining affordances, that is, constraints that both delimit and afford a range of possibilities. Those constraining affordances can be either semantic (legal normativity) or operational (technological normativity). So, the issue at stake is how such constraining affordances deal with the crucial question of human indeterminacy: namely, how the construction of knowledge that mediates between us and the world leaves room for a behavior understood as a creative response to the constraints of either legal or technological normativity. The aim of the paper is to investigate the conditions of possibility of this creative response, which entails a self-construction, whose narration we cannot, however, entirely accomplish by ourselves: it depends on the relation with the others and with the fundamental freedom of self-expression and circulation of information.

8.1 The Semanticization of Being

We undergo an *information revolution* or information turn that has been named, after Luciano Floridi (2008a), the 'fourth revolution', following the Copernican, the Darwinian, and the Freudian ones. What is the sense of this progression? Let us sum it up, by quoting Floridi (2010: 8–9):

M. Durante (✉)
Department of Law, University of Turin, Turin, Italy
e-mail: massimo.durante@unito.it

M. Hildebrandt and J. Gaakeer (eds.), *Human Law and Computer Law: Comparative Perspectives*, Ius Gentium: Comparative Perspectives on Law and Justice 25,
DOI 10.1007/978-94-007-6314-2_8, © Springer Science+Business Media Dordrecht 2013

> After Nicolaus Copernicus (1473–1543), the heliocentric cosmology displaced the Earth and hence humanity from the centre of the universe. Charles Darwin (1809–1882) showed that all species of life have evolved over time from common ancestors through natural selection, thus displacing humanity from the centre of the biological kingdom. And following Sigmund Freud (1856–1939), we acknowledge nowadays that the mind is also unconscious and subject to the defence mechanism of repression. So we are not immobile, at the centre of the universe (Copernican revolution), we are not unnaturally separate and diverse from the rest of the animal kingdom (Darwinian revolution), and we are very far from being standalone minds entirely transparent to ourselves, as René Descartes (1596–1650), for example, assumed (Freudian revolution).

This process of the reassessment of human nature is indeed *eccentric* and makes us conceive ourselves no longer as 'standalone entities, but rather [as] interconnected informational organisms or *inforgs*, sharing with biological agents and engineered artifacts a global environment ultimately made of information, the infosphere' (Floridi 2010: 9). We are part of a global environment made of information, the *infosphere*, which is constituted, at its turn, by 'all informational processes, services, and entities, thus including informational agents as well as properties, interactions, and mutual relations' (Floridi 2003, 2010: 9). It may be useful to recall that such an informational universe is constituted by both *analogue* and *digital* data (Floridi 2010: 24). This is a crucial aspect of this reassessment of human nature and universe in terms of data that is often underrated, if not overlooked. For this reason, this aspect, which is central to Floridi's *Philosophy of Information* (Floridi 2011a) is meant to be the starting point of my reflection in this chapter, since too many scholars do not sufficiently distinguish between data and information, and they treat them as synonymous. This is a big mistake. This crucial aspect, which enables us to distinguish between data and information, is the *semanticization of Being*. Let us expound it, by giving a reference to Floridi (2011a: 7):

> In order to emerge and flourish, the mind needs to make sense of its environment by continuously investing data (understood as constraining affordances) with meaning. (…) This giving meaning to, and making sense of reality (semanticization of Being) (…) consists in the inheritance and further elaboration, maintenance, and refinement of factual *narratives*: personal identity, ordinary experience, community ethos, family values, scientific theories, common-sense-constituting beliefs, and so forth. These are logically and contextually, and hence sometimes fully, constrained and constantly challenged both by data that they need to accommodate and explain and by the reasons why they are developed [italics MD].

According to Floridi (2011a: 8), this brings about four main consequences:

1. *a meta-semanticization of narratives*: not only the identity of the Self is narrative, it is also meta-narrative, namely, narration constantly becomes subject to reflection like in a *mise en abîme* (a rhetorical figure that means 'putting into infinity': a novel about a novel, a picture appearing within a picture as Magritte's well-known pipe, a dreamer encountering a dream within a dream, and so forth; this idea poses the philosophical question of the nature of the semantic content of a proposition);
2. *a de-limitation of culture*: we are 'produmers' (producers and consumers) of specific narratives defined by the semantic space we wish to inhabit: we culturally redesign the global environment by erasing old limits and creating new ones;

3. *a de-physicalization of nature and physical reality*: this generates two effects affecting objects and individuals in space and in time: (3.1) 'objects and individuals become fully replaceable and often absolutely indistinguishable tokens of ideal types' (Floridi 2011a: 8); (3.2) 'past, present, and future are reshaped in discrete and variable intervals of current time. Projections and indiscernible repetitions of present events expand them into the future; future events are predicted and pre-experienced in anticipatory presents; while past events are registered and re-experienced in re-playing presents' (Floridi 2011a: 8);
4. *a hypostatization (embodiment) of the conceptual environment designed and inhabited by the mind*: narratives themselves can be 'shaped and reified into "semantic objects" or "information entities", now coming closer to the interacting Selves', with the result that both 'the physical and the cultural are re-aligned on the line of the virtual' (Floridi 2011a: 9).

What does Floridi intend to suggest us? A reality constructed by information becomes the constantly re-shaped, displaced and re-situated, decomposed and recomposed, narrative content of information. The world of meaningful experience (which is subject to *the semanticization of Being*) is no longer 'an infra-subjective and anthropocentric construction' but an 'increasingly inter-subjective and de-anthropocentrified reality' (Floridi 2011a: 8). Data and hence information are produced by multiple, distributed sources, in addition to traditional centralized devices. What does this challenge? It challenges our capacity to re-appropriate ourselves as 'individuals discernable by others' (Floridi 2010: 15) or, in other terms, it challenges *our capacity to speak about ourselves*, which constitutes, in our view, the fundamental conceptual core of autonomy in the narrative era of information (Durante 2011a). Here lies our basic idea: this capacity can be better guaranteed if we sufficiently distinguish between (a) the production of data and (b) the semanticization of data. These two processes are interrelated but they are not the same: data *condition* but do not *determine* the process of semanticization. In this distinction – between conditioning and determining – lies the concept of normativity that will be investigated in the present contribution. Let us start with the role of data.

In this perspective, data play a fundamental, twofold role: they constitute both the *subject* and the *limit* of the process of semanticization of Being. This complex role is thus to be evaluated in relation to the conception of semantic information we endorse. An *objective* conception of semantic information (Dretske 1981), according to which the meaning of data is independent from any informee, can support the idea that the life-cycle of data (production, transmission, storing, management, erasure, etc.) is able to directly and fully affect the life-cycle of meaningful information. A *subjective* conception of semantic information (Checkland and Scholes 1990), according to which the meaning of data is entirely dependent on an informee, hardly supports the same idea; on the contrary, the life-cycle of meaningful information (production, emission, transmission, interpretation, etc.) is dependent on the situation of the informee. These views can be mediated by endorsing a third conception of semantic information that aims to reconcile the objective and the subjective ontology of information.

Floridi's conception of semantic information offers a third option, since data, being constructed as *constraining affordances*, 'may count as *resources* for (namely inputs an agent can use to construct) information, and hence for knowledge, rather than *sources*' (Floridi 2011a: 77). This means that 'the world is neither discovered [i.e. strong objectivism] nor invented [i.e. strong subjectivism], but designed by the epistemic agents experiencing it. This is neither a realist nor an anti-realist but a *constructionist* view of information' (Floridi 2011a: 78).

Data are both constraints and affordances and constitute the essential resources an epistemic agent can use to construct information and hence knowledge (Floridi 2011a: 278–279):

> There is a difference between relevant semantic information and knowledge (…). The difference is that relevant semantic information lacks the necessary structure of relations that allow different packets of information to account for each other. It follows that, for relevant semantic information to be upgraded to knowledge, it is necessary to embed it in a network of equally relevant questions and corresponding correct answers.

We cannot expound Floridi's conception of the network theory of account and epistemic constructionism in its full (see Durante 2011b), but it suffices here to say that the epistemic agent, when constructing information and hence knowledge, is *creatively responsive* to the constraining affordances of data. Furthermore, the semanticization of Being does not only involve investing data with meaning and constructing information, but it is also essential to the production of knowledge. This point is crucial, since knowledge is indispensable, in order to construct both legal and technological normativity, if normativity is conceived as *a set of constraining affordances*. This way of conceiving normativity allows us to put into communication epistemology, technology, and the law. This is a constructionist view of the world, according to which 'knowledge neither *describes* nor *prescribes* how the world is but *inscribes* it with semantic artifacts' (Floridi 2011b: 285). It is exactly this last point that we have to investigate and develop in the following paragraph.

8.2 Legal and Technological Normativity

According to us, both legal and technological normativity depends on *episteme* (knowledge), and they are deeply intertwined since the beginnings of modernity, as Mireille Hildebrandt (2008: 169) has pointed out:

> Since the beginnings of modernity law has become the most important instrument for the regulation of human society, amounting to a rule *by* law. Its success can be attributed in part to its alliance with the technologies of the written script and the printing press, which extend the reach of modern law both in time and space, allowing an ever more detailed design of human intercourse.

Legal normativity constructs our knowledge of the (legal) world through the mediation of the written and this mediation is meant to bring about four main consequences (Hildebrandt 2008: 171):

1. it extends the reach of legal rules beyond face-to-face relationships;
2. it introduces a linear sense of time due to the need to read from beginning to end;
3. it asks for a rationalization and a systematization, in order to cope with the explosion of available texts;
4. it introduces a distance between the author and the public, which no longer needs to share time and place with the author to access the text.

This last point is indeed crucial: the written distances the world from itself and makes it subject to predictions (legal provisions) and interpretations (legal norms, which require, as interpreted legal provisions, the semanticization of Being). According to Hildebrandt (2008: 171):

> Written text is the externalization and objectification of the spoken word, bringing about the need for interpretation. (…) This provides for an inevitable latitude in the use of texts and turns law-making (enactment of legal codes as well as their application) into a *creative process* rather than mechanical application. (…) Written law thus generates a dynamic, autonomous law that depends on and nourishes legal doctrine to provide continuity and flexibility in the application of law. Such continuity and flexibility are the conditions of possibility for the demand that law combines legal certainty, justice and effectiveness in the face of recurrent changes in the social and technological infrastructure of contemporary society [italics MD].

This means that the mentioned epistemic process of externalization and objectification (i.e. the representation of the world in legal terms by means of the distance and the delay introduced by written law) is more essential than any further classification of norms into constitutive or regulative norms, since both of them do require a constructionist view of the world. Floridi's constructionist view of information, which underlies the above-mentioned semanticization of Being, may thus apply to legal knowledge, precisely because of the importance of the written dimension of law. (Legal knowledge neither *describes* nor *prescribes* how the world is but *inscribes* it with semantic artefacts, namely, the legal norms.) We will return to this key point. At present, let us turn our attention to technological normativity. Again, we will take advantage of Hildebrandt's analysis of the topic. As she remarks, in her comparison of legal and technological normativity (Hildebrandt 2008: 174):

> Technological normativity does not depend on coercive authority but on the socio-technical arrangements that constitute or regulate specific practices like consuming electricity, driving a car, etc. Arrangements that generate practices that are *constituted* by specific technologies artifacts enforce compliance with the norms embodied by these artifacts, while arrangements that generate practice that are *regulated* by specific technologies artifacts *invite* compliance with the norms they embody.

Some considerations can be drawn, in order to assimilate or to distinguish legal and technological normativity:

1. Technological normativity can be described in terms of constitutive and regulative technologies as well as legal normativity can be described in terms of constitutive and regulative rules;
2. Technology 'does not necessarily rule out choice in comparison to law' (Hildebrandt 2008: 174), since regulative technologies merely *invite* compliance with the norms they embody, unlike constitutive technologies that directly *enforce* compliance with them;

3. Technological normativity does not *formulate* norms, as legal normativity does, but *embodies* them: this implies that technological normativity not only can determine the competence of an agent but also her capacity to behave in a given way (Hildebrandt 2008: 175)
4. The enactment of legal normativity is *legitimized* by democratic procedures and is subject to judicial review, whilst the endorsement of technological normativity may lack such legitimization. This specifies in three directions: legal normativity admits (a) interpretations; (b) exceptions; and (c) revisions, while technological normativity may exclude all of them, because the possible automated application of the law by means of technology may elude the difference between data and information, which implies the semanticization of Being and the meta-semanticization of narratives, as it has been noted, for instance, by Jonathan Zittrain (2008: 151), even if in a different context:

> Perfect enforcement collapses the public understanding of the law with its application, eliminating a useful interface between the law's terms and its application. Part of what makes us human are the choices that we make every day about what counts as right and wrong, and whether to give in to temptations that we believe to be wrong. In a completely monitored and controlled environment, those choices vanish.

However, despite these similarities and dissimilarities, there is one crucial aspect that ties legal and technological normativity. Technological and legal normativity are based on *episteme* (knowledge). In fact, they both rely on inferences, namely, in their capacity to foresee and anticipate behaviours (ours is the society of *anticipation*), in order to construct devices or norms that invite, constraint, afford or make us to behave (or not) in a given way. This also entails that both legal and technological normativity need data, in order to infer from them profiles, patterns of interactions, types of behavior, and habits. A knowledge base is necessary for every normative process of inference required either to regulate or to constitute a competence or capacity (a knowledge base and an inference engine are the necessary components of any device that is aimed to incorporate artificial intelligence (Durante 2007)).

The process of data production and/or of data mining – which are necessary to upgrade data into information and information into knowledge, in order to construct knowledge bases and inference engines – is nowadays increasingly technological. Data science, profiling, intelligent ambient, smart environments, autonomic computing, etc., participate in the construction of knowledge bases, by making available enormous amount of data to different agents. These agents are enabled to invest those data with meaning and infer from them profiles, patterns of interactions, types of behavior, habits, and so forth, with all risks involved (Hildebrandt and Gutwirth 2008).

As it has also been remarked (Kallinikos and Tempini 2012: 18):

> Data tokens as carriers of cognitive or cultural content are involved in the redefinition of personal living, including personal identity, in less conspicuous ways that necessitate the deconstruction of the commercial and institutional contexts within which data are gathered and assembled to digital content and services. Nowhere is this shown more clearly than in what is called profiling, that is, the assembly of personal data drawn from the Web into coherent patterns that reveal specific behavioral profiles.

Furthermore, we must observe that a *data-intensive paradigm* is emerging as a novel epistemological model. Jim Gray has argued, as recently also brought forward by Michael Nielsen (2011), that we face an historical breakthrough involving a new paradigm in scientific discovering (Hey et al. 2007: xix):

> The world of science has changed, and there is no question about this. The new model is for data to be captured by instruments or generated by simulations before being processed by software and for the resulting information or knowledge to be stored in computers. Scientists only get to look at their data fairly late in this pipeline. The techniques and technologies for such data-intensive science are so different that is worth distinguishing data intensive science from computational science as a new, *fourth paradigm* for scientific exploration.

We cannot underestimate the importance of all these phenomena, which are going to characterize many of the future debates on the issue of big data (i.e. difficulties concerned with collection, storage, sharing, analysis, management, and deletion of large sets of data). Even if we have taken into consideration that, according to the theory of semantic information, technologies make available large quantities of data and *not of information as such* (since information requires, at least from us, a process of semanticization, through which we invest data with meaning), we cannot fail to remark that, in the aforementioned scenario, it is exactly our capacity to invest data with meaning that is challenged, since data are the necessary primary *resources* for the construction of information.

This brings us back to the third option relative to the process of semanticization. Whether or not we are the only intelligent living entities capable to semanticize data, this does not mean that we have to stick to the pretended alternative between an *externalist* (there is information in the world independently of all forms of life or intelligent informee capable to extract it) and an *internalist* notion of semantic information (information strictly depends on intelligence). As Floridi says (2011a: 43): 'Could information be neither here (intelligence) nor there (nature) but on the threshold, as it were, as a special relation or interface between the world and its inhabitants (constructionism)?'. In this perspective, we have to understand whether or not legal and technological normativity are consistent with a conception of data conceived as *constraining affordances* (Floridi 2011a: 77), and, therefore, what it means and implies for a legal and a technological normativity to be conceived in terms of constraining affordances.

8.3 Constraining Affordances

Both legal and technological normativity face two interrelated and fundamental questions, namely, the *nature* of their impact over agents' behavior and the necessary *indeterminacy* of this behavior. These questions are the two sides of the same coin.

Legal and technological normativity are expected to have an impact over agents' behavior and hence over the society at large. Conceptually, this impact is at some point situated between the two opposite poles of a mere incitement, on the one hand,

and a strict determinism, on the other. What is more, normativity is not to be understood only in empirical terms. To put it differently, it does not merely belong to the chain of causation but it is rather inherent to the mental sphere of reflexivity. Against this backdrop, we have to remark that, whatever is our conception of normativity, it has to be consistent with the primary and crucial requirement of human freedom: this is an essential tenet of democracy. However difficult is to define human freedom, we must clarify this idea in the present context, by making reference to the following notions of autonomy.

We know that it is possible to command an agent to act only to the extent to which an agent is free. It is meaningless to command a stone to fall, when released it does. An agent should be able, at least, to choose between alternatives or to change state without direct response to interaction (*strict autonomy*, that is consistent with artificial agents). In a wider sense, an agent should be able to discern and judge that a course of action could have been different and hence to be able to offer reasons to follow a possible course of action instead of another (*counterfactual or reflexive autonomy*, that belongs to the sphere of reasons). In these cases, it is meaningful to command an agent to act, since the agent has necessarily to invest data with meaning, in order to behave in a determined way. Normativity involves the semanticization of Being.

Therefore, the emergence of normativity requires three conditions:

1. A *relation of conditioning* between possible, different states of the world, that displays some regularity and therefore can be subject to inference and prediction;
2. A free agent that *mentally establishes* and practically endorses such a meaningful relation of conditioning between states of the world;
3. A meaningfulness that expresses *a sort of adaptation* to the environment.

Norms are thus *semantic artefacts* through which we transform what is possible into what is meaningful to an autonomous agent, called upon to behave in a determined way in an environment that may be designed to this aim. (What conception of normativity is consistent with such requirements and with the constructionist view of semantic information that underlies these requirements?)

In this perspective, both legal and technological normativity may be conceived as a set of constraining affordances, namely, constraints that both delimit and afford a range of possibilities. Hildebrandt seems to share this view, by stating what follows about legal normativity (2008: 172):

> Normativity is associated with social norms that have been either deliberately issued *for* or tacitly developed *in* the practices of a certain community/collective. In both cases norms can be equated with constraints that induce or enforce certain types of behavior while inhibiting or ruling out other types of behavior.

She also states what follows about technological normativity, by making the concept of constraint more detailed (2008: 173):

> When speaking of technological normativity I do not focus on the intention of the designer, I simply refer to the way a particular technological device or infrastructure actually constrains

> human actions, inviting or enforcing, inhibiting or prohibiting types of behavior. (…) As to the use of the term 'constraint', this should not be understood as a negative term: constraints are the conditions of possibility of (inter)action, they do not only inhibit or rule out certain behavior, they also create or induce certain types of behavior.

We share this view, while adding that legal and technological normativity can be understood as a set of constraining affordances, not only because they induce certain types of behavior but, first and foremost, because they require us to be involved in a process of semanticization of data, according to a philosophy of semantic information that conceives data as constraining affordances (Floridi 2011a).

This philosophy of semantic information bridges epistemology and technology (Durante 2011b), since it endorses an epistemic conception of constraint (affecting the design or the *conceptual engineering* of the reality (Floridi 2011b)), that can be illustrated in the terms of Ilya Prigogine and Isabelle Stengers (1981: 1076):

> A constraint (…) does not merely delimit the possibilities; it is also an opportunity. It is not simply imposed from the outside onto a pre-existing reality, but participates in the *construction of an integrated structure* and determines in the light of a particular occasion an entire spectrum of intelligible new consequences [italics MD].

Once more: 'knowledge neither *describes* nor *prescribes* how the world is but *inscribes* it with semantic artifacts' (Floridi 2011b: 285). Let us explain this point in more details and remark the basic role of data in the process of semanticization of Being. Data require levels of abstraction (Floridi 2008b) to be processed and levels of abstraction require data as constraining affordances to delimit the possible range of information constructs. This mutual relation is not that of infinite regress. On the contrary, it defines Floridi's constructionism (2011b: 282–283) and makes us understand why knowledge is not some sort of picture of the world, i.e. of the intrinsic nature of the system it analyses. Rather, it is a way to construct models of systems that delimit the range of consistent answers that might be offered to relevant questions (Floridi 2011b: 302).

Indeed, it is Floridi himself that remarks what we may call the *normative* dimension of data, namely, that data can be an 'external anchor' (2011a: 85) for our information, since (2011a: 87):

> Understood are relational entities, data are *constraining affordances*: they allow or invite certain constructs (they are *affordances* for the information agent that can take advantage of them) and resist and impede some others (they are *constraints* for the same agent), depending on the interaction with, and the nature of, the information agent that process them.

Data are constraining affordances as *relational entities*, being this relatedness the reason why data cannot be accessed or elaborated independently of a level of abstraction. In other terms, data understood as constraining affordances are 'answers waiting for the relevant questions' (Floridi 2011a: 77, 2011b: 294). Here lies the foundation of Floridi's constructionism that is rooted in the *relational* nature of data conceived in terms of constraining affordances. This means that constructionism is entrenched with human responsibility (Floridi 2011b: 300), because data are not intended as *sources* of information but as *resources* for information. This distinction is crucial, since it forges a robust, although not always patent, link between constructionism and responsibility. Let us, first, quote Floridi (2011a: 77) and elucidate, afterwards, this point:

> Note, however, that the fact that data may count as *resources* for (namely, inputs an agent can use to construct) information, and hence for knowledge, rather that *sources*, leads to constructionist arguments against mimetic theories that interpret knowledge as some sort of picture of the world. (…) Whether empirical or conceptual, data make possible only a certain range of information constructs at a given level LoA for a particular purpose, and not all constructs are made possible equally easily.

So, the distinction between resources and sources of information leads to a constructionist view, and it forges a link between constructionism and responsibility *for the same reason*, namely, because the informational epistemic agent cannot have a passive attitude towards data: it cannot be a passive receiver of information. Data are inputs that always need to be processed in order to construct information. This construction makes us responsible for the creative responses (Durante 2011c) we can devise within the constraining affordances that design our own environment at different levels of abstraction.

The normativity of constraining affordances may be consistent with both human indeterminacy (freedom) and accountable behaviours (responsibility). What Floridi makes us understand is that normativity is not only a matter of Code (as suggested by Lawrence Lessig 1999), law or social norms, but it is initially concerned with the nature of data and hence with the construction of information, which in turn constructs ourselves as epistemic, informational agents experiencing the world in terms of well-formed and meaningful data (Floridi 2011b: 283).

So, the issue at stake now is to better understand how constraining affordances deal with the crucial question of indeterminacy: namely, how the construction of knowledge that mediates between us and the world leaves room for a behavior which is still understood as a creative response to the constraints of either legal or technological normativity. The conditions of possibility of this creative response, which is a construction of ourselves, bring us back to the question of semanticization of Being, that is, of how we invest data with meaning.

8.4 The Meta-semanticization of Narratives

We have, first, to recall, by reference to Floridi's theory of semantic information, that, in the self-construction process, the world of meaningful experience, subject to the semanticization of Being, 'moves from being a private, infra-subjective, and anthropocentric construction to being an increasingly inter-subjective and de-anthropocentrified reality' (Floridi 2011a: 8).

This means that, as *produmers*, namely, as producers and consumers of specific narratives that form a community of speakers (this may also evoke, from the standpoint of the relation between law and literature, Stanley Fish's idea of an *interpretive community* (1980) and his understanding of text and context, even if in the digital environment text and context are both made only of data), our main, essential task is twofold: we have to share 'the precious semantic *resources* needed to make sense of the world' (Floridi 2011a: 8; italics MD) and to appropriate 'narratives as well, now perceived as further data-affordances that the Self is forced to semanticize' (Floridi 2011a: 8).

In other terms, the needed process of semanticization of Being also entails a process of meta-semanticization of narratives, according to which 'reflection turns to reflection and recognizes itself as part of the reality it needs to explain and understand' (Floridi 2011a: 8). Making sense of the world (semanticization of Being) is always coupled with making sense of ourselves (meta-semanticization of narratives) in the sphere of reflexivity. We have to invest data with meaning (data that are produced by multiple, distributed sources, in addition to traditional centralized devices) by means of narratives. Afterwards, we have to appropriate narratives as well, by means of meta-narratives, in the sphere of reflexivity, which redesign the semantic space, i.e. the world of meaningful experience, which is once again subject to the semanticization of Being.

However, this process of semanticization is not a sort of circularity, if circularity is taken to mean the repetition of the same. It is a narrative process of self-construction, that is part of the constructionist view of reality, according to which we have to provide relevant questions with consistent answers (Floridi 2011a) or, in our terms, with creative responses (Durante 2011c). This self-construction depends on the openness to the autonomous reality of the future (*the otherness of time*), which is not the mere development (namely, the 'modified form') of our present, as if the future would be merely understood through a chronological representation of time (*continuity*). The reality of time has always been debated both in the philosophical and in the scientific discourse, and the reality of future, understood as an autonomous mode of temporality, has been even more disputable. However, this is the conceptual core of constructionism: *the reality of the future is inherent in our present lives*. We will come back to this point. At present, we have to clarify the conceptual meaning of the term 'meta' in the expression 'meta-semanticization' of narratives.

What, on this view, is the function of the preposition 'meta'? This is an important point that has characterized much of the history of philosophy but, nowadays, should not be taken for granted. The preposition 'meta' does not only say something about the nature of the semantic content of a proposition. In other terms, it does not only tell us that narratives are subject to a process of re-semanticization. It tells us much more. It poses the philosophical question of why and how something becomes subject to a process of re-semanticization.

Floridi's conception of the term 'meta' can be illustrated by making reference to Stanislas Breton's analysis of the so-called 'function meta' (Breton 1982), even if we do not intend to make any direct and explicit comparison between Breton and Floridi. We simply believe that what Breton says can shed some light on Floridi's conception of the *meta*-semanticization of narratives (and about his *meta*-physics). According to Breton, the term meta shows 'an active movement of displacement' (Gilbert 2011: 533), which is articulated in three moments corresponding to three linguistic determinations: *metastasis*; *metaphor*; *metamorphosis*. Each of them illustrates a main aspect of the 'function meta'.

The function meta is firstly characterized, through the notion of metastasis, by 'the idea of instability or that of impatience that shakes the solidity of things that appeared to be stable' (Breton 1988: 41): the term meta involves a questioning that 'awakens our dogmatism' (Breton 1988: 41). Breton's dogmatism is what Floridi calls 'scholasticism'. It is exactly when scholasticism reaches its full that the function meta operates (Floridi 2011a: 11):

> Scholasticism, however, can perform one progressive task: it can indicate that philosophical research has reached a stage when it needs to address new topics and problems, adopt innovative methodologies, or develop alternative explanations. It cannot specify which direction the innovation should take. Historically, this is the task of two other positive forces for innovation, external to any philosophical system: the substantial novelties in the environment of the conceptual system occurring also as a result of the *semantic work* done by the old paradigm itself; and the appearance of an innovative paradigm, capable of dealing with them more successfully, and thus of *disentangling* the conceptual system from its stagnation [italics MD].

Secondly, the function meta of the metaphor indicates 'a unity of the whole' (Gilbert 2011: 536), since the metaphor can put into communication 'the matter and the spirit, the organic and the inorganic, the solid and the fluid' (Breton 1982: 51). The displacement brought about by the metaphor has a positive meaning and it signifies that 'all levels of the universe communicate' (Breton 1982: 52). This makes us understand that the *meta*-semanticization of narratives is meant to express, according to Floridi, a universalistic dimension: i.e. the informational treatment of all instances constituting the universe.

Here, the function meta is designed to put into communication different worlds within a single representation of the universe. It is the informational construction of an object that allows an epistemic agent to vary the levels of abstraction at which the object may be experienced (Durante 2011b). Let us make an example: the same car, understood as a set of information, may be viewed as a 'token' (that car belonging to me [*owner's viewpoint*] or the one subject to an incident [*insurer's viewpoint*] that has to be fixed [*mechanic's viewpoint*]), or as a 'type' (that model of car [*the designer's viewpoint*]), or as a 'type-token' (that car that needs to be provided with new tires, brakes, windscreens, or lamps, substituting the old ones [*the manufacturer's viewpoint*]). Every piece of the car (*observables*) may be viewed as a piece of information (an *interpreted typed variable*) that allow different people to have different points of view about the same car (Floridi 2011a: 48).

Thirdly and lastly, the function meta of the metamorphosis displays, according to Breton (1982: 52–53), the power of 'transformation, (…) the passage of a form (*morphé*) into another one' (Gilbert 2011: 540). This idea is pertinent to Floridi's constructionist view of the world and is inherent to the idea of meta-semanticization of narratives. It means that, at the same time, we transform our world and we are subject to this transformation: world and self are mutually constitutive. This inner process of transformation, signaled by the function meta, makes us be intrinsically 'open towards a future' (Gilbert 2011: 541), which is not yet determined: this is the crucial meaning of the meta-semanticization of narratives. It is because our future is not yet determined that we are responsible for the transformation of both the world and ourselves. This happens when we invest our data with meaning and our 'reflection [semanticization of Being] turns to reflection and recognizes itself [meta-semanticization of narratives] as part of the reality it needs to explain and understand' (Floridi 2011a: 8).

In a world made of data, the first and most essential thing to protect is thus our own capacity to invest data with meaning at the double level of semanticization of Being and meta-semanticization of narratives. As pointed out, it is highly debatable whether this capacity belongs only to human beings or to all (natural or artificial) living entities. In the latter case, would it mean that all entities accomplish the process of semanticization in the same way or with sharable results?

For sure, it is a process that engages all of us in a constant narration (*mise en abîme*). In this sense, let us focus on Paul Auster's profound reflection about the nature of narration, that is exactly conceived in these terms, as a never lasting self-construction. This idea is explored in the novel *Oracle Night* (Auster 2004). We believe this investigation can shed some light on the act of writing, and what is implied by the most difficult element of the narrative process: i.e. the narration of ourselves.

8.5 Narration as 'mise en abîme': Paul Auster's *Oracle Night*

In its narrative structure, *Oracle Night* is a *mise en abîme* (a narration that implies a meta-semanticization of narratives). This book is a thoughtful exploration 'on why we write, and what kind of power that writing actually holds' (O'Connor 2011: 1). Let us refer to O'Connor's review of the complex plot of *Oracle Night* (2011: 1):

> Auster's protagonist, Sidney Orr, is a marginally successful Brooklyn author who finds himself in a writing dry spell [...]. It is on one of these daily trips that Sidney stumbles into The Paper Palace, a curious paper shop. [...] Following the purchase [of a notebook], Sidney finds himself reinvigorated with the need to write. On the advice of his mentor, John Trause, Sidney appropriates the story of Flitcraft, a minor character from Dashiell Hammet's *The Maltese Falcon* as his first project. The theme of the Flitcraft story is how a random occurrence can completely shift the path of a person's life. Hammet's character has a good job and a good family life, then one day gives it all up and disappears after a near tragic accident as he is passing a construction site. Both Sidney and Trause find Flitcraft's tale to be a compelling enough story with innumerable possibilities. Sitting down with his notebook, Sidney creates his Flitcraft in the form of Nick Bowen, a high-profile New York book editor. Bowen, Sidney decides, has just received an unpublished manuscript entitled *Oracle Night* from the granddaughter of the late Sylvia Maxwell, a major literary figure. On his way home from work, Bowen is nearly decapitated by the dislodged head of stone gargoyle, thus beginning his Flitcraft tale. Bowen hightails it on the first plane out of New York, bringing with him only the clothes on his back and the copy of *Oracle Night*.

The central theme of Paul Auster's literature is the role of chance in human affairs. A random occurrence (chance) not only shifts the path of a person's life but makes us perceive how indeterminate is the fabric of our own reality (2004: 12):

> The world is governed by chance. Randomness stalks us every day of our lives, and those lives can be taken from us at every moment – for no reason at all.

However, this indeterminacy is not as meaningless as it could appear. On the contrary, it is an opportunity to invest data with meaning. In other terms, it reveals to us that we never follow a given path but we are taken in the indeterminate process of *constructing* the path of our personal life, like a novelist does, being aware of the fundamental fact that both the means and the materials we use in this construction do not entirely belong to us (Auster 2004: 12):

> So I removed the cap from my pen, pressed the point against the top line of the first page in the blue notebook, and started to write. The words came quickly, smoothly, without seeming to demand much effort. I found that surprising, but as long as I kept my hand moving from left to right, the next word always seemed to be there, waiting to come out of the pen.

The blue notebook, which seems to dictate words to Auster's character, resembles a sort of automatic writing that reminds us of the constant need to *re-appropriate* the produced data, by constantly re-investing them with meaning, since narration splits time and reality into equal parts: the novelist's life and the life of his own characters. Let us go back to the synopsis, in order to appreciate this point (O'Connor 2011: 2):

> From here on in, Auster's *Oracle Night* splits time inside and out of Sid's creation, describing, in equal parts, Sid's own life, and the life of his character. Sid finds the words pouring out of him at a [rapid] pace. Could the newfound verve be due to the mysterious notebook? Sid seems to think it has helped him, but can't believe that it has some kind of power over his writing. That is until he finds that Trause has been using the very same notebooks for his own novels. 'Those notebooks are very friendly, but they can also be cruel, and you have to watch out you don't get lost in them' warns Trause.

The automatic writing also reminds us that narrating a story is not just a self-centered activity: it is not only dependent on our own creativity (self-determination). On the contrary, it always requires us to make use of something else, notably a notebook (a magic, technological, device), that *helps* us invent what we are. However, Auster warns us against the possibility to lose oneself in automatic narration, as O'Connor reminds us (2011: 2):

> And the notebook soon shows its cruelty. Sidney sends Bowen off to Kansas City and sets him up with an eccentric named Ed Victory, a newly retired cab driver who inhabits an underground bunker full of historical phonebooks. Bowen becomes Victory's apprentice of sorts, spending his days helping out in the Bureau and obsessively reading and rereading *Oracle Night*. But then Sidney gets stuck. He's got Bowen set in this bunker with nowhere to go, and he's running out of pages in the notebook. Not to mention that his wife, Grace, has pulled a Flitcraft of her own disappearing and leaving no trace of where she's got off to. Could it be that Sidney subconsciously predicted this whole chain of events, and entered them into his own fictionalized story? Auster takes this on as the central question in *Oracle Night*. Auster plays this out in a number of ways as several characters in Sidney's novel mirror those in his real life and Auster drops hints connecting Sid's reality and his fiction throughout *Oracle Night*. (…) But with all of this fraternizing going on between author and characters and characters and other characters, the line starts to blur about who it is that is actually doing the talking?

Gradually, Auster comes to confront us with the crucial question: who it is 'that is actually doing the talking'? 'Who' is it that narrates one's 'own' life? How can our life (or identity) consistently emerge out of these multiple narratives that seem to conceal, at all times, the dividing line between what is fictional and what is real?

This is an important point in today's world of new technologies, since technologies mediate to a growing extent both our relation with reality and our encounters with others. In the words of Auster (2004: 25–26):

> It seemed to belong as much to the world of fiction as to the world of solid objects and flesh-and-blood human beings. Unexpectedly, this feeling didn't go away. (…) It's not unusual for a person to be so preoccupied as to appear absent – but the point was that I wasn't absent. I was there, fully engaged in what was happening, and at the same time I wasn't there – for the there wasn't an authentic there anymore. It was an illusory place that existed in my head, and that's where I was as well. In both places at the same time. In the apartment and in the story. In the story in the apartment that I was still writing in my head.

As already noted above, Auster's question gains significance as far as the virtual and the physical realities converge (*onlife*) and our personal identity also emerges out of the technologically mediated (automated, intensive or autonomic) production, collection, and selection of data constituting our own profile (Hildebrandt and Rouvroy 2011). When personal identity is conceived in terms of data, it becomes hard to recognize this identity as a unity (i.e. what are the data that form our identity?) and to protect this unity against the (automated, intensive or autonomic) production, rearrangement and de-contextualization of data (i.e. what are the real sources of data?). This unity can be only the result of the process of semanticization of data, and such a unity is protected as far as the capacity to invest data with meaning is concerned. On the one hand, we are called upon to manage the data that construct our own identity (freedom of self-determination); on the other hand, this self-construction (that is increasingly framed in terms of the right to identity or in terms of the right to be forgotten) cannot disable people from having access to our data (freedom of expression), for a simple but crucial reason. The construction of the self is always achieved in the relation with others: it is a *hetero-self-construction*, that makes use of materials (data plus meaning) that do not entirely belong to us. The idea itself of re-appropriation means that we always need to refer to something else coming from the others. This brings us back to the questions raised above: who it is that is actually doing the talking? What is real?

Trause (whose anagram is Auster), whom Sidney consults throughout the whole novel as a mentor, provides us with the following statement, which is the conceptual core of the novel, and serves as a good illustration of the basic idea that underlies our contribution (Auster 2004: 189):

> 'Thoughts are real', he said. 'Words are real. Everything human is real, and sometimes we know things before they happen even if we aren't aware of it. We live in the present, but the future is inside us at every moment. Maybe that's what writing is all about, Sid. Not recording events from the past, but making things happen in the future'.

A decisive consideration is formulated. Notably, writing is not about recording events from the past, but it is about making things happen in the future. Here lies the authentic nature of writing: writing is not just a reconstruction of meaning through the registration of events from the past. It is a construction of meaning, based on the fact that our present is orientated towards a future that is inside us at every moment. Writing (giving form to our identity) is not just to retrieve or to be restored of something lost: it is being engaged in the construction of our future. Auster's 'at every moment' is, more or less unknowingly, Heidegger's 'everydayness' of the 'being-toward-death' (2008: 233, orig. 1927), that does not qualify the future but, first of all, our own present.

According to the German philosopher, at every moment, we know we will die, albeit we do not know when. Death is not only a certainty: it is the certainty par excellence, from which all other certainties are drawn. We know from the very beginning that the future of death is inside us at every moment. Therefore, we live our time in the horizon of such a certainty, which concerns an event (*death*) that never occurs in the present that we call our own. It is in this horizon that we can project our lives: what we are not yet is the time we have to live and that makes our lives meaningful at present. In more philosophical terms, there is not a clear-cut separation between present and future (like in Hesiod's cycle of seasons), as if the present time would simply transform itself into the future: the future is already inside us at every moment.

We are made of this tension, that seems to defeat the traditional logic of narration based on the connection between the before and the after: what we are not yet constructs, from the very inside, what we are at present. It is this tension towards what we are not yet that requires us to invest data with meaning. The process of semanticization of data is triggered by the inherence of future into our present lives: our identity is not much made of what we already are but, primarily, of our relation with the future, i.e. of what we are not yet (otherness is inside us). This tension renders our lives indeterminate (open to the future) (Auster 2004: 189–190):

> Is there a connection between the *before* and the *after*? I don't know. (…) More than twenty years after the fact, I now believe that Trause called it right. (…) The future was *already inside* me [italics MD].

What does Auster's undecided answer (*I don't know*) mean? It signifies that human indetermination has more to do with meaning than with courses of action. We are indeterminate, not so much because our courses of action are not entirely predictable (since prediction is already part of the process of semanticization of data), but rather because we need to invest data with meaning. This idea rejoins an evolutionary conception of semantic information (Floridi 2011a: xiv):

> The mind does not wish to acquire information [data+meaning] for its own sake. It *needs* information to defend itself from reality and to survive. So information is not about representing the world: it is rather a means to model it in such a way to make sense of it and withstand its impact [italics MD].

On the views expressed above, human indetermination is the condition of possibility of (both legal and technological) normativity: norms condition but do not directly determine human behavior; if it weren't so, human beings wouldn't be autonomous and free agents. The process of semanticization of data (*semanticization of Being* and *meta-semanticization of narratives*) is the real condition of possibility of human indetermination: data are such constraining affordances (the constituent parts of those semantic artefacts that are legal norms) that require our capacity to invest them with meaning.

Investing data with meaning is a creative response to the constraints of data: it is an open, indeterminate hetero-self-construction within the realm of affordances enabled by those constraints. Such a construction is an evolutionary process that is brought about by the inherence of future into our present lives. This seems to me a plausible interpretation of Paul Auster's wonderful, yet counterintuitive account of the nature of writing: 'that's what writing is all about. Not recording events from the past, but making things happen in the future' (Auster 2004: 189).

This line of reasoning provides us with a critical conclusion. Get rid of the inherence of future from our present lives, and you will have destroyed normativity. Is this possible? The short answer is yes. A longer answer is sketched out in the following paragraph.

8.6 Data Tokens and the 'Digital Habitat'

The question is whether or not the integration of future into our lives is fundamentally inherent in our comprehension of the present and the normativity thereof. Our comprehension of the present is guided by a future still to be accomplished to the extent that data are understood as constraining affordances that design the environment as an epistemic space. In other terms, the question is not only about how to design legal or technological norms in order to protect our data (which still is a crucial aspect of the problem), but, first and foremost, how to design and understand the epistemic space: what Jannis Kallinikos has defined 'digital habitat' (Kallinikos and Tempini 2012: 3) or Floridi has extensively called 'infosphere', in which data can be invested with meaning and interpreted (Floridi 2003: 287).

The point is that, in a digitalized environment, data not only serve to construct our *texts* (identities, profiles, or legal provisions) but also the *contexts*, in which those texts are invested with meaning and interpreted. A context or epistemic space is 'a sum of information that characterizes a specific situation' (Dey 2001: 3), and allows us to interpret it. We are used to believe that a constructionist view of semantic information only concerns the interpretation of texts: that just the meaning of a text is indeterminate and it invites us to provide it with interpretation. On the contrary, the constructionist view of semantic information is more radical and it affects the construction of the epistemic space or context in which our texts are produced. As a sum of information characterizing a situation, the epistemic space or context involves meaning and hence it is meant to be, at least to some extent, indeterminate. This may not be the case, if the epistemic space is constructed by the automated mediation of technologies which gather and assembly data in our own. Let us explain this point by making reference to the idea of a computationally driven digital habitat (Kallinikos and Tempini 2012: 3):

> It is vital to understand the embeddedness of single digital devices within broader networks of data relations from which they gain their utility. The computational devices that populate everyday living and institutional practice alike are made potent through the growing transactivity (as opposed to connectivity) they acquire, as the outcome of being embedded within widely distributed and standardized data and information sources. In this regard, the developments we pinpoint construct a comprehensive, computationally driven *digital habitat*,

whereby social and cultural states and relationships are increasingly mediated by data and information tokens.

Our self-construction may be challenged when our texts (narrative self-representations) are held to be *indeterminate*, whereas their contexts are constructed as *determinate* epistemic spaces (i.e. they are not constructed by our interactions), in which our capacity to invest data with meaning is defied by technologies that mediate our interactions (by determining the range of informational resources we have access to) (Kallinikos and Tempini 2012: 3–4):

> As digital devices diffuse and become omnipresent, they embed human behaviour in an environment dominated by surrogate technical images and information tokens in which the description and depiction of life situations result from procedures and strategies of data processing and assembly. The relationship between the sensible and the intelligible, what can be perceived by the senses and what can be thought without immediate access to tangible reality is thereby refigured.

When data that concern us are gathered and assembled on a large scale and hence invested automatically with meaning, our capacity to appropriate or re-appropriate these narratives is challenged, if not displaced. As already remarked, the construction of both texts and contexts (*meta-semanticization*) may be technologically embedded, mediated, and therefore pre-determined (Kallinikos and Tempini 2012: 12):

> A commensurable data and information space is thus established making possible the sharing and elaboration of data across the traditional (culturally and technologically based) divides of text, image and sound, and the boundaries of distinct institutional conventions through which these have been produced and consumed such as films or video, books, photographs, games, journals or magazines. Such a sharing and elaboration of data and the information-based culture and knowledge they mediate are not a common or natural offspring of human activities. Rather, they are the outcome of a range of longstanding technological and institutional developments operating at different levels of aggregation. Through the standardization of data and the procedures by which they are acted upon, these developments have made possible the rendition of a growing range of social and cultural practices as interoperable digital content.

The 'rendition of a growing range of social and cultural practices as interoperable digital content' (Kallinikos and Tempini 2012: 12), in which personal data are increasingly gathered, assembled, de-contextualized, disposed of or even manipulated, has brought many to feel as if they were losing control over their data: this has concerned not only individuals but also states.

This thesis has provoked manifold reactions. One typical reaction is to entrust law with the claim of protection. A reaction to the loss of control over data has given rise, for instance, to the current legal elaboration of the right to be forgotten (as a part of our identity), conceived as a form of protection of one's self-construction. It is a significant legal elaboration intended to protect individuals. However, this elaboration is often more concerned with the prevention of someone's else behaviour rather than with self-protection, on the one hand, and the construction and understanding of the digital habitat or the infosphere, on the other.

This right is to be correctly constructed as a form of self-protection, that does not have to excessively reduce someone's else fundamental right to freedom of expression.

In other terms, we cannot disable other people from having access to information that concerns us, unless we prove that their access corresponds to an infringement of our individual rights. The burden of the proof remains with us.

It is dangerous to state (as in the recent proposal for a General Data Protection Regulation 2012/0011) that people have a right to be forgotten, according to which they are entitled to obtain from the controller of data the erasure of personal data, without having to prove that someone's else is infringing their rights (art. 17, sect. 1: 'The data subject shall have the right to obtain from the controller the erasure of personal data relating to them and the abstention from further dissemination of such data, (…), where (…) (a) the data are no longer necessary in relation to the purposes for which they were collected or otherwise processed').

This construction – still based on the traditional and old-fashioned idea that narration is about recording events from the past – overturns the burden of proof and shifts it from the data subject to the controller of data, with the result of conceiving the fundamental right of freedom of expression as a mere restriction of the right to be forgotten (art. 17, sect. 3: 'The controller shall carry out the erasure without delay, except to the extent that the retention of the personal data is necessary: (a) for exercising the right of freedom of expression').

The struggle for self-construction is not to be conceived in a reactive but, on the contrary, in a proactive manner, that is concerned with our capacity to manage and rearrange personal data, and it requires from us to constantly negotiate our identity in the relation with the others (*hetero-self-construction*). In this sense, we are called upon to re-contextualize and re-integrate our data in co-constructed narratives, even if this may modify our identity in two directions, both as subjects and as agents of such a process of re-contextualization (Kallinikos and Tempini 2012: 21):

> The individual or collective appropriation of these life styles and patterns inevitably entails the re-contextualization and situated interpretation of abstract and freely circulating data tokens. It is beyond any doubt that individuals and groups transform and complement the generic and de-contextualized solutions mediated by technologies. Yet, by the same token, they become accomplices in the framing and sampling of the world these technologies and the services they enable mediate. *Re-contextualization (and interpretation) is double act that changes not only what is re-contextualized but also the agents of re-contextualization.* Seen in this light, the tasks and patterns of daily life that have predominantly been shaped by all those qualities and faculties we associate with human experience are subject to change, as computational techniques infiltrate the everyday living habitat [italics MD].

We are nowadays proactively called upon to manage personal data (i.e. the informational resources or constraining affordances trough which we co-construct our texts and contexts) and to make them subject to a constant process of semanticization, increasingly confronted with their technologically mediated de-contextualization and re-contextualization, which challenge our capacity to invest data with meaning beyond what we are generally inclined to optimistically recognize:

> These generic attributes which we have identified with the prominence of cognition over perception, the preponderance of information and computational principles in defining reality cannot be wished away by the widespread rhetoric of technological appropriation, technological malleability or contextual adaptation that has become common over the last

few decades. They need to be conceptually deconstructed and studied empirically with the view of exposing the distinctive forms through which they are manifested, change and fuse into the fabric of social practice (Kallinikos and Tempini 2012: 21).

8.7 Conclusion

In conclusion, how to appropriate or re-appropriate our narratives in the *digital habitat* (Kallinikos) or *infosphere* (Floridi) is a serious challenge, which will engage us in the close future. However, it might be dangerous (and perhaps illusory) to believe that this challenge should be dealt with by disabling other people from having access to information or by merely preventing data from being gathered and assembled according to the data-intensive paradigm. Freedom of expression and the circulation of information are the conditions enabling the informational hetero-self-construction of personal identity, and thus they are the core value in the construction of the digital environment. The essential key, in order to judge the soundness and legitimacy of a legal and technological normativity, lies in what the construction of a digital environment preserves the human capacity to invest data with meaning, namely, the capacity to co-construct our lives according to that productive tension towards a future that is *already inside us at every moment*. We can no longer be mere reactive subjects, who wish to defend their pretended identity as a stable enduring fortress. We are called upon to be proactive agents: "that's what writing is all about. Not recording events from the past, but making things happen in the future" (Auster 2004: 189).

References

Auster, P. 2004. *Oracle Night*. London: Faber & Faber.

Breton, S. 1982. Réflexions sur la fonction *méta*. *Dialogue. Canadian Philosophical Review. Revue Canadienne de Philosophie* 21(1): 45–56.

Breton, S. 1988. *Poétique du sensible*. Paris: Editions du Cerf.

Checkland, P., and J. Scholes. 1990. *Soft systems methodology in action*. Chichester: Wiley.

Dey, A.K. 2001. Understanding and using context. *Personal Ubiquitous Computing Journal* 5(1): 4–7.

Dretske, F. 1981. *Knowledge and the flow of information*. Oxford: Blackwell.

Durante, M. 2007. Intelligenza artificiale. Applicazioni giuridiche. IV ed., *Digesto Italiano. Discipline Privatistiche, Sezione Civile*, II, 714–724. Torino: UTET.

Durante, M. 2011a. Rethinking human identity in the age of autonomic computing: The philosophical idea of the trace. In *Law, human agency and autonomic computing. The philosophy of law meets the philosophy of technology*, ed. M. Hildebrandt and A. Rouvroy, 85–103. London: Routledge.

Durante, M. 2011b. How to cross boundaries in the society of information: Vulnerability, responsiveness and accountability, In: *Proceedings of Computer Ethics Philosophical Enquiry (CEPE) 2011*, University of Wisconsin-Milwaukee, Milwaukee, 31 May–3 June 2011.

Durante, M. 2011c. Normativity, constructionism, and constraining affordances. How Luciano Floridi's semantic philosophy of information bridges *Techné* and *Episteme*, *Ethics & Politics*,

Symposium on Luciano Floridi, *Philosophy of Information*. Retrieved from: http://www2.units.it/etica/. Accessed 6 Apr 2012.
Fish, S. 1980. *Is there a text in this class?* Harvard: Harvard University Press.
Floridi, L. 2003. On the intrinsic value of information objects and the infosphere. *Ethics and Information Technology* 4(4): 287–304.
Floridi, L. 2008a. Artificial intelligence's new frontier: Artificial companions and the fourth revolution. *Metaphilosophy* 39(4–5): 651–655.
Floridi, L. 2008b. The method of levels of abstraction. *Minds and Machines* 18(3): 303–329.
Floridi, L. 2010. *Information. A very short introduction*. Oxford: Oxford University Press.
Floridi, L. 2011a. *The philosophy of information*. Oxford: Oxford University Press.
Floridi, L. 2011b. A defence of constructionism: Philosophy as conceptual engineering. *Metaphilosophy* 42(3): 282–304.
Gilbert, P. 2011. Metafisica e 'funzione meta'. *Giornale di Metafisica* XXXII: 529–552.
Heidegger, M. 2008, orig. 1927. *Being and time*. Trans. J. Macquarrie and E. Robinson. London: Harper.
Hey, T., S. Tansley, and K. Tolle. 2007. Jim Gray on eScience: A transformed scientific model. Available at: http://www.research.microsoft.com/en_us/collaboration/fourthparadigm. Last accessed 6 Apr 2012.
Hildebrandt, M. 2008. Legal and technological normativity: More (and less) than twin sisters. *Techné: Research in Philosophy and Technology* 12(3): 169–183.
Hildebrandt, M., and S. Gutwirth (eds.). 2008. *Profiling the European citizen. Cross-disciplinary perspectives*. Dordrecht: Springer.
Hildebrandt, M., and A. Rouvroy (eds.). 2011. *Law, human agency and autonomic computing. The philosophy of law meets the philosophy of technology*. London: Routledge.
Kallinikos, Y., and N. Tempini. 2012. Post-material meditations: On data tokens, knowledge and behaviour. Available at: http//:www.tigair.info/docs/kalltemp_egos11.pdf. Last accessed 6 Apr 2012.
Lessig, L. 1999. *Code and other laws of cyberspace*. New York: Basic Books.
Nielsen, M. 2011. *Reinventing discovery: The new era of networked science*. Princeton: Princeton University Press.
O'Connor, M. 2011. The review of Oracle Night by Paul Auster. Available at: http://www.contemporarylit.about.com/od/fiction/fr/oracleNight_2.htm. Last accessed 22 Nov 2011.
Prigogine, I., and I. Stengers. 1981. Vincolo. *Enciclopedia einaudi*, vol. 14, 1064–1080. Torino: Einaudi.
Zittrain, J. 2008. Perfect enforcement on tomorrow's internet. In *Regulating technologies. Legal futures, regulatory frames and technological fixes*, ed. R. Brownsword and K. Yeung, 125–156. Oxford/Portland: Hart Publishing.

Chapter 9
When a Robot Can Love – *Blade Runner* as a Cautionary Tale on Law and Technology

Shulamit Almog

Did I request thee, Maker, from my clay to mould me Man?
Did I solicit thee from darkness to promote me?

(Milton 1821, orig. 1667: 315)

Abstract This paper examines Ridley Scot's 1982 film *Blade Runner* as a cautionary tale relating to the role of law in a technology augmented environment. *Blade Runner* presents a regime that uses law first in order to create beings with superior abilities and pre-determined longevity, and then to define them as non-human or non-beings, devoid of legal personhood, and thus exploitable. *Blade Runner*, alongside other cultural representations created within the science fiction genre, serves as illustration of a society that brings together technology and law, in order to maintain unaccountable and arbitrary employment of authorized power. It provides a warning against uninhibited use of technology in order to crate genetic inferiority, and calls for careful scrutiny of the overt and covert functions of law, as new technologies gradually become available.

9.1 Introduction

The film *Blade Runner* was released in 1982. Its acclaim was built gradually, and at the same time the circles of influence and inspiration it ignited widened, both within popular culture and among researchers and thinkers (Bukatman 1997: 41). *Blade Runner* continues to inspire the creation of various cultural products, such as computer games, television and novel series, debate groups, and ever growing internet

S. Almog (✉)
Faculty of Law, University of Haifa, Haifa, Israel
e-mail: Salmog@law.haifa.ac.il

M. Hildebrandt and J. Gaakeer (eds.), *Human Law and Computer Law: Comparative Perspectives*, Ius Gentium: Comparative Perspectives on Law and Justice 25,
DOI 10.1007/978-94-007-6314-2_9,

discourse. Some of them touched upon legal issues, such as the definition of human and non-human implied by the film (Gwaltney 1991), to issues of racism (Booker 2006), ecology and environmental contamination (Fischer 1989), and gender equality (Barr 1991).

The reading suggested here aims to examine the place of the law in the film from a wider perspective, and present it as an important, though clandestine actor in the intricate narrative. In the following, after describing the plot, I will analyze the role of law in denying human status to certain parts of the population. Such denial is represented in the film not as an ethical or moral practice, but as serving the purpose of harnessing technology in order to create human-like individuals that will be subjected to (real) humans. This practice is facilitated and backed by legal instruments.

After elaborating upon *Blade Runner*'s narrative, the next two sections will describe how *Blade Runner* breaks thorough the old rooted discourse, focuses on perceiving artificially created beings as risk sources, and introduces a new moral and pragmatic challenge – a claim that such beings could and should be considered as new humans, entitled to legal personhood. The following section and the conclusion will explicate how *Blade Runner* can serve as a warning against using legal instruments by institutional, violent employment of authorized power that abuses technological abilities.

The central text discussed here is the film *Blade Runner-Director's Cut* (Ridley Scott 1992).[1] In certain points I will also refer to Philip K. Dick's novel *Do Androids Dream of Electric Sheep?* (1968). The book's plot was the primary basis for the film, and though there are major differences between the two, juxtaposition of the literary text to the film enriches the discussion in certain points, and enhances some of the film's themes.[2]

9.2 *Blade Runner*: The Story

Since the narrative and its visual production are highly significant for a presentation of the intricacies of *Blade Runner*, I will start with a rather thorough description of both.

The following opening is presented at the beginning of the film:

> Early in the 21st Century, THE TYRELL CORPORATION advanced robot evolution into the NEXUS phase – a being virtually identical to a human – known as a Replicant. The NEXUS 6 Replicants were superior in strength and agility, and at least equal in intelligence, to the genetic engineers who created them. Replicants were used Off-World as slave labor, in the hazardous exploration and colonization of other planets. After a bloody mutiny by a NEXUS

[1] It should be noted that *Blade Runner* has several versions. Two of the others are the 1982 version (Domestic Cut), and the 2007 version (Final Cut). For elaboration, see Bukatman (1997: 33–40).

[2] The correlation and the differences between the film and the novel gained much attention, see for example Heldreth (1991: 40–52).

> 6 combat team in an Off-World colony, Replicants were declared illegal on earth - under penalty of death. Special police squads – BLADE RUNNER UNITS – had orders to shoot to kill, upon detection, any trespassing Replicant, this was not called execution. It was called retirement.

The time is November 2019 and the place is Los Angeles. The first images introduce the view of the metropolitan area from above. From the weave of lights, the pyramid of the Tyrell Corporation stands out. Inside, a new employee, Leon Kowalski, is undergoing a security check aimed at discovering whether he is a person or a Replicant.[3] A moment before the test reveals his true identity he shoots the examiner and escapes.

Following this event, Rick Deckard, is approached by Gaff, a policeman sent to bring him to the office of Bryant, Captain of the *Blade Runner* unit. It turns out that Deckard is a policeman who recently left his job. Bryant informs Deckard that four Replicants have infiltrated the city, and that Deckard is required to eliminate them, despite having left the service. Deckard refuses, but ultimately succumbs to the pressure and takes on the assignment. He is presented with the fleeing Replicants: Roy Batty 'Battle Model', the group's leader; Zhora who was trained to murder; and Pris, a 'Basic Pleasure Model'. The Nexus 6 Replicants, as Deckard finds out, were created with a lifespan of 4 years.

In the beginning of his investigation, Deckard arrives at the management offices of the Tyrell Corporation. There, he meets Rachael, who is introduced as the niece of Dr. Eldon Tyrell, the head of the corporation and the scientist who designed the Nexus type Replicants. Tyrell requests Deckard to give Rachael the Voight-Kampff test. The test reveals that Rachael was created as an experiment: she thinks she is human while she is actually a Replicant. Rachael was implanted with artificial memories in order to structure her emotional system, and to gain better control over her. Later on, Deckard reveals that Leon, like Rachael, was implanted with artificial memories of family life.

At the same time, Leon and Roy Batty discover that the information they seek is solely in Tyrell's possession, and that J.-F. Sebastian, a genetic engineer may help them reach Tyrell. Deckard, alone in his apartment, dreams of a unicorn running in a forest. The camera moves to the old family photos on his Piano.[4] When Deckard wakes up, he manages to locate Zhora. After finding out she has been discovered, she runs off but Deckard chases after her and shoots her, while Leon is watching in terror from across the street. When Leon nearly kills Deckard, Rachael suddenly appears and shoots Leon, saving Deckard's life.

Roy Batty, after Pris, arrives at Sebastian's apartment and together they reveal to Sebastian that they are Replicants. Sebastian agrees to set up a meeting between Batty and Tyrell. At the meeting, Batty demands a longer life. Tyrell claims that for technical reasons, a Replicant's life span cannot be lengthened. Batty then kills

[3] For a discussion on the test, which is called "Voight-Kampff test", see Francavilla (1991: 12–13).

[4] 'The unicorn hallucination' was added to the Director's Cut version of 1992. Some maintain it implies that Deckard is a Replicant, see Bukatman (1997: 81–82).

Tyrell and Sebastian and escapes into Sebastian's building. When Deckard arrives at Sebastian's apartment, he kills Pris and chases after Batty. Batty overtakes him and towards the end of the chase, Deckard is at his mercy, hanging in the air. Batty decides to spare Deckard and pulls him to a safe place. Before dying Batty says:

> I've seen things you people wouldn't believe. Attack ships on fire off the shoulder of Orion. I watched C-beams glitter in the dark near the Tannhäuser Gate. All those moments will be lost in time, like tears in rain. Time to die.

Deckard goes back to his apartment, where Rachael is waiting for him. In the last scene, they both leave the apartment, probably to run away together.[5]

9.3 And Personhood to All

The Replicants in *Blade Runner* are named robots, or androids in *Do Androids Dream of Electric Sheep?* Robots, Androids, Replicants and Cyborgs, posits Bukatman, are all technological objects which reflect human fears (Bukatman 1997: 72).[6] They evoke dark visions of the destructive potential released when an android turns against its creators.

Such apprehensions can be gleaned from a report published in 1982 by a U.S. presidential committee, regarding the advantages and risks of genetic engineering. The report mentions, among other things, the Frankenstein myth, and warns against reversal of technological innovations, that will turn the slave into a master.[7] 'You are my creator, but I am your master – obey!' (Shelley 1974, orig. 1818: 165), demands the artificially created malevolent creature from its terrified creator, Victor Frankenstein, in a conceptualizing narrative, echoing the collective human fear from the fateful consequences of hubris-like artificial creation of life.

---

[5]In the 1982 version Deckard and Rachael are floating over natural scenery in the last scene, and in the background one can hear Deckard say that Rachael has no expiration date. See the screenplay by Fancher and Peoples (1981: 23).

[6]The Webster dictionary (online) defines a robot as a machine able to perform a complex series of actions, sometimes resembling a human in outer appearance, but always incapable to human emotion. A Cyborg is a bionic human, a combination of flesh and blood and machine. An android is defined as a mobile robot, usually with a human form. The word 'android' derives from the Greek word *androids*, meaning 'similar'. The similarity to humans makes the android more than a machine, but because it is similar and not identical, it remains less than human. In The American Heritage Dictionary of the English Language (online) an android is defined as an artificial creature made of biological material and having human characteristics, also called a humanoid. The android theme is present in the seminal Frankenstein narrative. The novel *Frankenstein* is considered as an inspirational source for several science fiction constituting themes. Among them is the notion that creating life in a lab is a dangerous, Hubris-laden act, which is bound to lead towards disastrous consequences.

[7]President's Commission for the Study of Ethical Problems in Medicine and Biomedical Behavioural Research (1982: 27–28).

Blade Runner challenges the presumptions and fears that are embedded in the narrative of the slave turning into master, and puts forth reverse queries, dealing with situations in which the slave becomes human, or in which humans are denied humanity by being defined as non-human or slaves. *Blade Runner* does echo the old rooted fear of an android as a source of risk, but at the same time it introduces a new moral and pragmatic challenge: a claim that androids could and should be considered as new humans. The denial of the Replicants' human status is represented in the film not as an ethical or moral practice, but as a plain manifestation of force, backed by concealed law. Law is the back-stage factor that facilitates and serves a regime in which government and capital form an unholy alliance that creates exploitable beings.

In his *Force of Law*, Jacques Derrida explains the common practice of marking subjects and of casting them outside the protective definitions of the law (Derrida 1990: 951):

> There have been. There are still, many 'subjects' among mankind who are not recognized as subjects and who receive this animal treatment (...) What we confusedly call 'animal', the living thing as living and nothing else, is not a subject of the law or of law. The opposition between just and unjust has no meaning in this case.

Derrida exposes the arbitrary and artificial characteristics of the practice of exclusion, and the way in which arbitrary classifications and definitions render the discussion about 'justice' or 'injustice' irrelevant with regard to outcasts. Only deconstruction and reconstruction of the manner in which basic terms are defined, can reverse the picture (Derrida 1990: 953):

> If we wish to speak of injustice, of violence or of a lack of respect toward what we still so confusedly call animals (...) we must reconsider in its totality the (...) axiomatic that dominates, in the West, the thought of just and unjust. From this very first step we can already glimpse the first of its consequences, namely, that a deconstructionist approach to the boundaries that institute the human subject (preferably and paradigmatically the adult male, rather than the woman, child or animal) (...) does not necessarily lead to (...) the effacement of an opposition between just and unjust (...) but may (...) lead to the reinterpretation of the whole apparatus of boundaries within which a history and a culture have been able to confine their criteriology.

What Derrida describes is a system of criteria which excludes certain 'subjects' from the protection of the law, or from the discourse related to justice, morality and rights. According to Derrida, this system complements the determination to turn an adult male into the initial, most meaningful representative of the human subject. The reasons for the creation of such a system of criteria are not embedded in firm views regarding ethics, morality or justice. They derive from the wish to maintain the advantage and the powers which are attributed to those who are defined as 'human'. 'Humans' are able to enjoy the benefits of their status, and to profit from the unprotected, or weakened status of those defined as 'non-human' or less human.

Derrida's discussion ties in with the *Blade Runner* theme, where it draws on the contemporary discourse on the nexus between novel technologies and legal personhood issues. For example, the notion that highly sophisticated computer programs, known as intelligent agents (IA) will be termed as 'autonomous artificial agents' and become legal persons has gained attention within the discussion on interactions between humans and IA. According to Gunther Teubner, 'there is no compelling reason to restrict the attribution of action exclusively to humans and to social systems (…). Personifying other non-humans is a social reality today and a political necessity for the future' (Teubner 2006, quoted by Koops, Hildebrandt and Jacquet-Chiffelle 2010: 14). Yet, past experience demonstrates that personification of non-humans might serve as merely a tool for the reproduction of current power structures and for the supremacy of 'genuine humans'. Samir Chopra aptly explains this point (Chopra 2010: 38–40):

> The law has never considered humanity a necessary or sufficient condition for being a person. For example, in 19th century England, women were not full persons; and, in the modern era, the corporation has been granted legal personhood. The decision to grant personhood to corporations is instructive because it shows that granting personhood is a pragmatic decision taken in order to best facilitate human commerce and interests. In so doing, we did not promote or elevate corporations; we attended to the interests of humans.

The novel *Do Androids Dream of Electric Sheep?* comes to mind in this context. It describes a society which has deconstructed the traditional system of definitions regarding the status of animals. Because they are so rare and valuable, animals have become superior subjects, with an especially protected and well-kept status, both by social conventions and by the law, which obliges every human to take care of an animal. Not taking care of an animal is also considered as immoral behavior within the social reality described by the novel (Dick 1968: 10). Because real animals are so scarce, most people must settle for 'raising' artificial animals, which are electronically operated. Yet, the protected status of animals is not derived from acknowledgment of their moral right. Rather, it is, again, a pragmatic practice, used in order to distinguish between humans. Those humans who own rarer and more expensive animals are perceived as more successful and important, and are therefore granted more power. The protection of animals promotes human commercial markets that sell animals, and serves the interests of humans. The privileged status of animals in *Do Androids Dream of Electric Sheep?* (which is also alluded to in *Blade Runner*) that mainly serves human interest, emphasizes the artificial nature of the exclusion, when the circumstances are different and it is the exclusion of certain beings that serves the human interest. As the film and the novel illustrate, the human interest counts, and not the inherent rights of any subject. What matters is not whether one is defined as a 'Replicant', 'human' or 'animal', but the power to decide who is protected and who is not. The following quote from the novel, relating a conversation between Pris and Sebastian stresses this point (Dick 1968: 140):

> B-b-because things like that don't happen. The g-g-government never kills anyone, for any crime…
>
> 'But you see', Pris said, 'if you're not human, than it's all different.'
>
> 'That's not true. Even animals – even eels and gophers and snakes and spiders – are sacred.'
>
> Pris, still regarding him fixedly, said, 'So it can't be, can it? As you say, even animals are protected by law'.

Blade Runner challenges the practice of such an interest-based system of legal protection. It confronts us with the potentially forceful demand of Intelligent Agents for legal status. It presents the artificial creation of such agents as insufficient rationale for a denial of legal status. An approach that seeks to address such a challenge will have to take a moral standing; it will assert that a being that achieves self-consciousness is morally entitled to legal personhood, and that biological processes, usually interwoven with self-consciousness, are not a *sine qua non* when legal personhood is granted.

As Lawrence B. Solum explains this notion (Solum 1992: 1286):

> If AIs behaved the right way and if cognitive science confirmed that the underlying processes producing these behaviors were relatively similar to the processes of the human mind, we would have very good reason to treat AIs as persons. Moreover, in a future in which we interact with such AIs or with intelligent beings from other planets, we might be forced to refine our concept of human.

Blade Runner is not the first cultural representation that echoes a demand for granting legal personhood and human rights to artificial creations. Roy Batty's claims resonate, for instance, Frankenstein's creation's demand for a spouse: '"Shall each man" cried he, "find a wife for his bosom, and each beast have his mate, and I be alone?"' (Shelley 1974, orig. 1818: 165). The artificially created being phrases his demand in terms of a right that he is entitled to: 'You must create a female for me, with whom I can live in the interchange of those sympathies necessary for my being. This you alone can do; and I demand it of you as a right which you must not refuse' (Shelley 1974, orig. 1818: 140).

Like *Frankenstein, Blade Runner* became a cultural benchmark. As Bukatman (1997: 8) suggests, its idiosyncratic nature is perhaps located in its visual density and in its layering effect, which produces 'an inexhaustible complexity, infinity of surfaces to be encountered and explored'. *Blade Runner* evolved into a visual icon of the fear for the implications of technology on society. It has become an important hallmark, relevant to the present and to the future, cautioning against the potentially devastating nexus between technological innovation and exploitation.

9.4 Replicants: The Construction of the Non-human

All the Replicants' actions in the film are part of a survival struggle. Their main aspiration is actually the deconstruction of reigning definitions, and the reconstruction of a new system that will define them as humans, who are entitled, first and foremost, to a natural life-span, and to other human rights.[8]

[8]Human, in this context is a signifier of entitlement to legal rights, and not a signifier for biological uniqueness that is required in order to deserve the legal rights. In that way the Replicants' aspiration is not to become humans but to gain human rights.

See the short and loaded dialogue Leon exchanges with Deckard, before Rachael shoots him:

Leon:	How old am I?
Deckard:	I don't know.
Leon:	My birthday is April 10, 2017. How long do I live?
Deckard:	Four years.
Leon:	More than you. Painful to live in fear, isn't it? Nothing is worse than having an itch you can never scratch.
Deckard:	Oh, I agree.
Leon:	Wake up! Time to die.

It is Leon, and not Deckard, who dies at the end of the interchange, but not before having shattered the barriers separating himself and Deckard. First, he refers to himself with semantics usually linked to humans. He uses words and phrases like 'birthday', 'how old am I?', 'painful', and 'fear'. By doing this, Leon succeeds in defying the legalistic definition that qualifies him as not human and authorizes Deckard to kill him. The legal norm does not classify such killing as murder. On the contrary, it is perceived as a commendable and financially beneficial fulfillment of one's job.[9] Leon also tries to demonstrate his humanity and his fear of death, during his allotted life span, using a metaphor that might invoke Deckard's empathy and solidarity. His last outcry to Deckard: 'Wake up!' is also a demand for the annulment of the arbitrary definition that qualify him and the other Replicants as inhuman.

Roy and Pris take similar action. Sebastian recognizes them as Nexus 6 type Replicants, and asks them to demonstrate some of their abilities. Roy answers: 'We are not computers Sebastian, we are physical'. Pris uses the famous Cogito sentence: 'I think, therefore I am'.[10] Pris, who is defined as a 'Basic pleasure model', ironically uses one of the most well-known icons of Western philosophy, in order to challenge all who labeled her as inexistent.

Before his death, Roy Batty mentions living in fear, as does Leon before he is shot. When Deckard is sure Batty is going to kill him, Batty shatters the wall separating himself from Deckard, thus deciding to spare the life of the person who killed his friends.

Similarities between the exploitation and oppression of Replicants in *Blade Runner* and other forms of exploitation and oppression have been mentioned in a number of contexts. Francavilla describes the situation of Replicants in terms of

---

[9]The authority to 'kill and triumph' the created entities is a fundamental element in *Blade Runner* as well as in *Frankenstein*: 'You, my creator, would tear me to pieces, and triumph; remember that, and tell me why I should pity man more than he pities me? You would not call it murder, if you could precipitate me into one of those ice-rifts, and destroy my frame, the work of your own hands' (Shelley 1974, orig. 1818: 141).

[10]'I think, therefore I am' are the famous words of seventeenth-century French philosopher Rene Descartes, also known as the 'Cogito' (meaning 'I think' in Latin).

human rights, and compares their oppression to a denial of rights experienced by certain races and nations throughout human history (Francavilla 1991: 9):

> the Replicants in *Blade Runner* have virtually no right to life, liberty, or the pursuit of happiness. Contemporary fiction's view of the android or Replicant as a persecuted being deprived of human rights may reflect our culture's projected guilt over the exploitation, conquest, enslavement, and extermination of other races and nationalities in history: the Aztec Indian, the American Indian, the African Slaves, the Jews in World War II and many more.

Judith Kerman juxtaposes the Replicants' lack of legal agency and their demolition with the catastrophic historical events of the holocaust and the dropping of the atom bomb on Japanese cities, maintaining that such events occur when humans perceive other humans as inhuman, in order to pursue power and political ends (Kerman 1991: 1). This dimension of systematic extermination for political goals is represented in *Blade Runner* alongside the dimension of exploitation. Kerman adds that the exploitation of the Replicants who are used as soldiers is comparable to the exploitation of soldiers as canon-fodder and to the exploitation of third world's inhabitants as cheap workers: 'The political critique is inescapable, pointing to our world, in which soldiers are "cannon fodder", workers and native peoples expendable (...)' (Kerman 1991: 22).

Situations which entail plain slavery are indeed not merely fictional, futuristic dark visions. They occur today, within the domain of the current labor market, in which there is no need to create artificial Replicants who will serve as slaves, since masses of people are already available for slave-labor defined as 'work'. The film invites a critical confrontation with the present, as well as speculations about the future. Anyone who is enslaved and exploited, ignoring his or her humanity, is in fact a Replicant. *Blade Runner*, than, confronts its audience with the acute question of what it means, ethically, technologically, and most of all – politically, to live such a life not only in the future, but also in the immediate present.

9.5 Law as an Invisible Maker

In a short story titled *Human is?* by Philip K. Dick, the author describes a society in which aliens, named after their home planet Rexor – 'Rexorian', try to invade the earth and disguise themselves as humans. The hero is a Rexonian who takes over the body of a human scientist named Lester Lerik, stealing his identity and invading the earth.[11]

The person in charge of exterminating Rexorians, the 'Clearance Director', explains to the scientist's wife, that her declaration in court regarding the differences between her husband and the one impersonating him, is needed for the purpose of eliminating the suspect: 'We must work within legal channels', he declares (Dick 2007: 259–269). In contrast to outer space, in which there is a separate legal system called 'martial law', on earth, 'regular civil law' applies (Dick 2007: 267).

[11] *Human is?* is both the title of the novel and the story. For elaboration on Philip K. Dick's great interest in androids, see Barlow (1991).

The legal process becomes the Rexonian's savior. Jill decides that the infiltrator-imposter is a much more preferable partner than her original husband. She decides not to provide the legal system with the declaration required for the destruction of the Rexonian. At the crucial moment in court, the scientists wife uses legal rules to morph the imposter into a human. The imposter becomes Jill's husband within Lester Lerik's body, for good. The law, the tool which is most often used to declare against inhumanity, becomes, in this case, the instrument through which the inhuman is redeemed and turned into a human.

This short story, like *Blade Runner*, brings out the arbitrary nature of the classifications 'human' and 'inhuman', and of the attempt to defy their borders. But while in *Blade Runner* the Replicants aspire to gain their own legal personhood, the Rexorians aspire for a false one. In *Blade Runner*, the pseudo-legal procedure determining humanity is the allegedly scientific Voight-Kampff test. Legal rules enable the automatic implementation of the test and the convenient and fast elimination of those declared to be Replicants after failing the test. The authority given to those executing the test is absolute. It seems unaccompanied by legal or other critical processes. An option of appeal or a petition for a new trial or judgment is not mentioned as available.

Replicants are constructed with limited longevity, or 'sentenced to death' without any due process or access to mitigation. Roy Batty believes that the person that is able to reverse this state of affairs is Dr. Eldon Tyrell. His demand for a reconstruction that will turn him into a 'human', entitled to a life span which is not predetermined, leads him to confront who he thinks of as his 'maker' Tyrell. When Tyrell's replies: 'Death. Well, I'm afraid that's a little out of my jurisdiction', he ironically inflicts upon himself the defenseless fate he designed for his creations. The disenchanted Batty kills the failing maker, in a scene that brings to mind the threat of the disenchanted monster in Frankenstein towards its maker, when he understands he is doomed, by his creator, to live a lone life with no companion by his side (Shelley 1974, orig. 1818: 141):

> I will revenge my injuries: if I cannot inspire love, I will cause fear; and chiefly towards you my arch-enemy, because my creator, do I swear inextinguishable hatred. Have a care: I will work at your destruction, nor finish until I desolate your heart, so that you curse the hour of your birth.

Yet, though Tyrell is Roy's 'maker' in one sense, he is not the only one. Another 'maker', that remains obscure, is the one who has the power to permit and facilitate the creation of pre-determined longevity. The identity and nature of this meta-maker, who uses the law as a tool, remains indefinable.

The corporation can act within a legal regime that defines what is permitted and what is not, while enjoying a total lack of accountability, and while remaining absolutely inaccessible. Roy Batty has no chance to reach the lawmaker that shaped his fate. In contrast to the infiltrating Rexoinan, the hero of *Human is?*, who managed to get his 'day in court', a day that saved his life, Roy Batty is prevented from achieving legal deliverance.

In an article dealing with the construction of social meaning and the use of legislation to achieve a change of prevailing meanings, Lawrence Lessig mentions *Blade Runner* while attempting to demonstrate how social meaning evolves. In the beginning of the film, Deckard views Replicants (Lessig refers to them as 'creatures') as machines, and treats them as such. Further on he begins to treat Replicants as human. Established social meaning which was not questioned in the past is being reversed. Deckard learns that Replicants are not machines, commodities or merchandise, and his personal insight could represent a far-reaching shift. Doubts and misgivings as to the status of Replicants, can gradually proliferate and create new social meaning, overruling the legal dictate (Lessig 1995: 960).

One of the most powerful points raised by *Blade Runner* is the following claim: it is uncertain who is Replicant and who is human, and yet this does not really matter. The inferiority of the Replicants is presented as artificially contrived by using legal definitions; it is not derived from relevant differences between Replicants and humans. Rachael, who believes she is human, and is presented as having human-like consciousness, memories and feelings, finds out that according to the legal definition she is a Replicant. Deckard probably views himself as human, but is (perhaps) a Replicant.[12] Yet, as the narrative suggests, what matters is self-awareness and not arbitrary definitions.

The danger of exploiting beings by using exclusionary definitions is what one should be wary of. Reality confronts us with those who have, in practice, been defined as 'Replicants', undeserving of the legal defenses provided for those defined as human. In this sense, *Blade Runner* is a sophisticated vision of a possible future, which could serve as a useful alert against exploitation of current 'Replicants'.

9.6 Conclusion: What Does It Mean if a Robot Can Genuinely Love?

Artificial Intelligence (also known as *A.I.*), a 2001 science fiction film directed by Steven Spielberg is also focused on the creation of beings that can be perceived as Replicants. It tells the story of David, a child-like android programmed with the ability to love, that was created in order to replace a human child. A student asks the scientist who created David the following question: 'If a robot can genuinely love a person, what responsibility does this person hold towards this robot?'

At this point, I wish to dwell briefly on the invaluable importance of literature, with its wealth of narratives, when it comes to tackling the complex questions of

[12] The question whether Deckard is a Replicant is the most common one among viewers. Some maintain that the 1992 director's cut includes clues ascertaining that Deckard is indeed a Replicant. However, as Bukatman aptly posits, the question 'who is human?' is more about us than it is about Deckard, and in any case ambiguity about "real" status is essential to the narrative. See Bukatman (1997: 80–83), for elaboration see Žižek (1993).

human responsibility to sentient beings. One of the main sources that illustrate the intricate links between the ability to love and the essence of humanity is literature (Almog 2007: 765):

> Literature presents the uniqueness of every consciousness; indeed, it may offer the richest, most precise, and most accessible representation of the essence of human consciousness that is available to us.

This aspect of literature is profoundly tied to law's basic underlying principle. Any system of law is based, first and foremost, on recognition of the uniqueness of individual consciousness. Such recognition is a prior condition to the idea that one is capable of choosing between good and evil, or between what is right and what is wrong. It likewise underlies the obligation to respect and defend the individuality and autonomy of every self. The premise that every person has an autonomous consciousness, possessing distinctive features, allows for choice and justifies the assignment of responsibility, and the entitlements of rights.

A constant flow of meaningful narratives which create representations of consciousness is essential for law's functioning. I referred to this reciprocal relationship as *the literature alongside law paradigm* (Almog 2001: 59):

> The *literature-alongside-law paradigm* depicts both law and literature as social practices in constant interaction. It contends that aesthetics and poetics are an inextricable part of law, just as legal and ethical structures are an essential part of aesthetic expression. Narrative, as a basic component of human experience, continually provides one of the formative as well as change-inducing forces of cultural activity, including legal activity.

Layered narratives such as *Blade Runner* and *A.I.* that skillfully present the types of consciousness of androids, Replicants and their ilk, as well as their being sentient and their ability to love, to hate and to remember, resonate two complementing claims. The first focuses on their alleged humanity; the second on the responsibility of the society that created them to grant them legal personhood, and the ensuing rights, duties and protections.

A.I. offers a bleak illustration of an absolute lack of responsibility towards 'loving robots', inter alia by presenting the 'Flesh Fair', an event where damaged Replicant-like androids (called 'Mecha') are abused and destroyed in front of cheering crowds. Later on the film, the narrative advances into a future in which humans are extinct, and non-humans have evolved into a highly advanced form. Ironically, these non-humans devote their intelligence to the task of reconstructing humans.

Blade Runner can be perceived as a contemporary variation of the ancient mythical warning about the dark fate that awaits humanity that by means of advanced technology creates 'a being virtually identical to a human' and 'superior in strength and agility, and at least equal in intelligence, to the genetic engineers who created them', as the exposition to the film declares. On the background of the entire plot, the opening declaration acquires a deep, ironical meaning: if we create beings that are better than humans, treating them as lesser than humans will forcefully backlash on 'real' humans.

Deckard's choices, as they evolve during the film, distill *Blade Runner's* saying: humanity must hone the awareness to possible consequences of technologically creating beings. One important consequence is indeed taking full responsibility to the fate of robots that can love.

Blade Runner takes us a few steps further. It envisages not only the potential negative moral and practical results of evading responsibility. It envisages another scenario – the use of technology in order to create genetic inferiority by means of embryo planning (Robertson 2003: 480). In this sense, the expiration date after 4 years of the Nexus 6 Replicants is a purposeful construction of genetic inferiority (Robertson 1996, 2003: 480). The intentional creation of genetically inferior humans, for the sole purposes of other humans' interests, supported by law, which is the core of the *Blade Runner's* theme, is already here. Today, the possibility to choose an embryo with a specific disability, such as deafness or short stature is available, and sometimes chosen by parents with the same disability, that is to say parents who opt for similar siblings (Savulescu 2002; Murphy 2008).

To sum up, *A.I.* depicts the end of human life, and the artificial creations as the sole survivors. *Blade Runner* narrates an earlier stage, a stage when the use of technology can still be controlled and contained within certain limits. The key term that comes repeatedly to mind in this context is, indeed, responsibility. The answer to the student's question in *A.I.*: 'If a robot can genuinely love a person, what responsibility does this person hold towards this robot?' is then: full responsibility. Humans should be responsible towards their own creations. An essential part of that responsibility is the careful scrutiny of the roles and functions of law whenever new paradigm shifting technologies emerge.

References

Almog, S. 2001. Literature alongside law as a contemporary paradigm. *Cultural Dynamics* 13(1): 53–91.

Almog, S. 2007. Windows and 'Windows': Reflections on law and literature in the digital age. *University of Toronto Law Journal* 57(4): 755–780.

"android." Merriam-Webster.com. 2012. Available at: http://www.merriam-webster.com. Last accessed 16 Aug 2012.

"android." AHdictionary.com. 2012. Available at: http://ahdictionary.com. Last accessed 16 Aug 2012.

Barlow, A. 1991. Philip K. Dick's androids: Victimized victimizers. In *Retrofitting Blade Runner: Issues in Ridley Scott's Blade Runner and Philip K. Dick's Do androids dream of electric sheep?* ed. J.B. Kerman, 76–89. Bowling Green: Bowling Green State University Popular Press.

Barr, M. 1991. Metahuman 'Kipple' or, do male film makers dream of electric women?: Speciesism and sexism in *Blade Runner*. In *Retrofitting Blade Runner: Issues in Ridley Scott's Blade Runner and Philip K. Dick's Do androids dream of electric sheep?* ed. J.B. Kerman, 25–31. Bowling Green: Bowling Green State University Popular Press.

Booker, M.K. 2006. *Alternate Americas: Science fiction film and American culture*. Westport: Praeger.

Bukatman, S. 1997. *Blade Runner*. London: BFI Publishing.

Chopra, S. 2010. Rights for autonomous artificial agents? *Communications of the ACM* 53(8): 38–40.

"cyborg." Merriam-Webster.com. 2012. Available at: http://www.merriam-webster.com. Last accessed 16 Aug 2012.

Derrida, J. 1990. Force De Loi: Le "Fondement Mystique De L'Autorité"/Force of law: The "Mystical Foundation of Authority". *Cardozo Law Review* 11(5–6): 920–1045.
Dick, P.K. 1968. *Do androids dream of electric sheep?* New York: Ballantine Books.
Dick, P.K. 2007. *Human is?* London: Orion Publishing Group.
Fancher, H. and D. Peoples. 1981. *Blade Runner – Screenplay*. Available at: http://www.daily-script.com/scripts/blade-runner_shooting.html. Last accessed 16 Aug 2012.
Fischer, N. 1989. *Blade Runner* and do androids dream of electric sheep? An ecological critique of human-centered value systems. *Canadian Journal of Political and Social Theory* 13(3): 102–113.
Francavilla, J. 1991. The android as Doppelgänger. In *Retrofitting Blade Runner: Issues in Ridley Scott's Blade Runner and Philip K. Dick's Do androids dream of electric sheep?* ed. J.B. Kerman, 4–15. Bowling Green: Bowling Green State University Popular Press.
Gwaltney, M. 1991. Androids as a device for reflection on personhood. In *Retrofitting Blade Runner: Issues in Ridley Scott's Blade Runner and Philip K. Dick's Do androids dream of electric sheep?* ed. J.B. Kerman, 32–39. Bowling Green: Bowling Green State University Popular Press.
Heldreth, L.G. 1991. The cutting edges of *Blade Runner*. In *Retrofitting Blade Runner: Issues in Ridley Scott's Blade Runner and Philip K. Dick's Do androids dream of electric sheep?* ed. J.B. Kerman, 40–52. Bowling Green: Bowling Green State University Popular Press.
Kerman, J.B. 1991. Introduction. In *Retrofitting Blade Runner: Issues in Ridley Scott's Blade Runner and Philip K. Dick's Do androids dream of electric sheep?* ed. J.B. Kerman, 1. Bowling Green: Bowling Green State University Popular Press.
Koops, B.-J., M. Hildebrandt, and D.-O. Jaquet-Chiffelle. 2010. Bridging the accountability gap: Rights for new entities in the information society? *Minnesota Journal of Law, Science and Technology* 11(2): 497–561.
Lessig, L. 1995. The regulation of social meaning. *University of Chicago Law Review* 62(3): 943–1045.
Milton, J. 1821, orig. 1667. *Paradise lost.* London: Printed for John Bumpus, Holborn-Bars.
Murphy, C. 2008. Is it wrong to select a deaf embryo?. *BBC News*, March 10, 2008. Available at: http://news.bbc.co.uk/2/hi/health/7287508.stm. Last accessed 16 Aug 2012.
President's Commission for the Study of Ethical Problems in Medicine and Biomedical Behavioral Research. 1982. *Splicing life: The social and ethical issues of genetic engineering with human beings.* Washington, DC: US Government Printing Office. Available at: http://bioethics.georgetown.edu/documents/pcemr/splicinglife.pdf. Last accessed 10 Oct 2012.
Robertson, J.A. 1996. Genetic selection of offspring characteristics. *Boston University Law Review* 76(3): 421–482.
Robertson, J.A. 2003. Procreative liberty in the era of genomics. *American Journal of Law and Medicine* 29(4): 439–487.
"robot." Merriam-Webster.com. 2012. Available at: http://www.merriam-webster.com. Last accessed 16 Aug 2012.
Savulescu, J. 2002. Deaf lesbians, "designer disability" and the future of medicine. *BMJ* 325: 771–773.
Shelley, M. 1974, orig. 1818. *Frankenstein or: The modern Prometheus*, ed. J. Rieger. Chicago: The University of Chicago Press.
Solum, L.B. 1992. Legal personhood for artificial intelligences. *North Carolina Law Review* 70(4): 1231–1287.
Teubner, G. 2006. Rights of non-humans? Electronic agents and animals as new actors in politics and law. *Journal of Law and Society* 33(4): 497–521.
Žižek, S. 1993. *Tarrying with the negative: Kant, Hegel, and the critique of ideology*. Durham: Duke University Press.

About the Authors

Shulamit Almog is a Professor of Law at the University of Haifa. Her research focuses on law and culture, law and literature, law and film and on children's rights. She has published numerous books and articles in US, Canadian, European and Israeli law reviews. Alongside her academic work, she is appearing before the Israeli Knesset, drafting sections of Israel's report to the UN on the International Convention on Children's Rights, and participating in the committee reforming Israel's Adoption Law and in the committee endowing national award for combating trafficking in persons. She is also a member of the Israeli Press Council Presidency.

Bibi van den Berg has an M.A. and a Ph.D. in philosophy, both obtained from Erasmus University Rotterdam in the Netherlands. She specialises in philosophy of technology and philosophical anthropology. After completing her PhD Bibi had a postdoc position at the Tilburg Institute for Law, Technology and Society (TILT) of Tilburg University in the Netherlands. Currently, Bibi holds a position as an assistant professor at eLaw, the Centre for Law in the Information Society at Leiden University's Law School. Her research interests include (1) the regulatory effects of technologies, (2) social, legal and ethical issues in the deployment of autonomous technologies and robots, and (3) identity and privacy in online worlds.

Niels van Dijk obtained a LL.M. in law and an M.A. in philosophy at the University of Amsterdam. He works as a Ph.D. researcher at the Free University of Brussels within the research project "Law and Autonomic Computing: A mutual transformation process". He is currently finishing his Ph.D. thesis "Grounds of the Immaterial. A Transversal Approach of a Legal Philosophy in Intellectual Rights", which is concerned with devising new empirical approaches to the theory and practice of intellectual rights and an analysis of the consequences for some of its crucial concepts.

M. Hildebrandt and J. Gaakeer (eds.), *Human Law and Computer Law: Comparative Perspectives*, Ius Gentium: Comparative Perspectives on Law and Justice 25,
DOI 10.1007/978-94-007-6314-2, © Springer Science+Business Media Dordrecht 2013

Massimo Durante is Researcher in Philosophy of Law at the Department of Law of the University of Turin and holds a Ph.D. in History of Philosophy at the Faculty of Philosophy of the University of Paris IV Sorbonne. His main fields of research are: Philosophy of Law, Legal Informatics and Ethics. Author of several books, he has widely published articles in Italian, English and French. He has recently edited, with Ugo Pagallo, the book: *Manuale di informatica giuridica e diritto delle nuove tecnologie*, Utet, Torino, 2012.

Jeanne Gaakeer is endowed professor of legal theory and associate professor of jurisprudence at Erasmus School of Law, Erasmus University Rotterdam, The Netherlands. The focus of her research is on interdisciplinary developments in law and legal theory, more specifically on Law and Literature and Law and the Humanities, and their relevance to legal practice. She is co-founder, with Greta Olson (Giessen University), of the European Network for Law and Literature (www.eurnll.org). She also serves as a justice in the criminal law section of the Appellate Court of The Hague.

Mireille Hildebrandt holds the Chair of Smart Environments, Data Protection and the Rule of Law at the Institute of Computing and Information Sciences (iCIS), Radboud University Nijmegen. She is Associate Professor of Jurisprudence at the Erasmus School of Law, Rotterdam and Senior Researcher at the centre for Law, Science, Technology and Society, Vrije Universiteit Brussel. She works on the nexus of philosophy of law and philosophy of technology, combining research in positive law on privacy, data protection, liability, intellectual property, cybercrime and legal personhood for non-human agents with research into the normative impact of smart environments on the foundations and assumptions of the law.

Ronald E. Leenes is full professor in regulation by technology at the Tilburg Institute for Law, Technology, and Society (Tilburg University). His primary research interests are regulation by (and of) technology, specifically related to privacy and identity management. He leads different research teams in the field of privacy-enhancing identity management and Online Dispute Resolution. He is also involved in research in ID fraud, biometrics and e-government. Ronald has extensive research experience in the fields of Artificial Intelligence and Law, E-Government and since he joined TILT, technology (primarily ICTs) and law. Since 2012, Ronald is academic director of the Privacy & Identity lab (PI.lab), a joint venture of Tilburg University, Radboud Universiteit Nijmegen, TNO, and SIDN.

Ugo Pagallo is Professor of Jurisprudence at the University of Turin, Law School, since 2000, faculty at the Center for Transnational Legal Studies (CTLS) in London and faculty fellow at the NEXA Center for Internet and Society at the Politecnico of Turin. Chief editor of the *Digitalica* series published by Giappichelli in Turin and co-editor of the AICOL series by Springer, his main interests are AI & law, network theory, robotics and information technology law (specially data protection law and copyright).

Katja de Vries is a Ph.D. student at the *Centre for Law, Science, Technology, and Society* (Vrije Universiteit Brussel). Her research is focused on the collisions and interactions between legal and technological modes of thinking. More in particular she studies the differences and continuities between the role of probabilistic equality and rationality in the construction of machine learning/data mining algorithms and in the legal protection granted through the semantics of privacy, data protection and antidiscrimination law. De Vries obtained four masters degrees (Civil Law, Cognitive Psychology and Philosophy at Leiden University; Magister Juris at Oxford University).

Index

A
AA. *See* Artificial agents (AA)
Accountability, 37–39, 41, 49–51, 53, 56, 59, 60, 62, 63, 168, 190
Affordances, 2, 3, 5, 14, 15, 17, 19, 70–76, 131, 160, 162, 165–169, 174, 175, 177
  constraining, 73, 131, 160, 162, 165–168, 174, 175, 177
Agency, 7, 18, 19, 36–42, 51, 52, 57, 59, 61–63, 78, 91, 92, 189
AI. *See* Artificial intelligence (AI)
Androids, 4, 54, 182, 184–186, 189, 191, 192
Anthropomorphism, 20, 69, 78–81, 83
Artificial agents (AA), 4, 17–19, 36, 40, 52, 55, 56, 58–62, 166, 185
Artificial intelligence (AI), 4, 17–19, 24, 25, 29, 31, 34–36, 42, 49–51, 53, 58–60, 62, 63, 80, 126, 164, 191
Artificial legal subjects, 37–42
Attachment, 33, 56, 104, 106–107, 109–111, 115, 116
Auster, P.B., 7, 131, 171–175, 178
Austin, J.L., 93, 101, 104, 107
Autonomy, 4, 17, 39, 40, 43, 49, 51, 52, 59–62, 91, 131, 136, 137, 139, 142, 147, 150, 151, 154, 161, 164, 166, 173, 192
Awareness, 20, 27, 41, 71, 74, 75, 80, 81, 138, 141, 191, 192

B
Blade Runner, 7, 131, 132, 181–193
Blade Runner Director's Cut, 182
Bleak House, 91
Brain
  digital, 2, 154
  reading, 2, 32
Brownsword, R., 68, 90–92, 113

C
Captology, 71, 72, 74
Clef de lecture, 107–108
Code
  as law, 6, 7, 13, 17–21, 47–49, 51, 61, 62, 92, 127, 128
  region, 19, 68, 69, 83
Cogito, 188
Cognition, 2, 4, 14, 25, 30, 34–36, 41, 53, 61, 129, 142, 164, 177, 187
Computational, 3–6, 16, 17, 28, 30, 31, 33, 35, 36, 42, 126, 165, 175–177
The Concept of Law, 20, 91, 93, 97–100, 106, 107, 112
Constraining affordances, 73, 131, 160, 162, 165–168, 174, 175, 177
Constructionism, 162, 165, 167–169
Contracts, 4, 19, 36, 38, 42, 49, 53, 54, 56–62, 93, 95, 104, 137, 145, 150
Control, 14, 16, 40, 41, 58, 74, 84, 96, 106, 126, 131, 135–154, 176, 183
Corporations, 37–41, 43, 59, 60, 93, 182, 183, 186, 190
Corpus Delicti, 7, 131, 143, 144, 147–150
Council of State, 99, 101–105, 110
Culture
  popular, 181
  representation, 25, 129, 154, 187
Cyborgs, 17, 184

M. Hildebrandt and J. Gaakeer (eds.), *Human Law and Computer Law: Comparative Perspectives*, Ius Gentium: Comparative Perspectives on Law and Justice 25,
DOI 10.1007/978-94-007-6314-2, © Springer Science+Business Media Dordrecht 2013

D

Data, 4, 28–30, 34, 35, 39, 55, 57, 60, 129–131, 136–140, 142, 144, 149, 150, 153, 160–162, 164–169, 171–178
  data-intensive paradigm, 165, 178
Deep Blue, 18, 26–30, 37
Deleuze, G., 111, 131, 151
Demarcation, 90, 95, 97, 99–100, 103–108, 111
Design choices, 68, 74, 141
Dewey, J., 18, 37–39, 43
Dickens, C.J.H., 91
Digital habitat, 175–178
Disciplinary society, 131, 151
Do Androids Dream of Electric Sheep?, 182, 184, 186
DVD industry, 68, 83

E

Eisenstein, E., 94, 96
ELIZA, 78–80
Embodiment, 34–36, 90, 161
Embryo planning, 193
Emotion, 4, 34–36, 42, 51, 61, 69, 78–80, 127, 183, 184
Enunciation
  legal trajectory of, 111–113
  mode of, 106, 107, 114, 118
  regime of, 96, 102–104, 106–119
Epistemology, 34, 127, 129, 130, 136, 141–143, 146, 148, 152–154, 162, 165, 167
Ethnography, 95, 99, 101–103, 114

F

Facts, 4–7, 15, 16, 20, 27, 30, 32, 35, 36, 39, 48, 50, 54, 59–63, 69, 70, 74, 78–80, 82, 93, 98–101, 110, 127, 137–139, 143, 146, 150, 154, 164, 168, 172–174, 189
  institutional, 93, 100, 110, 138
Felicity, 103–107, 112, 118
  conditions of, 103–107, 112, 118
Files, 20, 21, 96, 97, 102–106, 114, 115, 128, 130, 144, 149, 164
Frankenstein, 126, 184, 187, 188, 190

G

Gaakeer, J., 34, 48, 125, 126, 128, 129, 131, 135, 140
Galatea 2.2, 7, 18, 23–43
Genetic
  engineering, 184
  inferiority, 193
Greimas, A.J., 20, 21, 103
Gutwirth, S., 29, 92, 103, 104, 113, 136, 164

H

Hart, H.L.A., 20, 90, 91, 93, 95, 97–101, 106, 107, 109, 112
Heidegger, M., 138, 151–153, 174
Hermeneutics, 7, 137, 139, 144
Hildebrandt, M., 1, 13, 17, 18, 23, 25, 29, 36, 42, 48, 49, 51, 62, 69, 74, 77, 84, 92–94, 113, 128, 136, 137, 139, 162–164, 166, 173, 186
Human
  human-like individuals, 35, 38, 40–42, 62, 70, 72, 137, 150, 154, 177, 182
  new human, 182, 185
  non-human, 4, 35, 37–39, 41, 42, 91, 132, 182, 185–189, 192
Human Is?, 132, 189, 190
Humanities, 3–5, 7, 16, 25–27, 29, 33, 48, 91, 126, 128–130, 136, 141, 147, 152–154, 160, 185, 186, 188–192
Human rights, 149, 154, 187–189

I

IA. *See* Intelligent agents (IA)
Indeterminacy, 131, 159–178
Information, 2, 4, 5, 16, 17, 25, 29, 32, 48, 52, 55, 71, 90, 93, 118, 119, 128, 131, 136–139, 141, 142, 147, 150–152, 159–168, 170, 174–178, 183
  revolution, 159
Inhuman, 188–190
Institution, 37, 72, 93, 98, 102–104, 107–111, 127
Intelligent agents (IA), 185–187
Intelligent machines, 18, 26, 37, 40–43, 49, 51
Intentional, 5, 14, 19, 37, 55, 57, 62, 68–70, 72–76, 81–84, 90, 148, 193
  influencing, 68–70, 72–76, 81

K

Kafka, F., 137, 146, 149, 151

L

Language
  computer, 6–7, 13, 15–17
  human, 6–7, 13–15, 17, 32
Latour, B., 20, 21, 68, 91, 95–97, 99–111, 113–119

Law
ambient, 92
as code, 6–7, 13–21, 47–49, 51, 61, 62, 92, 96, 127, 128, 150
command theory of, 48, 54, 93
computer, 1–7, 41
criminal, 18, 36, 39, 49–51, 53–55, 61–63, 146
and literature, 6, 7, 33, 48, 49, 51, 54, 64, 125–132, 136–138, 140, 141, 168, 192
passage of, 100–103, 105–107
as a practice, 2, 20, 90, 91, 93–95, 97–108, 112, 129, 130, 141, 185
as a regime of reattachment, 103–108
as a system of rules, 93, 97, 99–100, 109, 112, 116, 137, 138
Leenes, R., 3, 19, 20, 67–69, 83, 90, 92
Legal
definition, 191
medium of, 96, 109
norms, enforcing of, 16, 68
personhood, 17, 18, 25, 26, 36–39, 41–43, 60, 61, 131, 182, 185–187, 190, 192
positivism, 93, 101, 109
practice of, 91, 95, 99, 101, 107, 109, 112, 116
rules, 3, 6, 15, 20, 36, 55, 58, 69, 82, 90, 93, 99, 100, 106, 107, 113, 152, 163, 190
status, 34–42, 61, 187
subjectivity, 17–19, 36–38
Lessig, L., 7, 20, 68, 90, 92, 93, 126, 129, 153, 168, 190, 191
Lex informatica, 92
Liability, 17–19, 36–42, 49, 51–54, 56–58, 60, 62–64
Limited longevity, 190
Literature alongside law paradigm, 192

M
MacCormick, N., 91, 93, 95, 98, 100, 109
Machine learning, 4, 25, 29, 30, 34, 56
The Making of Law, 20, 102–104, 106–107, 112
McLuhan, M., 2, 94, 96
Media equation, 20, 79–81, 83
Mediality, 91, 96, 109
Medium, 20, 81, 90, 91, 93–97, 109, 113, 118
Methodology, 2, 38, 39, 77, 82, 98, 103, 130, 137, 139, 145–147, 153, 170
Mode
of enunciation, 20, 106–108, 113, 114, 118
of existence, 107, 115

N
Narration, 131, 160, 171–175, 177
Narrative
knowledge, 130, 140–143, 154
layered, 192
Non-beings, 78
Normativity
legal, 7, 19–21, 131, 162–168, 174, 178
technological, 19–21, 131, 162–168, 174, 178
Nudge, 69, 72–74

O
Oracle Night, 7, 131, 159–178

P
Personhood, 17, 18, 25, 26, 36–39, 41–43, 60–62, 131, 143, 154, 182, 184–187, 190, 192
Persuasion, 19, 20, 69–75, 81, 83
Poiésis, 152, 153
Postmodern, 18, 32, 131, 141, 143
Practice turn, 20, 91, 95, 101
Privacy, 36, 131, 139, 142, 144, 145, 147, 148, 154

R
Reidenberg, J.R., 92
Replicants, 182–193
Responsibility
thesis, new strong, 49, 59–63
thesis, new weak, 49, 53–60, 63
thesis, no new, 49–53, 63
Robots, 3, 4, 18, 19, 47–64, 71, 126, 181–193
Rules
incorporeal, 20, 91, 93–94, 109, 118
primary, 100
of recognition, 100, 106
secondary, 100

S
Science fiction, 3, 47–49, 51, 54, 62–64, 126, 184, 191
genre, 184
Scripts, 2, 20, 31, 76–78, 80, 81, 83, 94, 118, 119, 153, 162
Searle's Chinese room argument, 18, 26, 30–32
Self-expression, 173, 177, 178
freedom of, 173, 177, 178

Semanticization
of being, 159–169, 171, 174
of narratives, 160, 168–171, 174
Semiotics, 2, 20, 95, 101, 103–105, 107, 111, 127
Smart agents, 36–37
Snow, B., 25–26
Speed bump, 68, 83, 92, 113–118

T

Technè, 125, 152, 153
Techno-effects, 19, 20, 67–84
Technology
implicit influence of, 75–81
robotics, 18, 48, 49, 52, 53
unintentional influence of, 69, 70, 75–81, 83–84
Techno-regulation, 5, 17, 19–21, 67–84, 90–93, 104, 112–114, 116–119
Tien, L., 90, 92, 93
Turing
machine, 18, 25–27, 30, 32
test, 24–27, 36
Two cultures, 25–26, 126

V

Value object, 102, 104–106, 111, 112, 114, 115
Vismann, C., 21, 90, 94, 96, 97, 102, 128, 149
Voight-Kampff test, 183, 190

W

Watson, 17, 18, 23–43, 59
Weizenbaum, 18, 26, 27, 33, 78–80
Writing, 2, 15, 24, 31, 54, 84, 90, 92, 95–98, 101, 106, 110, 127, 131, 159–178

Z

Zeh, J., 7, 131, 136, 140, 141, 143, 144, 146, 148–150

Printed by Printforce, the Netherlands